PROUD TO PUNISH

PROUD TO PUNISH

*The Global Landscapes
of Rough Justice*

GILLES FAVAREL-GARRIGUES

AND

LAURENT GAYER

Translated by Cynthia Schoch and Trista Selous

STANFORD UNIVERSITY PRESS
Stanford, California

Stanford University Press
Stanford, California

English translation © 2024 by the Board of Trustees of the Leland Stanford Jr. University. All rights reserved.

A previous version of this work was published in French in 2021 under the title *Fiers de punir: Le monde des justiciers hors-la-loi* © 2021, Éditions du Seuil.

No part of this book may be reproduced or transmitted in any form or by any means, electronic or mechanical, including photocopying and recording, or in any information storage or retrieval system, without the prior written permission of Stanford University Press.

Printed in the United States of America on acid-free, archival-quality paper

Library of Congress Cataloging-in-Publication Data
Names: Favarel-Garrigues, Gilles, author. | Gayer, Laurent, author.
Title: Proud to punish : the global landscapes of rough justice / Gilles Favarel-Garrigues and Laurent Gayer ; translated by Cynthia Schoch and Trista Selous.
Other titles: Fiers de punir. English
Description: Stanford, California : Stanford University Press, 2024. | Originally published in French under the title: Fiers de punir : le monde des justiciers hors-la-loi. | Includes bibliographical references and index.
Identifiers: LCCN 2023039395 (print) | LCCN 2023039396 (ebook) | ISBN 9781503636569 (cloth) | ISBN 9781503637672 (paperback) | ISBN 9781503637689 (ebook)
Subjects: LCSH: Vigilantes. | Vigilantism. | Punishment—Social aspects. | Criminal justice, Administration of.
Classification: LCC HV7419.F39 2024 (print) | LCC HV7419 (ebook) | DDC 364—dc23/eng/20230921
LC record available at https://lccn.loc.gov/2023039395
LC ebook record available at https://lccn.loc.gov/2023039396

Cover design: Daniel Benneworth-Gray
Cover photograph: Rawpixel
Typeset by Newgen in Source Serif Pro 9.25/13pt

In memory of Jean-Pierre Masse (1967–2015)

CONTENTS

INTRODUCTION
Breaking the Law to Maintain Order   1

1   The Vigilante Show   9

2   Lynch Law   34

3   Cop Killers   60

4   Popular Justice, Revolutionary Justice   80

5   Cleaning Up Society   105

6   Punishers in Uniform   127

CONCLUSION
The Rough Justice Continuum   154

Notes   161

Selected Bibliography   203

Index   221

INTRODUCTION
BREAKING THE LAW TO MAINTAIN ORDER

There is no greater law firm than Smith & Wesson, especially if it's backed up by a 12-gauge injunction.

MEMBER OF THE US MILITIA MOVEMENT
POSSE COMITATUS (1978)[1]

A PHOTOGRAPH, SHARED MORE THAN three thousand times and eliciting 1,200 comments in the hours after it was put online in June 2016, shows a man wearing a baseball cap lying face down on the ground, his feet and hands bound in a hogtie, with a hunting knife a few inches from his face. The image was posted on the Facebook page of a group calling itself Darwin Crime Rally Protest. "Tired of the courts soft approach on criminals," the group targets residents of the Australian city eager to "get involved and make the community a safer place." The text accompanying the image claims the person shown in this humiliating posture was captured in the suburb of Palmerston as he was about to steal a car and threatened passersby with a knife. "His mates got away, and until we find them, this guy's new home is in the boot of our car," the author added and then suggested that there would be more vigilante action to come: "Get word out we aren't here to fuck around anymore, and we will be taking action into our own hands from now regardless of the outcome."[2] A number of people visiting the page lauded this social prophylaxis and encouraged the group in its efforts to clean up Palmerston. "Good job, hope you get a great collection of these scumbags," one of the comments read. Others criticized the vigilantes for being too lenient, with one commentator suggesting that the suspect should have been flogged and another that they "should have tied him behind the car and made him run." The local police took a diametrically opposite view, stating that "Northern Territory Police do not support or condone" any form of vigilantism and that ordinary citizens should refrain from "taking the law into their own hands." Clearly flustered by this challenge to their authority, law enforcement officers gave assurances that they were duly investigating the matter. The veracity of the photo was, however, soon called into question by informed commentators who derided the amateurish way that the suspect had been tied up: "Look at his hands, don't need to be Houdini to get outta that," one noted sarcastically.[3] The administrator of the Facebook page himself fueled doubts, first telling the police that the photo had been faked but then claiming to have lied to avoid criminal charges. In the end, he left it up to the people of Darwin "to decide whether the alleged incidents [were] real or not."[4]

Doubt continued to hover over this affair, and most commentators, including the police, did not rule out the possibility that it was indeed an example of vigilantism: an initiative by ordinary citizens determined to enforce the law and mete out justice on their own terms, in response to a formal justice system deemed to be either wanting or ineffective.[5] Darwin's self-proclaimed crime fighters may not have been expert knot tiers, but in the eyes of a large segment of their audience, their performance was no less convincing. Indeed, in their statements of intent, their modus operandi, and the controversies they fueled, these enforcers determined to clean up the streets were without doubt exemplary of their kind.

PUNISHING WITH PRIDE

The uncompromising approach to justice endorsed by the Darwin activists led them to defy the law and impose outrageous penalties. Few parts of the world have escaped such controversial improvised justice, administered by amateurs who, hands on hearts and heads high, proudly claim the right to punish. The iconic figure of the superhero, made popular through comics, pulp fiction, and Hollywood movies, continues to feed the global imagination of what vigilantes are, alongside more vernacular figures of punishers.[6] But whereas pop culture favors lone avengers, the Darwin vigilantes and their ilk tend to hunt in a pack, in the name of their people.

Physical punishment is a vindictive act of communication. When a mob gets hold of an alleged rapist to lynch him, it throws down a challenge to the authorities by appropriating sovereignty's ultimate attribute, the "right of death."[7] The message to governments and populations can be read on the battered bodies, in the edifying notices that death squads pin on the publicly displayed corpses of their victims: "I was a robber," "I was a dealer, don't become like me." Their communiqués, leaflets, or filmed stunts can take a more elaborate form than notes on corpses, but vigilantes always take delight in leaving their audience in a state of shock and awe. Yet to stand out from assassins drunk on revenge, they constantly seek legitimacy through approval of their actions by recognized authorities (the police, the government, political parties, the community, the people).[8] Vigilantes invoke the right of self-defense extensively and proactively for the sake of society at large, unlike those who claim it when under personal and immediate threat.

Dominant interpretations of rough justice tend to equate it with a form of establishment violence.[9] For US scholars, who pioneered the study of extralegal violence, the iconic vigilante is a reactionary and xenophobic White male, aiming to defend the natural order of things and, more prosaically, vacillating social, racial, and sexual hierarchies.[10] However, this archetype by no means exhausts the portrait gallery of self-styled enforcers on the fringe of the law. Sexual and racial minorities, revolutionary organizations, and dominated classes spawn their own whip-wielding, gun-toting avengers, and police and paramilitaries may also disregard the law to liquidate those branded as enemies of the state and the dregs of society. Whatever the cause they champion, vigilantes of all stripes share a critique of the judicial system—they resent undue delays, quibbling, rights granted to the accused and convicts, and leniency of sentences. This critique of procedure is coupled with a vitriolic indictment against the correctionalist ideal of the justice system, with its focus on rehabilitating criminals. In recent decades, this ideal has lost momentum in the face of public discourse advocating harsher sentences on the pretext of a supposed social demand for security.[11] Reflecting these punitive trends, vigilantes do not believe that deviants and criminals can mend their ways. Rabidly hostile to programs promoting the reintegration of ex-offenders, they claim the right to banish incorrigibles or even put them to death in the name of a community—from the poor and the marginalized to the more privileged "law-abiding citizens"—that varies from one vigilante group to another.

Although vigilantes take popular support for granted, it is difficult to measure. The intimidation they exert leaves little room for outright protest against their actions, and the failings of the state foster endorsement by default, in the absence of a credible alternative. Still, the embedding of protectors into the neighborhood or the village lends them credibility. The promise of restoring order also resonates with anxious and vulnerable populations. Vigilante justice often appears as a revolt against the law,[12] but it is also the vehicle for social demands and collective assertion. Defending private property and protecting one's family are not confined to the dominant classes; for the most vulnerable they take on an existential dimension. These concerns are heightened in societies damaged by decades of neoliberal reforms that, with their trail of privation and alienation, have intensified the specter of dispossession. Vigilante justice, then, partakes in the power

4   INTRODUCTION

struggles between marginalized populations, political authorities, and law enforcement institutions.

Vigilantes cut to the chase; they provide a cheap solution within everyone's reach and are not ashamed of their amateurism.[13] They are not immune to harrowing blunders, even if they often are "specialists in coercion"[14] with hunting skills, combat experience, or a background in law enforcement. At the same time, their propensity for rough justice does not imply wholesale rejection of the law. On the contrary, the legitimacy of these movements also relies on their ability to refer to positive law when need be, mimicking its procedures and appropriating its rituals. The ambition of this book is to demonstrate that, in its various forms, rough justice thrives on "the dense interweaving of arms and law."[15]

Pierre Bourdieu notes that a vigilante is like a "self-mandated legal prophet . . . who opposes a personal and private justice to juridical common sense," believing himself entitled to "[express] the collective morality" in the name of a group.[16] He is a "juridical creator"[17] who also oversees the entire penal chain: he is at once detective, interrogating officer, prosecutor, judge, and executioner. He may deliver justice here and there in the event of an obvious offense. More frequently, however, he produces evidence that is based on a victim's complaint or coerced confessions of an alleged perpetrator and also occasionally draws on indigenous rituals for establishing guilt (trials by ordeal, divination, oaths, etc.).[18] His versatility enables him to reach verdicts and hand down sentences in record time. However, his primary role is to administer punishment, and this he does with boundless imagination. Favoring spectacular and exemplary justice targeting the body, he degrades and tortures his victims for edification, dissuasion, and entertainment. Such resolutely corporal punishments resurrect the criminal justice system's past of torture and spectacle, which persists despite the advent of "the age of sobriety in punishment," as noted by Michel Foucault.[19] Whereas Foucault sees a "shame in punishing" that prompted contemporary penal institutions to hide punishment from the public eye,[20] the self-styled justice dispensers who fill these pages are proud of their actions and rejoice in their omnipotence. They orchestrate new "festivals of punishment"[21] that revive the excesses of the oldest forms of public execution for a global audience attained through social media. The more enterprising among them, such as Russian vigilantes,[22] even make a profit from these violent spectacles, providing sensational content for their YouTube channels, which they turn into business assets.

Vigilante actions serve two different conceptions of punishment. The first involves publicly humiliating deviants before returning them to society, as happens in village justice rituals such as charivari in France,[23] "rough music" in the United Kingdom,[24] and *vozhdenie* in Russia.[25] The second is intended to expel or eliminate those beyond redemption, in accordance with a hygienist agenda that seeks to cleanse society of its dregs. In every case, the vigilantes' prey are sanctioned for straying from legal or moral norms. They are punished for not only what they *do* but also who they *are* in terms of ethnic origin, social status, or sexual orientation. Their perceived identity makes them vulnerable to scapegoating by lynch mobs and vigilantes, who deliver their verdicts in the name of both positive law and an ideal conception of justice that predates or overrides the legal rules of the state. Indeed, positive law is not the only normative framework recognized by self-appointed punishers. As "moral entrepreneurs,"[26] they also penalize behavior deemed to be deviant even if not criminalized (such as homosexuality, adultery, and witchcraft). And when they put their strong-arm tactics in the service of the dominant classes, punishers hunt down trade unionists, political activists, and other champions of human rights disturbing the established order.

PRECARIOUS JUSTICE, SCANDALOUS JUSTICE

Extrajudicial punishment is premised on a presumption of impunity. Self-appointed law enforcers bank on the authorities' inadequacies or complicity to escape prosecution. As a number of cases discussed in this book show, the outcome is never a foregone conclusion, and advocates of rough justice sometimes cross the path of uncompromising judges, tenacious journalists, or competitors prepared to fight it out. These constraints oblige vigilantes to strike a balance between publicity and secrecy. Some groups opt to work underground, whereas others act in the open, proudly embracing their prophylactic mission and the inevitable dirty work that comes in tow. While pursuing spectacular justice, vigilantes strive to keep some details offstage. They readily exhibit their exploits, their victims, and expressions of popular support but often conceal their personal identities, unsavory feats, and hidden motives—even if these are "public secrets."[27]

The self-righteousness of vigilantes, their certainty of being in the right, does not prevent them from quickly running out of steam. This is particularly true for lynch mobs, associated in the public mind with sudden and explosive action. But more routine vigilante operations, such as patrols to keep watch over a territory or border, can also founder. The longevity of these ventures depends on their legitimacy at the local level and, especially, on the benevolence of official and customary authorities. This precarious accreditation endows them with a temporary right to exercise legal authority, thus paving the way for plural policing.

When their operations go beyond mere publicity stunts, vigilantes present their audience with a fait accompli. Their claim to realize the will of the

6 INTRODUCTION

people or the community is inherently divisive. The ensuing controversies revolve first of all around the appropriateness of the punishments, particularly when their unbridled violence seems to more moderate spectators to be disproportionate to the offense. Their conception of corporal punishment is intrinsically inclined to excess and responds to the crime with a surfeit of severity, "a sort of surplus on the side of punishment"[28] by which the vigilantes proclaim their sovereignty loud and clear. Additional layers of meaning may aggravate the imbalance between offense and sanction in these rituals of degradation. Crime fighting may thus combine with a reassertion of racial and sexual order, with a project of social cleansing, or with an attempt to disenfranchise certain categories of the population.[29] The propensity of vigilantes to make exceptions to their own rules also fuels controversies regarding their art of punishing. In shedding institutional constraints governing the use of violence and the right to judge, vigilantes let loose with exhilaration or delight in their own dilettantism, like the mercenaries hired to crush strikes and restore employer justice in 1970s France, who found factory life depressing and preferred to spend their time "partying wildly" and committing robberies for their own profit.[30]

As illustrated by the controversy over the Darwin Crime Rally Protest, both the sham of vigilante justice and the methods used to enforce it are condemned. In posing as paragons of virtue, vigilantes are bound to come under public scrutiny and expose themselves to judicial risks. Their claim to serve the common good and their professions of integrity are liable to arouse suspicion. They are therefore open to accusations of duplicity: under the cover of the law, they allegedly enrich themselves or conceal a political agenda. Also, their claim of autonomy in their determination to implement an alternative form of justice is puzzling. Are they really the vengeful arm of the people, as they proclaim, or are they secretly serving the interests of major corporations, criminal organizations, or political groups? The dissimulation strategies used by vigilantes themselves, their blurring of the line between law enforcers and troublemakers, and doubts surrounding the veracity of the images they produce and disseminate reinforce these suspicions of imposture. The specter of fakery looms over twenty-first-century vigilantes, whose pretentions to capture the moral high ground expose them to counterinvestigations and flurries of fact-checking.

This book draws on our respective fieldwork—in India, Pakistan, and Russia—and on a bibliography that takes an inclusive approach to the social sciences, drawing from sociology, political science, anthropology, and history.

Although firmly grounded in an analysis of the contemporary era, our investigation is nevertheless sensitive to the specific yet connected historicities of rough justice. Thus, the universal revulsion toward lynching has been fueled by the controversies surrounding racial violence in the United States since the second half of the nineteenth century, which have spread far beyond the country's borders. Although defending a comparative approach, we do not propose a term-by-term analysis or typological classification. Rather, we explore how, beyond idiosyncrasies, each case may refine the overall inquiry, shed light on other situations, and suggest potential circulations of narratives, practices, and controversies. The expansion of social media has strengthened these connections and contributes to a formal convergence of these narratives and practices through the circulation of global templates. Hence the striking similarities among contemporary lynching scenes from India to Mexico or among "pedophile hunts" from the United States to Russia.

The opening scenes introducing each chapter aim to capture the combination of sensorial overdrive, exhilaration, and routine practices that characterize rough justice in action. By observing the protagonists in their social environment, exploring their practices, and listening to their vindictive discourse and the reactions of their audience, we start drawing the contours of punitive configurations. These opening scenes also outline the realm of possibilities in which relations between private enforcers and public authorities are negotiated. Finally, these vignettes vividly convey the confusion that permeates rough justice, hinting at a world of subterfuge in which radical stances do not suffice to dispel suspicions of imposture.

Violent, controversial, and confusing, the subject matter of this book invites caution in the gathering and treatment of documentary sources. Press accounts, nongovernmental organization reports, and judicial investigations are often marred by sensationalism and political biases. Besides, most of these sources tend to make victims invisible and inaudible. The survivors are reluctant to publicize their ordeal and, at best, voice their grievances through authorized spokespersons. While engaging with this problematic corpus, we do not seek to set the record straight but instead analyze on their own terms the actors' statements (including messages and press releases, videos, exchanges on social media, and possible confessions) and unpack the controversies arising from their wrongdoing.

Proud to Punish follows two threads: One leads from seemingly autonomous citizens taking the law in their own hands to punishers in uniform. The other leads from crime fighting to social cleansing. The first two chapters tackle the most iconic representations of do-it-yourself justice: the vigilante, a private enforcer who breaks the law to maintain order, and the lynch mob, a vindictive horde acting with method, assuming the right to put the guilty

8   INTRODUCTION

to death without further ado. The next two chapters venture into less well charted territory, on the trail of cop killers and revolutionaries experimenting with a more subversive brand of popular justice. The last two chapters dive into the murky waters of political domination, where death squads and punishers in uniform set out to cleanse society. And when the political patrons of these executioners, such as Rodrigo Duterte in the Philippines, Jair Bolsonaro in Brazil, and Narendra Modi in India, elevate extrajudicial violence into an art of government, they hasten the advent of a vigilante state.

1 THE VIGILANTE SHOW

Preacher Casey was just a workin' man,
And he said, "Unite all you working men."
Killed him in the river some strange man.
Was that a vigilante man?

WOODY GUTHRIE, "Vigilante Man" (1940)

THEY ARE HERE TO "MAKE HIS LIFE HELL." Lying in a bathtub, Andrey tries to keep his head down, but Tesak, the gang leader, prevents him so that the camera doesn't lose a moment of his humiliation. Andrey, believing he had a date with a minor, sees the trap close in on him and now faces his tormentors, stuck with them in a gloomy Moscow apartment. Once the prey has been captured, the "safari" gives way to the punitive show. After sharing sexually explicit messages with his audience, Tesak brings in the adolescent who served as a decoy to testify. Familiar with the drill, the gang leader is bent on extracting a confession and undertakes a mock psychiatric evaluation designed to entertain his audience. Following a well-rehearsed script, his performance involves a gradual descent into degradation. Using a dildo in the place of a microphone, he questions the alleged pedophile about his sexual orientation and traumatic experiences to expose his monstrosity to the audience. Then comes a series of punishments: the would-be molester is forced to show his ID papers, call his employer or his family to confess, and then submit to a string of humiliations. Depending on their inspiration, the self-styled enforcers may partly shave the alleged perpetrator's head, draw a rainbow on his forehead, adorn it with slogans such as "I fuck children" or "FUCK LGBT," or force him to adopt grotesque poses or sing nursery rhymes. As a master of ceremonies carefully managing his brand image, Tesak usually ends with his signature punishment: "urotherapy," which involves dousing the victim with urine or making him drink it.

10   CHAPTER 1

The spectacle described here was not the first sadistic performance by Maxim Martsinkevich, "Tesak" (Hatchet). After about 2005, at a time when racist crimes were peaking in Russia, the neo-Nazi skinhead was already known for the ultraviolent films he produced and posted online, depicting beatings and even murders of immigrants, about which he boasted publicly.[1] Jailed for "extremism" and for "inciting racial hatred" in 2009, he was back to his old ways the following decade with his Occupy Pedophilia project, which fell in step with a moral crusade resulting in the Russian Duma's adoption of a law banning the "propaganda of non-traditional sexual relations among minors."[2] Though inspired by other initiatives against pedophiles, Tesak stood out by his radical nature, commercial ingenuity, and showmanship. At once inquisitor, tormentor, and MC of a "vigilante show," he laid the groundwork for a new genre. In his wake, dozens of copycat projects flooded Russian social media during the first half of the 2010s.[3]

With a following among youth whom he greeted in his videos as "fans of extremism," Tesak turned his activism into a business venture by charging a fee for participating in "safaris," developing online merchandising, doing advertising for gyms and protein drink brands, and offering lectures, workshops, and publications. Such outlets might cast doubt on the veracity of Tesak's performances: what if these punitive expeditions were merely staged? Although it is difficult to gauge the impact of the neo-Nazi's safaris from a judicial standpoint, the authenticity of at least some of them appears beyond question. For instance, Andrey, the man lying in the bathtub in the opening scene, held a senior position in the Moscow Regional Court Bailiffs Service. Arrested in September 2013, he was sentenced in August 2014 to a thirty-month prison term for acts of pedophilia.[4] However, the prosecution and conviction of Tesak's victims did not ensure his impunity. He was again jailed in 2014 for having posted messages calling on Russians to take up arms against foreigners in reaction to ethnic riots in a Moscow suburb. Restrukt, his new movement, was dissolved and the videos of its safaris were taken down. The content could still easily be accessed online, however, in 2020, when Tesak was found dead in his cell at age thirty-six.[5]

Occupy Pedophilia fits within a particular context in Russia, that of the 2010s, when punitive practices were being reinvented with the spread of digital tools. At the start of this decade, an increasing number of self-styled enforcers were filming their exploits and designing new projects promoted on social media and YouTube. Their "raids"[6] targeted reckless drivers, illegal immigrants, shopkeepers contravening liquor sales laws, alcohol drinkers in public places, drug dealers, and alleged pedophiles. Although not all of them went as far as Tesak in meting out punishment, they shared his modus operandi, which was based on the desire to take the law into their own hands,

THE VIGILANTE SHOW   11

the ability to use force to achieve this goal, and the nearly instant broadcast of their activities. From the viewpoint of these self-proclaimed "responsible citizens," a successful raid was above all a successful film shoot: the aim was to produce appealing scenes that encouraged the audience to click on the video the gang had edited and posted on social media. Russian vigilantes can often be heard shouting, "Don't touch the camera!" to deter their recalcitrant prey from harming the key element of their setup. This unusual combination of civic claims, moral policing, and commercial concerns is specific to contemporary forms of Russian vigilantism, but it nevertheless fits in with a longer, more global history.[7]

———

Although symptomatic of the proliferation of self-styled law enforcers in Russia in the 2010s, Tesak's performances can be related to the idiosyncratic style of policing and dispensing justice associated with vigilantism. Closely linked to the history of the United States since the nineteenth century, the practices vigilantism covers are currently being debated in many other countries. As a social science concept, *vigilantism* refers to a voluntary and apparently autonomous practice, minimally routinized, involving the use of force to right wrongs or enforce norms (both legal and moral precepts) in the name of a community of reference that is the primary audience of the self-styled law enforcers. Vigilante activity has a temporality of its own: it is not eruptive, as in some cases of lynching, or stable over the long term, as are the regular police. Having various sociological profiles, but usually linked to conservative or reactionary circles, vigilantes have no qualms about breaking the law to maintain the order in the name of which they patrol, hunt, and punish their prey.[8] By resorting to coercion, vigilantes enact a form of "capillary power"[9] that deploys itself at street level against illegal or immoral behaviors. Although they generally move in some sort of gang—such as "regulators," "vigilance committees," or "self-defense groups"—they may also act alone, as responsible citizens bursting with initiative. In the age of the Internet, pedophile hunters often appear as lone avengers, thus playing on the superhero imaginary. When Tesak had a page on VKontakte (Russia's Facebook equivalent), a drawing actually showed him dressed in cape and tights, flying through the air as if Superman—a well-worn cliché in the vigilante imagery.

In its contemporary forms, vigilantism is a global phenomenon with digital ramifications, resulting in the proliferation of Internet-mediated policing initiatives. In addition to the protection of private property and community boundaries, vigilante practices challenge the boundary between activism and rough justice. Naming and shaming practices in the digital era share

12   CHAPTER 1

with classic vigilantism a mimicking of the judicial process (identification of the culprit, evidence gathering, sentencing, and instant punishment) and an amateurism that leaves the groups open to controversy regarding the legality of their acts, their autonomy, and their ulterior motives. Internet mediation, however, reveals tensions that are specific to contemporary vigilante enterprises, which hover between collective action and lone crusade, selflessness and profit seeking, pseudonymity and overt action, reactionary causes and struggles for emancipation.

"AS AMERICAN AS APPLE PIE"

The scene is set in an African American neighborhood of an anonymous city in the early 1970s. For Oscar and his friends of the Anti-Slavery Committee, it is time to move into action. Drug pushers in the ghetto pose the threat of a new form of slavery—addiction to hard drugs—with the violence and social alienation in their tow. Corruption has anesthetized the police and politicians, and hoping for help from the authorities would be in vain. The time has come for this neighborhood committee to take action, catch the drug dealers, and banish them from the city. Foxy Brown and her boyfriend, Michael, witness one of these heavy-handed expulsions and comment on it. "Vigilante justice. . . . Honestly, I dunno," says Michael, the legalist. But the explosive Foxy retorts that this expedient method is "as American as apple pie."[10]

Taken from one of the best-known blaxploitation films,[11] this scene bears witness to the central role of vigilante justice in US history and popular culture. From the armed gangs of Whigs fighting Tories in the eighteenth century to the Minutemen of the first decade of the 2000s hunting down illegal migrants on the Mexican border, the United States has spawned countless social mobilizations claiming to make up for the government's law enforcement inadequacies. According to Richard Maxwell Brown, a pioneer in studies on vigilante justice in the United States, its history began in South Carolina in 1767 with the founding of the first group of Regulators, a term often used subsequently by other vigilantes over the following decades.[12] Recruiting among colonists determined to fight the Tories and gangs of outlaws, Regulators assumed the role of both police and the courts: they captured, tried, and punished their prey, matching the sentence to the gravity of the offenses the perpetrators were accused of—flagellation for petty theft, exile or forced labor for more serious crimes.

During the nineteenth century, capital punishment predominated in the punitive repertoire of self-appointed lawmen who joined forces in vigilance committees. The history of vigilantism in this instance intersects with the history of lynching, without entirely overlapping it (see Chapter 2). Even if vigilance committees were guilty of summary executions, they should not be likened to the mobs enraged by court delays or leniency who broke into the local jail to remove a prisoner—usually Black and often accused of molesting a White woman—and hanged him forthwith in front of a vindictive audience, galvanized by the spectacle of punishment. In contrast to these lynch mobs, vigilance committees were better established, carrying out regular patrols[13] and using violence with greater restraint on the delinquents who fell into their hands. Although they were a favorite target of vigilantes, horse thieves and counterfeiters were not the only ones to bear the brunt of rough justice. Vigilance committees also considered themselves a bulwark for the community against threats from abroad (Mexicans on California farms, for instance) and minorities gaining social and political ground (Black people in the South, the Irish in San Francisco, Italians in New Orleans, and so on).

On the western pioneer frontier, especially, vigilance committees claimed that the justice they meted out made up for the deficiencies of law enforcement bodies. They also criticized the rules of due process as part of a liberal regime that protected the rights of offenders more than upright citizens.[14] These historical forms of vigilantism reflected a concern for self-preservation—"the first law of nature," according to a common expression among these movements—and also invoked the "right of revolution" to contravene federal law by dispensing justice outside the legal framework.[15] According to Illinois governor Thomas Ford, Regulator actions in 1816 and 1817 to deal with horse thieves and counterfeiters started after the people "formed themselves into *revolutionary tribunals*."[16] Among vigilantes, popular sovereignty was enshrined as the answer to the cost and inadequacy of the courts. *The Vigilantes of Montana*, written by Thomas Dimsdale, a journalist of British stock, famously narrates the exploits of a "league of safety and order" that carried out "popular justice" in the Rockies in the 1860s. It justified recourse to a procedure that was "shorter, surer, and at least equally equitable" to that of the courts.[17] The vigilantes of Casper, Wyoming, enforced popular justice when in 1902 they pinned a warning jingle to the body of an outlaw they had just hanged:

> *Process of law is a little slow*
> *So this is the road you'll have to go.*
> *Murderers and thieves, Beware!*
> PEOPLE'S VERDICT.[18]

Yet there is nothing plebeian about the popular justice dispensed. Meeting in Masonic circles and lodges, in San Francisco, for instance, where the vigilance committee founded in 1851 chose the all-seeing eye as its symbol,[19] or in

1860s Montana, local notables not only started such movements but directly participated in operations. Their determination to dispense justice tended to reinforce their authority. In Rawlins, Wyoming, in 1881, Dr. John E. Osborne, a wealthy breeder and banker destined for a brilliant political career—he would be elected state governor in 1893—seized the body of George "Big Nose" Parrott, a criminal freshly hanged, to carve it up and have personal items made out of his skin: a medical bag, a pair of shoes. These were exhibited for years in the lobby of Rawlins National Bank, a reminder of the community's commitment to defending its citizens' life and property.[20]

Vigilantes stoked controversy right from the start. They were accused of improvising cheap justice on a par with their amateurism. The rules followed for producing evidence and holding a public trial served as a facade for punishments that wrapped up fast-tracked and fundamentally biased proceedings. Thus the South Carolina Regulators were quickly accused of being brutally vindictive and abusing their position to give free rein to their impulses. This criticism, moreover, explains the emergence of a rival group that appropriately took the name Moderators. Another criticism had to do with the racist underpinnings of vigilante justice. For abolitionists and early leaders in the civil rights movement, vigilantism was often synonymous with the lynching of Black people in the South.[21] To this day, Arizona's Minutemen,[22] who patrol the US border with Mexico in pickup trucks, peering through binoculars to flush out illegals, remain one of the bêtes noires of anti-racist activists.[23]

Although these movements' commitment to defending existing racial hierarchies is a distinctive feature of US vigilantism, it certainly does not exhaust the modalities of constructing the enemy within these groups. Defending property and protecting the interests of local elites are central to the vigilantes' concerns, predisposing them to join counterrevolutionary struggles.[24] Thus, between 1909 and 1919, vigilante groups supported by and occasionally including bankers, merchants, and other members of the economic elite conducted a deadly countersubversive campaign against the Wobblies[25] and other radicals. This counterrevolutionary violence culminated with the lynching of Wesley Everest in Centralia, Washington, on November 11, 1919. Among the assailants were prominent businessmen and members of the American Legion, a patriotic vigilante group formed at the end of World War I.[26] Rarely has vigilantism so blatantly been used to maintain through violence the gains of the propertied classes, to enforce labor discipline, and to defend prevailing relations of production. In turn, this blurring of boundaries between vigilantes and capital's henchmen has inspired a radical critique of rough justice.

Referring to a character in the novel *The Grapes of Wrath*, published a year earlier, Woody Guthrie's song *Vigilante Man* (1940)—in this chapter's epigraph—denounced the role of vigilantes in crushing this major labor struggle of the early twentieth century. The singer portrays self-styled lawmen who tyrannized poor migrants—in this case farmers fleeing to California, to escape the ecological disaster of the Dust Bowl in the 1930s—and also hobos and activists such as Jim Casy, the former preacher in Steinbeck's novel who is murdered when he attempts to form a union. Could the "strange man" who killed him by the river have been a "vigilante man"?

In the collective imagination and in US academic research, the emblematic vigilante is a White, Protestant, racist male defending his family, his property, or his neighborhood, and women are confined to the role of innocent victim.[27] Since the 1960s, however, minority communities have poked holes in this stereotype. Exasperated by inadequate police protection in their neighborhood, some groups have decided to take the law into their own hands to shield their people from delinquency. The Jewish Defense League, founded in New York in 1968 by Rabbi Meir Kahane, patrolled the streets of Brooklyn to defend Jews against perceived threats from Black people and Puerto Ricans.[28] The Black Panther Party, established two years earlier, mounted armed patrols in Oakland's Black neighborhoods to keep an eye on police activity.[29] A few years later, journalists discovered that blaxploitation films' fascination with vigilantes mirrored a social reality. In Chicago's ghettos, for instance, groups of African Americans and Hispanic Americans spread out through the neighborhood to prevent drug dealing and called for rough justice.[30] Such initiatives, and unsolved murders of dealers linked to them, have also been observed in African American communities in New York and Washington, D.C. Although the 1970s was a particularly intense period in this regard, racial minorities have not given up their fight. During the summer of 2020, as White supremacist militias stepped up attacks against the Black Lives Matter movement,[31] African American security forces popped up in Minneapolis, Atlanta, Detroit, and elsewhere.[32] These armed groups portray themselves as intermediaries between their community and the police, and as defenders of businesses vulnerable to looting and vandalism in their neighborhoods. The Minneapolis Freedom Fighters, for instance, was formed following a call from the local chapter of the National Association for the Advancement of Colored People (NAACP) advocating self-defense in response to the attacks committed by outside troublemakers. As explained by one NAACP activist taking part in these night patrols after the death of George Floyd, "Black people in America have always had to survive. . . . Superman doesn't apply to us, he's not coming to save us. We have to save ourselves."[33] There is always a risk of matters escalating, as reflected in a series of shootings in Atlanta and an incident in Louisville, Kentucky, when the Not Fucking Around Coalition, founded by

16   CHAPTER 1

Grandmaster Jay, reported several injuries owing to stray bullets during an armed demonstration.[34]

VIGILANTE JUSTICE EVERYWHERE?

Structuring the imaginary of vigilante justice across the world, the "American vigilante tradition"[35] has dominated academic attention. Since it emerged in the 1970s, this literature has constantly probed the US exception in this area, which is believed to be rooted in the preponderance of racial issues in US history, the enduring myth of the Wild West, and the long-lasting critique of due process. However, in recent decades, vigilantism has been adopted as an analytic framework and a commonsense category the world over. This is particularly the case on the African continent, even if the term's usages vary from one country and period to another. In South Africa in the 1950s, for instance, the term first referred to a tolerated form of self-policing in Black neighborhoods. In response to the growing role of gangs in local social life, groups of residents mobilized under the banner of the Vigilante League of Decency, the Vigilante Association, or the Peacemakers, aiming to combat theft and other offenses while playing a part in the moral rehabilitation of the townships.[36] The term, however, took on a derogatory meaning in the 1980s, coming to refer to violence perpetrated by the most radical opponents to the African National Congress.[37] Four decades later, it remains hotly contested and can be used both to praise popular security initiatives and to condemn the enforcers' abuses.[38]

The situation is considerably different in Nigeria, where since 1987, *vigilante* has officially designated "state-recognized citizen organizations that are more or less remotely controlled by the police or the army."[39] Far from being derogatory, it encompasses counterinsurgency groups enlisted to combat Boko Haram in the Lake Chad region; organizations such as the Vigilante Services of Nigeria, which are financed by state governors and patrol in uniform alongside the police; and at the local level, citizens involved in social control and surveillance, sometimes with total autonomy. Official recognition of vigilante initiatives reflects a double movement through which the "commodification of protection" is combined with the reinforcement of state control, resulting in the formation of "parapublic institutions."[40] One of the most notorious vigilante groups, the Bakassi Boys, was set up in the late 1990s at a market in Aba, southeastern Nigeria, by shoemakers and traders in leather goods seeking to defend themselves against criminality. Favoring merciless "instant justice"—the condemned are usually hacked apart by machetes and then burned—these vigilantes claim to use supernatural powers to expose the offenders. At first commanding respect owing to their integrity and their adherence to a "strict code of conduct," they spread throughout the states of Abia and Anambra and were soon being wooed by politicians to handle their dirty work.[41] Initially funded by traders and entrepreneurs, since 2000 they have been bankrolled by public funds and known as Vigilante Services, even State Vigilante Services. In Anambra State, in June 2000, a local politician lauded the positive impact of the "extrajudicial execution" by the Bakassi Boys of more than a hundred suspected robbers, opining that an "unconventional problem"—armed robbery—called for an "unconventional solution." A little later in the year, the state's governor directed citizens to "kill instantly any confirmed robber" and publicly criticized lawyers and nongovernmental organizations (NGOs) for condemning the vigilantes' methods when they "should rather condemn armed robbers who maim and kill innocent civilians."[42]

Another, more recent development pertains to digital vigilantism, which aims to combat delinquent behavior by exposing alleged offenders on social media.[43] This contemporary form of vigilantism covers a wide variety of practices, reflecting the technical possibilities enabled by computer technology and social media. Digital platforms provide a means to collect and widely disseminate data pertaining to reprehensible acts, suspects, and alleged perpetrators. This evolution mirrors the public policy trend of involving the population in the fight against insecurity. Police forces have in fact increasingly encouraged responsible citizens to report infractions and antisocial actions they witness. Considered the "eyes and ears" of law enforcement bodies, these community guardians have contributed to the development of a form of liberal governmentality in which the population has a responsibility for policing itself.[44] In the United States, the mobile phone app Vigilante, renamed Citizen after Apple removed it from its app store,[45] connects citizens on a network to increase their safety.[46] Participants are informed of calls to the emergency line 911 and urged to film the scene while waiting for the police to arrive. This reticular form of "DIY policing"—to use the clever expression of a Dutch start-up in the same niche market—seeks to stop a crime by filming it, according to a sales pitch for the product.[47]

Social network platforms also enable ordinary citizens to become involved in prosecuting suspects and even in hunting them down. The bombing at the Boston marathon in 2013 was a landmark in this regard: the day after the bombing, three thousand amateur investigators got together on a Reddit forum to identify the perpetrators. After the Federal Bureau of Investigation put out photographs of two anonymous suspects, the crowdsourced investigation led to the mistaken accusation of a student, Sunil Tripathi, who had disappeared at the time of the crime and whose family was subject to angry abuse.[48] The search for and dissemination of personal data to damage a target's reputation occurs elsewhere, such as in China where "human flesh search" engines run at full steam.[49] Disclosure of damaging information in that case amounts to "naming and shaming," resulting in "visibility" that is "unwanted" for persons targeted and likely to mar their reputation.[50] Advocacy groups such as Anonymous also resort to this tactic—known as *doxing*—for instance by leaking the personal data of police officers, Ku Klux Klan members, or more recently, supporters of the QAnon conspiracy group.[51]

As discussed in Chapter 2, there is sometimes a very fine line between the feverish collective hunt for suspects and lynching. Although many would-be law enforcers eagerly carry out their policing responsibilities by reporting suspected or averred infractions to authorities, not all are satisfied with simply acting as informants. Indeed, vigilantes may also be incited to punish alleged offenders on their own, in the name of a civic ideal or a critique of state performance. In such cases, "responsible" citizens turn into "autonomous" citizens,[52] less inclined to play by the rules and free from all institutional supervision.

IN THE NAME OF LAW AND ORDER

Vigilantes join forces to carry out patrols, detect infractions, hunt suspects, hand down sentences, and even punish culprits. They assert an ethics of individual responsibility and self-help that justifies their claims of coercive prerogatives to fight crime.[53] Professing to act on their own in the name of a group under threat, they use force or the threat of it to defend the established order—in its legal, political, moral, economic, sexual, or racial manifestations. This commitment likens vigilantes to "moral entrepreneurs" who enforce rules for want of being "rule creators" themselves.[54] Whereas some self-styled rule enforcers refer to the law to justify their acts (for instance, when they claim to be combating thieves or pedophiles), others defend moral precepts and are more akin to a cultural police, eager to protect the community from foreign impurity.

The causes taken up by vigilantes can be broken down into three main missions: protecting private property, defending territorial integrity and community norms, and asserting rights. In the United States, as previously discussed, vigilance committees have historically been the armed wing of local elites determined to prevent the plebeians from harming their property. In many contexts today—for instance, in Peru[55] and in Tanzania[56]—farmers and breeders anxious to protect their livestock are the primary clientele for vigilantes and also fill their ranks. In Nigeria, the marketplace is the Bakassi Boys' preferred field of operations: one grateful trader believes that their "instant justice" means he can now sleep easy, whereas he never expected the slightest aid from the police, whom he suspected of releasing thieves in exchange for bribes.[57] Another trader is more ambivalent about his support for the vigilantes, whose objectionable methods he views as a necessary evil: "Killing human beings is not good. The Bakassi Boys will go to Hell, but we thank God they're here."[58] Beyond protection of private property and businesses, vigilantes can help gain market share, including for illicit goods and services. In the state of Michoacán, Mexico, the *autodefensas* movement has been driven by the exasperation of local populations with the Knights Templar Cartel, but it also serves the interests of other drug traffickers, who have used it as a vehicle for a new criminal hegemony.[59]

Although pioneer imagery and the attendant glorification of frontier justice may seem specific to the United States, in many other regions vigilantes can come to serve as a border police. Defending community boundaries—in both the geographic and the anthropological senses—is central to such law enforcement endeavors. This explains these movements' xenophobia, holding foreigners primarily responsible for the ills they see around them. Well beyond the United States, vigilantism and racism continue to go hand in glove, and it is often for this reason that the term has derogatory overtones in national debates. In most of its contemporary forms, vigilantism tends to pit the guardians of nativeness against outside forces viewed as threatening. The Minutemen defend the US-Mexican border against an "invasion";[60] the Soldiers of Odin (a xenophobic group formed in Finland in 2015 that has branched out into an international franchise[61]) and La Meute in Quebec[62] portray themselves as bulwarks against the migrant peril; far right Russian and Greek groups[63] hunt down illegal immigrants;[64] and the *gau rakshak*, Hindu nationalist extremists dedicated to cow protection, mainly attack Muslims.[65] The insecurity attributed to migrants and refugees is a matter of concern on both sides of the English Channel for the vigilante groups Calaisiens en Colère and Sauvons Calais in France and for political organizations and video activists in Great Britain.[66] Foreigners, who are the usual "property"[67] of amateur law enforcers, sometimes simply come from a neighboring area, as research on the *autodefensas* in Mexico and the *rondas campesinas* in Peru has shown. Sometimes subtle distinctions are made—for instance, when vigilantes hierarchize their targets: the Arizona Minutemen distinguish between Mexicans crossing the border to try their luck in the United States and "coyotes," the unscrupulous people smugglers who are vigilantes' most prized catch.[68]

Vigilantes also seek to rid the community of undesirable elements. Enemies from within include drug dealers, accused of leading youth astray. This common form of urban vigilantism, present in Northern Ireland back in the 1970s[69] or in Alevi communities in Istanbul, exists also in post-Soviet countries, such as in Ukraine.[70] Antidrug crusades appeared in Russia early in the 2000s, when a businessman—Yevgeny Roizman, who later became the mayor of Yekaterinburg—forcibly weaned drug addicts off drugs, tracked down dealers in the Uralmash district, and had the support of the most influential local gang.[71] The visibility of these crusades increased in the early 2010s. The Youth Antidrug Commando became known for violent online videos illustrating its punitive expeditions. The script was elementary: The initial footage shows vigilantes delighted to meet up at a metro station exit and eager to begin their raid. Dressed in hoodies, they carry gym bags and smugly exhibit the weapons stuffed in them: pickax handles, hammers, axes, cameras, smoke devices, and paint bombs. The gang soon sets off toward the kiosk or parked vehicle used by the dealers. Then comes the moment to incite the infraction and gain evidence: using a hidden camera, one of the protagonists buys a bag of "spice"—a cheap synthetic drug popular with youth—and then, having obtained what he was after, waves it for his friends, who are waiting a little farther away, to see. The soundtrack changes suddenly as the adrenaline mounts, and in place of the vigilantes' voices comes a loud, aggressive musical score. They cover the kiosk with defamatory graffiti such as "Death sold here" and "I kill children with impunity," but that is not enough. They then wreck the premises and drive out the terrified occupant. Before leaving the place and after having called the police, they tie their victim to a pole, rough him up, and even slather him with indelible paint, with total impunity.[72]

Antidrug vigilantes raise the specter of an insidious enemy draining the community's lifeblood. The same anxiety arises in health-scare-related vigilante campaigns. Eager to protect loved ones' health from contamination, righters of wrongs seek to flush out and neutralize anyone spreading the disease. In Haiti in 2010, dozens of voodoo priests were killed on suspicion of actively spreading the cholera epidemic ravaging the country.[73] In keeping with a popular belief that "the one who cures an ill is also the one who causes it,"[74] medical personnel are also exposed to popular wrath when a health crisis strikes. This has been the case for frontline health care workers in the COVID-19 pandemic: occasionally threatened in France,[75] they have been sprayed with chlorine, insulted, or ostracized in Mexico and the Philippines.[76] In India, medical teams have had stones thrown at them when they attempted to approach patients, and funerals for doctors who have died from COVID-19-related afflictions have been met with violence in some areas.[77] Several Indian Muslim villagers have also been attacked, accused of undertaking "corona jihad" by deliberately spreading the virus among the Hindu population.[78]

The fight against the enemy within includes stamping out behavior that is not criminal but is perceived as particularly detestable. This is true of witchcraft, which, along with cattle rustling, is one of the preferred targets of vigilantes operating in rural areas from India to Peru via South Africa (see Chapter 2). Religious fundamentalists, for their part, campaign against what they regard as blasphemous works of art: in France, in 1988, several movie theaters screening Martin Scorsese's *The Last Temptation of Christ* were victims of arson; in Russia, in 2017, screenings of the film *Matilda*, about the relationship between a ballerina and Czar Nicholas II, canonized by the Russian Orthodox Church, stirred the ire of extremist groups such as Christian State and resulted in an attack on a movie theater.[79] In India, in the late 1990s, Hindu nationalists went after one of the country's most famous painters, M. F. Husain, whose depictions of naked goddesses shocked, particularly because the artist was a Muslim.[80] Under the pretense of defending the holiness of the goddesses, they protested the composite culture that forms the very foundation of Indian society's deep-rooted pluralism. The Hindu nationalist offensive also carries a strong patriarchal dimension. Its moral police particularly target works and artists accused of bringing disgrace on the Indian family (like the film *Fire*, which shows a sexual relationship between a neglected housewife and her sister-in-law[81]) or containing excessive obscenity (such as a young painter from the University of Baroda depicted in his works as mating with goddesses[82]). These vigilantes conflated defense of Hindu goddesses with defense of women in general. Niraj Jain, a lawyer affiliated with the Bharatiya Janata Party (BJP; Indian People's Party) who led the 2007 raid against the end-of-year exhibition by art students at the University of Baroda, thus claimed to be defending the honor of "mothers and sisters" and then added, like a good vigilante, "I defend Hinduism because others are scared to do so. The person who [tolerates] injustice is worse than the person who commits it. So here I am."[83]

Although vigilantism is generally associated with the championing of reactionary enterprises by dominant groups, it can nonetheless be a vector of empowerment for marginalized groups. This is evidenced by the rather ambiguous participation of a handful of women in a predominantly male environment that cultivates an extremely conservative conception of gender relations. The case of female Hindu nationalist activists brought to light by Atreyee Sen is in this respect highly disturbing. Departing from the role of victim that women are usually assigned in vigilante statements, female activists with the Shiv Sena—an extremist Hindu party known for its propensity for direct action—hide behind the organization's scandalous reputation to police the Mumbai slums, intimidating and even punishing violent husbands and employers demanding sexual favors. The advances in terms of security, empowerment, and mobility wrested by these activists from an organization that professes a resolutely patriarchal ideology are also reflected in a

CHAPTER 1

change in police attitudes. Afraid of offending the top guns of the dominant party, the police have been more conciliatory toward the female activists, going so far as to turn a blind eye to their illegal activities.[84] India's Gulabi (Pink) Gang, for its part, has tens of thousands of mostly Dalit members,[85] who have risen up under the charismatic leadership of Sampat Pal against domestic violence, sexual aggression, and the corruption of local officials. The vigilantes in pink saris have learned to wield the lathi—a bamboo baton used by the police and brutal henchmen in the pay of the wealthy—which has become their emancipatory emblem. This weapon not only symbolizes the group's authority but also embodies it in beatings that are doubly transgressive, because the humiliation of being thrashed by a woman is compounded by that of being dominated by a pariah.[86]

Some vigilantes more explicitly take up an emancipatory cause by claiming membership of a dominated group. "This Is Lebanon" is a project using digital vigilantism to defend the rights of migrant workers employed as domestic servants in Lebanon, particularly by exposing violent employers on social media. Founded by a former domestic employee from Nepal now based in Canada, the project aims to combat this form of exploitation through naming and shaming campaigns.[87] Feminist initiatives that followed in the wake of the #MeToo movement also fall into the "digilantism" (digital vigilantism) category, using social media to publicize the names of men accused of predatory behavior. In 2017, a law student in the United States, Raya Sarkar, created an uproar by posting on her Facebook page a list of seventy-two men in academia, the majority of them Indian, whom she accused of sexual harassment and rape—grievances that Sarkar says she verified by carefully gathering and examining the evidence.[88] The trivialization of online misogyny is another focus of action, as illustrated by the case of the Australian gamer Alanah Pearce, who responded to threats of sexual violence received via the Internet by alerting her persecutors' mothers.[89]

In these instances, monitoring, investigating, and disclosing do not preserve a threatened social order but, on the contrary, reverse a relation of dominance by supplying new weapons to those subjected to it. The vigilante in that case tends to merge with the activist who openly steps in for the law to put an end to injustice. The press, for instance, has expressed alarm at the rise of climate vigilantes[90] and animal rights vigilantes[91] and noted that clashes between breeders and vegan vigilantes[92] have also increased. Using *vigilante* in news reports disqualifies the tactics adopted by some activists who prefer to describe them as civil disobedience. The actions carried out in the name of the Animal Liberation Front—an advocacy label that a constellation of highly diverse groups and individuals claim to fall under[93]— took a more radical turn in the early 1980s in the United Kingdom, when laboratories, butchers, livestock farms, circuses, and slaughterhouses were subject to arson attacks and parcel bombs.[94] The history of the movement is, moreover, full of debates on the legitimacy of direct action, pitting non-violent activists against hardliners.[95] Vegan vigilantes fueled controversy in Australia in the late 2010s, when they illegally entered farms and burst into slaughterhouses, releasing penned animals and engaging in potentially violent clashes with breeders.[96] Actions of these kinds, which mainly cause material damage, share with classic vigilantism a determination to right wrongs or prescribe norms without concern for the legality of the means used.

VIGILANTISM IN ACTION

In the Arizona desert, beneath the beating sun, the Minutemen are waiting for "José," symbol of the criminal army and the poverty flooding the United States, bringing it to the brink of the abyss. José is an elusive figure: each minuteman on average encounters a migrant once in every fifty hours of patrol, and when contact is finally made, the watchful citizen can do nothing more than notify authorities of the US Customs and Border Protection, which has never been keen on these amateur border guards.[97] The Minutemen are patient nevertheless. Owing to the military background some of them have, and more generally their extensive hunting experience, they are practiced in the art of waiting. Although tracking their prey provokes strong emotions when the chase begins, the long phases of idleness that come afterward are equally crucial for the group's cohesion and the integration of new recruits. The moments of camaraderie spent killing time, on patrol, or in the evening around the campfire are not at all unpleasant. For veterans nostalgic for their glorious past, these moments provide an opportunity to relive their military days and share collective values.[98] Their military and hunting experience has also taught them to read a landscape. More than their firearms, however overabundant and sophisticated they may be, their preferred tool is their binoculars, if possible the night vision variety. Whether patrolling in a vehicle or parked to watch a spot, the hunter of migrants is out to catch his prey off guard. Knowledge of the terrain gives him a tactical advantage over both the enemy and the official security forces. A former Green Beret who enjoys a legendary status among the Minutemen—they say he can predict storms—reputedly knows every inch of this desert area so well that he can drive at night with no headlights, one hand on the wheel and his binoculars in the other.[99]

The hunting skills of many vigilantes are directly applicable to their activities as justice dispensers. One example is the Minutemen's practice of "lighting up" illegal migrants by blinding them with their flashlights—a deer-hunting tactic.[100] In West Africa, especially in Benin, Côte d'Ivoire, and

24   CHAPTER 1

Burkina Faso, hunting organizations (e.g., Dambanga, Dozo, Koglweogo) play a prominent role in crime fighting, sometimes with the tacit support of the state.[101] The vigilante lexicon is full of hunting references, amply illustrated by initiatives against pedophilia. Whether deployed in North America, Europe, or the post-Soviet space, they all have a common terminology: the hunters use decoys to trap their prey. *To Catch a Predator* was a television program that stirred considerable controversy in the United States from 2004 to 2008 by unmasking alleged pedophiles. This program served as the matrix for a vocabulary and modus operandi that circulated in the English-speaking world. Launched in 2004 by host Chris Hansen on NBC in conjunction with the organization Perverted Justice, which hunted down child molesters on social media, the program used hidden cameras to film adults who arranged meetings with minors to have sex. The "minors" were adults who stated during online chats that they were between twelve and fifteen years old. The teenager who greeted the potential predator at the arranged meeting would find a pretext to leave the room, at which time Chris Hansen would walk in, detain the "predator," question him, and read out the most scandalous passages of his correspondence with the girl (or boy). In most cases, law enforcement was also on the premises to apprehend the suspect. Controversial from the start, the program was taken off the air after the November 2006 suicide of an alleged predator trapped by Perverted Justice when the police and a film crew from NBC rang his doorbell.[102]

The program, a partnership of a television channel, an NGO, and local police departments, inspired other such initiatives. In the United Kingdom, Letzgo Hunting, a group that aims to "flush out devious and unscrupulous individuals like pedophiles and child molesters, or anyone who may be a threat to our children,"[103] masquerades as twelve- to fifteen-year-old girls and save their conversations as evidence. The confrontation with the adult who believes he is showing up for a meeting is filmed, put online, and sent to the police. The British media took an interest in the group when one of its suspects hanged himself after having been caught by vigilantes.[104] Other similar British vigilantes include Stinson Hunter, the hero of a 2017 documentary, *The Paedophile Hunter*.[105] In Canada, the group Creep Catchers reportedly has representatives in some thirty cities.[106] It was founded in 2014 by Justin Payne, a former construction worker turned champion of child protection who was inspired by *To Catch a Predator*. His YouTube channel The Payneful Truth offers videos in which alleged criminals are exposed and identified and has 185,000 subscribers.[107] In Belgium in 2018, YouTuber Gary Ducran also started going after sexual predators. Having snared a twenty-five-year-old man and shot him with a Taser, Ducran forced him to confess his crime to the police or else be left tied up on a soccer field in his underwear, with "pedophile" written in felt-tip marker on his chest. The video was such a hit that the vigilante went on to further exploits.[108] In France, antipedophile vigilantes made headlines twice in 2020: In February in Mont-de-Marsan, after creating a fake profile of a teenager on Facebook and accepting a request to meet in a park, a local couple filmed, using a hidden camera, their meeting with a forty-eight-year-old man they had trapped. Once the video was posted on the Internet, the suspect turned himself in to the police and the public prosecutor launched an investigation.[109] The punitive pluralism espoused by antipedophile vigilantes—in supplementing the lawful punishment with that of their own devising—came more starkly to the fore a few months later in Sainte-Geneviève-des-Bois, near Paris: After thrashing a man who had a rendezvous with a teenager, two vigilantes called the police before vanishing into thin air. On arrival, the officers found a man tied up, his face swollen and, next to him, his cell phone, with the screen showing a naked minor. Two separate proceedings were initiated: one for possession of child pornography images and corruption of minors, the other for assault.[110]

The hunt for pedophiles is not always turned into a show. Jewish Community Watch, founded in Brooklyn in 2011 by the Lubavitch community, conducts its own investigations. When it believes it has gathered enough evidence, it reveals the alleged molester's identity on the Internet, posting his picture on a wall of shame, which included over two hundred names in 2019.[111] A similar wall appears on the website of Hand Over a Pedophile, a project launched by Anna Levchenko, a young activist with ties to the Kremlin.[112] In the Netherlands in 2013, the NGO Terre des Hommes made headlines by designing a computer model of a ten-year-old Filipina girl, called Sweetie. Her profile attracted hundreds of thousands of men, over a thousand of whom were identified and reported to Interpol. The first convictions resulting from this operation were handed down in 2014, most of them in Australia.[113]

Vigilantes do not confine themselves to tracking people down; they also tend to take the law into their own hands, transforming neutralized suspects into culprits on whom they inflict their own punishments. Not all of them bother to observe legal norms, but some are remarkable for their procedural approach: in her observation of *rondera* justice in northern Peru, Emmanuelle Piccoli describes in minute detail the work of "commissions," which first torture suspects to force them to confess and then put them on trial—with an audience or not, depending on the case—before deciding on a punishment to fit the crime.[114] Whether they are the outcome of a bogus trial or are administered when the presumed culprit is apprehended, the punishments imposed are neither improvised nor completely random; they are pondered, justified, and ritualized. They conform to the formal conventions of penal rationality. Although vigilantes sometimes seize their victims' property, the punishments administered by the justice enforcers themselves—in addition to possible judiciary proceedings—generally take the form of corporal punishment.

Although critical of the police and in competition with them, some vigilantes call on law enforcement officials to deliver their prey. Beyond this facade of legalism, however, lurks an alternative conception of retribution, compensating for authorities' lack of diligence and severity with immediate additional, self-decreed sanctions. The examples of antipedophile justice in particular show the emphasis vigilantes place on putting the offender's identity and the nature of his crime out in the open. Although amplified by the development of the Internet, exposure is not new: many times, the vigilantes' prey is forced to parade around or stand with a sign around his neck pinpointing the punishable act he is accused of. Some practices involving the public humiliation of deviants and alleged offenders are reminiscent of the charivari or rough music rituals that were part of village justice in the British Isles and continental Europe until the early twentieth century.

The punishment is proportional to the gravity of the deeds and to the circumstances in which they were committed or to the personality of the offender and his entourage.[115] The Irish Republican Army's fight against juvenile delinquency during the Troubles provides a prime example. In the 1970s, republican activists punished not only informers and traitors but also drug dealers, car thieves, joyriders, and other delinquents. Their punishments included beatings, bullet wounds, tarring and feathering, and banishment. The vigilante arsenal was made up of baseball bats, pickax handles, drills, and hacksaws. The most subtle method was punishment shootings, which are believed to have affected nearly two thousand people—mainly young men—between 1973 and 1994, and are still being used since the ceasefire.[116] The term *kneecapping* subsumes variants: the part of the body affected, the number of limbs shot, the caliber of the gun used, and the position of the wound relative to the joint. In lighter sentences, the fleshy part of the thigh might be hit, whereas a more serious crime might entail damage to arteries and bones, resulting in a longer-lasting handicap. Repeat offenders were liable to be shot in the back of the knee, in the popliteal artery, a wound that, if not properly treated, can result in amputation.[117] Punishments were so common that articles were written on the medical treatment of the specific traumas they caused,[118] the stigma attached to the victims, or the supporting role of their parents.[119] The penal rationality of the Northern Irish vigilantes was thwarted by their inability to completely depersonalize their verdicts, given the tightness of the community under their control. The sentences dispensed thus varied according to the disciplinary measures expected from the relatives of the young offenders.[120]

Acts of vigilante violence are always publicized. Historically, on the western frontier of the United States, vigilantes defended their reputation by showing or describing the treatment they inflicted on horse thieves. This aspect has moved to an entirely different scale today with the use of digital technology, which is as conducive to staging punitive performances as it is to mere hype and short-lived shows of force. For example, the posting of a Soldiers of Odin video showing a half dozen activists patrolling the streets of the major French city of Bordeaux in October 2016 turned out to be simply a publicity stunt, after which the group was never again heard from.[121] For contemporary vigilantes, communication strategies and bluffing are an integral part of their negotiations with public authorities.

When they go into action, vigilantes perform degrading acts—shaving heads, administering beatings, exhibiting their victims in ridiculous getups or humiliating postures—before an audience, either on the village square or over the Internet. The body is tortured to underscore the abomination of the offender, in a spectacle of supposedly pedagogical or disciplinary value. As Tesak and the Youth Antidrug Commando exemplify, echoing David Garland's findings on "public torture lynchings" in the US Deep South in the early twentieth century, the punishments can be deliberately excessive, endowing them with meaning beyond the mere intention to punish an alleged offender.[122] By torturing his prey on-screen and denying him any rights, the Russian neo-Nazi vigilante Tesak belittled his victim and sent a terrifying message to all his targets, well beyond pedophiles, especially to gay people. The same is true for the Youth Antidrug Commando when they cover an alleged dealer of non-Russian origins with paint and feathers, replicating a conventional technique used throughout the history of vigilantism.

Indeed, together with ropes and whips, punishment by tarring and feathering is emblematic of the arts of rough justice, and variants can be found on every continent. From the ports of Europe to the New World frontiers, the history of this punitive practice follows that of navigation. Before the advent of tar, pine pitch and resin had made ships watertight since Greek antiquity, and large quantities were stored in boat yards and on vessels setting sail for the Holy Land and later for the colonies. Sailors and soldiers were both the first exporters and the first victims of this torture—from unruly participants in Richard the Lionheart's crusades in the twelfth century[123] to the British soldier in Dominica in 1789 expelled from his regiment for unnatural acts with a turkey and sentenced to wear the bird's feathers around his neck and in his beard.[124] Similar forms of popular justice could be found in rural czarist Russia up until the nineteenth century,[125] but it was during the American Revolutionary War that this painful but rarely fatal form of punishment came to be known as tarring and feathering. The practice became emblematic of

28   CHAPTER 1

US-style vigilantism, although found in many other contexts, especially in Northern Ireland during the Troubles.[126] Other occurrences are less easily traceable to the British Isles: up until the twenty-first century, in Lyari, a working-class district of Karachi, it was customary to tie abusive husbands to a post and smear them with tar.[127]

VIGILANTES ON TRIAL

Near the fountain on Bolotnaya Square in central Moscow amid the Friday-night revelers, Mikhail "Misha" Lazutin, the young leader of Lev Protiv (Lion Versus), takes a break. Surrounded by henchmen, his cameras have just re-corded several altercations with young people whom he has reminded that it is illegal to drink and shout profanities in public. Having been alerted by Lazutin of the offenses, the police had intervened earlier in the evening to chase after an inebriated delinquent who had reacted with fury to the vigi-lantes' provocation. A lull occurs between two rushes of adrenaline following the inevitable brawl provoked by the arrival of Lazutin and his brigade of spoilsports on the square: disinhibited by drink, the less aggressive youths use the occasion to start a conversation with the self-styled lawman, airing their grievances. They try to reason with him: "You're right in principle, but why do you do this? We could talk things over, work something out. Why do you go right to the cops?" "In one way you're a normal guy, and we can un-derstand each other, but in another . . ." Others try to rattle him, bombarding him with arguments they have pulled off social media and that everybody knows: "You edit out half the images," "You do it for the money," or, as one staggering drunkard bellowed over and over, "Misha, where's the 12 mil-lion?" referring to government subsidies the group was granted. Others do nothing to hide their feelings: "Everybody hates you!" screams a drunken young woman, to which Lazutin retorts, "My channel has one million sub-scribers, and most of them are young people." And when she resumes her of-fensive, "That doesn't mean they like you," Lazutin answers, "It's always been 50/50: half support me, the other half insults me. There's good and evil."[128]

Every vigilante on a crusade against evil inevitably arouses controversy over the coercive means and the purpose of the crusade. Would-be law en-forcers often need to be restrained. Tesak himself regularly had to bring his most enthusiastic fans to heel when they began instigating their own safaris in provincial cities where they lived. He urged them not to "mess up" pedophiles too much, to avoid "hitting them too hard," to "cut incriminating passages when editing," and not to yield to the temptation of "fleecing" their prey, or they might face legal proceedings.[129] The vigilantes' propensity for excess can have serious consequences. Unable to control themselves, high

THE VIGILANTE SHOW   29

on omnipotence or egged on by their cronies, self-appointed amateur law enforcers easily spin out of control. If breaking the law to maintain order is an integral part of their practices, the sometimes enormous discrepancy between the ends and the means always draws criticism, even in the ranks of the vigilantes themselves.

The controversy over Tesak's methods revolves around the legality of the means used and the effectiveness of this voluntary crime fighting. Victims, observers, and human rights champions all criticize vigilantes for their excesses and their propensity to play the lawman to let off steam. In the hunt for pedophiles, vigilante action stirs debate when a suspect commits suicide, as happened in the United States in 2006 or in the United Kingdom in 2013.[130] Insofar as vigilantes disclose the identity of their prey against their will, protests are also frequent: Jewish Community Watch thus had to remove an alleged offender from its wall of shame, after charges against him were dismissed.[131] Pointing out that some vigilantes are themselves former offenders, the police often criticize their summary methods on the grounds that the means used to flush out or neutralize alleged offenders are illegal and might also interfere with an ongoing investigation. The Canadian police used this line of argument against the pedophile hunter group Creep Catchers, stating that they were "not professionals," did not "understand the case law," and used questionable evidence.[132] This criticism, which recurs throughout the history of vigilantism, obliges would-be law enforcers to justify the legality of their practices. Even though they systematically denounce the limits of due process and the inability of the courts to fight crime, they generally try to minimize their deviations from the law. Lev Protiv vigilantes are particularly adept at this game. Intimidating and provocative, they do not hesitate to rattle off the article numbers of the Code of Administrative Infractions to violators and even sometimes embed the legal reference as a subtitle to their videos. "I'm warning you," Lazutin solemnly tells a drunken punk furious at having a spotlight trained on his face, "according to the law on self-defense, I have the right to use physical force if you use it against me. You've been warned."[133] And the threat is acted on instantly.

Criticism of vigilantism has two additional allegations, one pertaining to the groups' supposed autonomy and the other to their motivations. In the public mind, vigilantes act spontaneously and completely independently, exasperated with the spread of delinquency and the inadequacy or lack of law enforcement. This view is reflected in stock phrases describing their actions—they "take the law into their own hands" and "administer justice themselves." These dominant representations, however, do not stand up to the facts: less critical of the state as such than of "the state's actual performance,"[134] vigilantes may have covert ties with government actors or a

30   CHAPTER 1

segment of the local elite. Like the Bakassi Boys, they may even enjoy the direct backing of the authorities, in which case the phenomenon is known as state-sponsored vigilantism.

The trajectory of the *sungusungu* movement in Tanzania studied by Ray Abrahams shows how a local and spontaneous initiative initially criticized by official law enforcement bodies can eventually be co-opted and backed by the government. *Sungusungu* roved villages in the Nyamwezi region in the early 1980s, armed with bows and arrows to protect their community from cattle raiders, highwaymen, and witches. Those caught were sometimes tried, had to publicly confess their crime, and had to set the amount of their fine themselves or else be ostracized. Sometimes, particularly if they were suspected of witchcraft, they were executed. Whereas Tanzanian police officers and magistrates were critical of their autonomy, the country's socialist president described them as a "revolutionary force," more familiar with the terrain than officers of the law, and deserving to be encouraged. *Sungusungu* groups finally won legal recognition in 1989, entitling them to arrest suspects. They then began carrying out missions for the government, particularly tax collection.[135] According to another ethnographic investigation conducted in the 1990s in the northern part of the country (Tarime District), they were more popular than the police owing to their local embeddedness. They were less costly than corrupt police officials, were accountable to the community, and saved villagers from having to air their disputes out in the open.[136]

In Russia, three social projects undertaken by youth volunteers to combat lawbreaking in Moscow in the 2010s reflect the sham of vigilante autonomy, because for two or three years, depending on the project, they received government subsidies in an effort to encourage the development of civil society. In addition to Lev Protiv, StopKham (Stop a Douchebag) and Khryushi Protiv (Piggies Against) received such aid. StopKham combats rude drivers by placing stickers on their windshield to shame them, often provoking brawls with the drivers. Disguised as pink pigs, the female vigilantes of Khryushi Protiv prevent stores and supermarkets from selling out-of-date products.[137] Lev Protiv's government subsidies amounted to 12 million rubles—approximately 180,000 euros—over a two-year period. Investigations into Lev Protiv and the money it received, sometimes conducted by well-known bloggers and YouTubers, explains why a drunken reveler asked Lazutin, during one of his raids, to account for those "12 million." The three projects, which were highly popular among Russian youth, were all instigated by activists in pro-Putin youth movements in the early 2010s, although the loyalty of these groups to the Kremlin is not devoid of ulterior motives and fades when subsidies dry up. Vigilante-government collusion is highly volatile: the StopKham group was funded by the government for three years but was subsequently taken to court after several scandals.[138] Russian vigilantes act primarily to increase their business profits, and their loyalty to the government is conditional on the benefits they expect from their allegiance.

The rewards of vigilantism can have a more personal dimension, which fuels further allegations. Although they claim to be a cohesive group, vigilantes are also individuals in search of gratification who rely on their involvement to find employment or turn a profit. Vigilantism can lead to more or less stable jobs in the security sector, in private security firms, or in government service. Laurent Fourchard shows how women involved in neighborhood watches on the periphery of Cape Town, South Africa, build "local acquaintanceship networks that can be put to use for more lucrative tasks,"[139] such as providing security for private social functions. The reputation and know-how acquired can also launch a political career. For example, Anna Levchenko, discussed earlier, offers an acceptable alternative to Tesak and his followers. Since 2011, she has worked with the ombudsman for children's rights and with Duma members known for their reactionary stances. She is a consultant for the Civic Chamber[140] and director of a child protection initiative, obtaining government resources earmarked for NGOs.[141]

The job opportunities opened up by vigilantism also include the illicit rewards characteristic of law enforcement professions. Instead of combating offenders, vigilantes can join forces with them. Michael Fleisher describes several instances in which *sungusungu* illegally profited from their surveillance and policing activities, extorting cash from victims by promising to recover their stolen goods, turning a blind eye to cattle raiders' activities, and even giving them valuable information to help them commit their crimes, such as herders' sleeping habits.[142] The hunt for pedophiles is particularly conducive to blackmail because the punishments tend to fit the degree of its opprobrium. Thus, the enforcer often becomes a racketeer, as several incidents in the United Kingdom[143] and in Russia have shown.[144] Acts of extortion tend to increase when vigilantes believe—rightly or wrongly—that they have the government's backing. As Christophe Jaffrelot found, cow vigilantism in India is spearheaded by the Gau Raksha Dal (GRD; Cow Protection Movement), a Hindu nationalist organization whose emblem is the head of a cow flanked by two AK-47s. Primarily made up of young unemployed men to whom the organization offers a meager salary and a chance to recover some self-esteem, the GRD patrols highways and inspects trucks that might be transporting cows. If the driver is Hindu, he receives a mere reprimand, but Muslims are severely beaten. The GRD works hand in glove with the police while extorting victims.[145] Despite the police's relative softness since the BJP came to power in 2014, Prime Minister Narendra Modi himself took exception to the *gau rakshak*, criticizing those who, "to hide their bad activities, . . . don

32   CHAPTER 1

the mantle of cow protectors."[146] And indeed, some of the movement's leaders have run into trouble with the law, such as the GRD chief in Punjab, arrested in 2016 and accused of rioting, extortion, and sodomy.[147]

Whether villainous or not, the rewards of vigilantism sow doubt about the honorability of vigilantes' motivations. Are they truly seeking only to fight crime and stem the tide of insecurity? Does their activity bring them only the "moral satisfaction" of a citizen's duty accomplished, as a Lev Protiv member assured one of us?[148] Criticism of the subterfuges of vigilantism now takes into account the economic opportunities that digital tools offer vigilantes. Online vigilantism is potentially a lucrative business. Lazutin makes no secret of this: because government subsidies have dried up, he no longer describes Lev Protiv as the social project of a responsible citizen but as a full-time job. With 1.7 million subscribers to his YouTube channel in June 2020, the Lev Protiv brand has become profitable. He lives on the hosting platform's payments and runs his own advertisements during his filmed raids. His channel is his main asset, which explains his meticulous attention to the editing, the posting cycle, and the titles and thumbnails of his videos, intended as clickbait to entice his audience. With Lazutin, the vigilante has become a self-assumed entrepreneur who does not shy away from turning his security mission into a business venture. Famous as the leader of Lev Protiv, the young entrepreneur admits to his fans that his biggest regret is not having started his vigilante career under his real name.[149] And if Lazutin has become an influential YouTuber, it is partly thanks to Tesak: while still a teenager, he began his career by organizing antipedophile safaris inspired by the neo-Nazi, whose influence he now blames on his youth. In any event, Tesak in retrospect appears as a forerunner, one of the first vigilante-entrepreneurs to have grasped the huge moneymaking potential of digital vigilantism.

With smiling bear cubs frolicking in a field, the childish graphic design of the poster could be misleading: in fact it is an invitation to attend an Occupy Pedophilia party held by Tesak in late 2012 in a Moscow nightclub. In a video posted on social media, the neo-Nazi describes what is on the program:

> Hello, my dear fans of extremism. You are invited to the Occupy Pedophilia party on December 17, 2012, from 7 p.m. to midnight. What awaits you? Premieres of new videos, videos you have never seen on the Internet . . . , my stand-up routines, my music, a fun atmosphere, competitions. And a surprise also awaits you, a [man] that doesn't even know yet that we're going to ask him and that we'll do everything to get him on

stage. The evening is open to those sixteen and older; no one below that age is allowed to enter, so there will be no bait on the premises, sorry! Admission is free for girls, as part of our propaganda in favor of heterosexuality. . . . For everyone else, it's three hundred rubles.[150]

Before being sentenced and having to watch the liquidation of his official means of communication, Tesak was seeking to maximize the income he derived from his activity. A resolutely divisive figure, he posed a dilemma for his audience: on the one hand, it was hard to find fault with a plan to neutralize sex offenders; on the other, the scandalous pedophile hunter's propensity for exploiting his punitive enterprise for fame and profit cast doubt on his integrity. By using the Internet for mobilization and crowdfunding, advertising, the sale of auxiliary merchandise, training, and even fraud and blackmail, Occupy Pedophilia shed stark light on the potential rewards associated with vigilantism in the digital era. The success of such an enterprise depends on its renown as a brand, which is sometimes confused with its originator. This business strategy severs digital vigilantism from its roots, replacing the vague contours of an anonymous posse with the face of the leader who manages the lucrative enterprise in his own name.

The Tesak case also shows that financial gains may combine with political rewards. Whether they seek to enforce the law or subvert it, vigilantes aspire above all to earn respect, by crudely asserting authority through the use of force and more subtly by seeking approval from a wide audience. In the latter effort, vigilantism is akin to collective action in pursuit of activist goals, with legitimation that enables violent actors and groups to achieve recognition and negotiate their place in society. By claiming to protect children and the social body as a whole, by posing as the vehement critic of a figure even more revolting than himself, and by relishing the game of attracting media attention, this neo-Nazi activist provocatively postulates his social usefulness and turns vigilantism into a political act. In this he is emblematic of self-styled rule-enforcers who, by contributing to the common good and by posing as responsible citizens, attempt to smooth the rough edges that spoil their image and to gain acceptance for their social project in the service of an established order, a racist agenda, or more rarely, the emancipation of dominated groups.

By turning his safaris into a lucrative vigilante show, Tesak may have outlined the future of vigilantism, in which justice is served with a click. The care he took in communicating and staging his antics is comparable to another classic form of vigilante justice—lynching—in which the punishment administered in public by an elusive crowd produces another form of punitive spectacle.

2 LYNCH LAW

> Talking about public opinion, it's not a pretty sight either. Take the day of the reconstruction [of the crime scene]. People came to watch, egged on by newspaper headlines: "Pauletto the monster. . . . The vile murderer, etc." You shoulda seen 'em! They were shouting at me and throwing stones. They were ready to string me up. . . . The crowd was rocking the police van. I was in chains, tied up and left to myself. A mob is a terrible thing, it's dangerous and crazy. Criminal, too.
>
> ANDRÉ PAULETTO, whose death sentence for murder in
> 1981 in France was commuted to life imprisonment[1]

"TONIGHT, THIS IS WAR, BROS," Souleymane swore[2] on Snapchat as he followed a suspicious white van on route RN3 heading toward a camp in Bobigny, France. In March 2019 a rumor was spreading on social media: Roma, also called Romanians, or people from Eastern Europe, at the wheel of vans—white or red depending on the version—were kidnapping children to abuse them, force them into prostitution, or harvest their organs to sell. Individual accounts accumulated: one woman swore that her "little sister" almost got abducted, a man claimed that a "guy with a stick" tried to "steal [his] baby," and a third said that "three of [his] colleague's nephews almost got kidnapped today coming out of class." Facebook pages created for the occasion—"Parents soyez vigilants" (Parents be vigilant), "Parents vigilants. Vigilance parentale. Mes enfants sont les tiens!!!" (Vigilant Parents. Parental vigilance. My children are yours!!!), "Balance ta camionnette" (Report the van)[3]—relayed accounts of Roma roving junior high schools, up to no good. Online ads in which "Romanians" stated they would give up a kidney in exchange for a few thousand euros proved, in the eyes of worried parents, that a vast international network of organ traffickers was in operation. The wannabe detectives shifted into action and photos started to circulate, showing the license plate of the "van that kidnaps children" or handing over "the asses of the guys driving the red van" to mob justice.[4] Communiqués addressed to the "soldiers of the Clichy/Montfermeil area" called for action and urgently warned "Children stay home." In addition to grievances against the "Romanians" came criticism of police indifference: "The cops don't do a thing," "If we don't do something, who's going to do it for us?" "We'll do the pigs' job, but we'll do it differently." Rivalry incited bragging and a proliferation of declarations of war: "Tonight we'll rough up some Romanians," "trample them," "make mincemeat out of them."

Operations sometimes backfire. When youngsters armed with pickax handles and "long objects" gather at the entrance to a camp, they are chased off by its residents, alerted by the police that an attack is imminent. Several videos, however, offer evidence of severe beatings and the torching of vehicles; in one of the most-viewed videos, a group of men dressed in black stone a person lying in the front seat of a van. Described by the press as "Roma lynchings," the incidents have been corroborated by law enforcement officials, who stepped up their interventions. On March 25, the police were called to a vacant house in Clichy-sous-Bois where dozens of people were "armed with sticks, shovels, and stones." They also came across a group raining blows on their victims and saw "a huge, highly excited dog" sicced on Roma in a supermarket parking lot. The officers who arrived on the scene were themselves targeted by stones and blows. They had to throw two sting-ball grenades and use their billy clubs to calm the mob down. The following day, the public prosecutor in Bobigny announced that, following the spread of false reports that led to "acts of violence against the Roma community" and "retaliation," nineteen people were detained in police custody for "assault, intentional fire damage and armed participation in an unlawful assembly."[5] The police reported that "two people were unjustly accused and lynched," and human rights lawyers mentioned practices that stood "halfway between racial attacks and pogrom." On March 29, the Council of Europe urged France to exercise "vigilance" regarding acts of hatred against the Roma community.[6] That same day, the managers of the "Parents soyez vigilants" Facebook page issued a statement apologizing for their "insensitivity" and any "inappropriate terms" they may have used. Claiming to have "nothing against Romanians," they dissociated themselves from the "purges against people of tzigane/Romani/gypsy or other origin."[7]

———

Of all the forms of rough justice, lynching is the most infamous. The origin of the term is generally associated with Charles Lynch (1736–1796), a Virginia tobacco planter and colonel in the local militia during the Revolutionary War.

36   CHAPTER 2

In 1780, Lynch set himself up as a magistrate to protect lead mines needed for bullet production and coveted by Tory loyalists. In the face of this imminent danger, he meted out swift, uncompromising justice. In a letter of 1782, he used the expression "Lynchs [*sic*] law" himself, referring to the expedient methods required against "lawless men," whether they were traitors or unruly miners. In this early form of lynching, the penalty applied followed the whims of the elite, dispensing with "the tedious and technical forms of our courts of justice."[8]

The term came into widespread use a half century later. In 1835 in Vicksburg, the local militia, assisted by several civilians, went into a rough part of town called Kangaroo to settle accounts with a bunch of inveterate gamblers who had publicly dared to defy the authorities. Following a shootout, they strung up five of the gamblers. The tabloid press, then just beginning to flourish, wrote about a "lynching," giving it national resonance. Henceforth associated with the murderous rampage of a vengeful mob,[9] it was in this inflammatory sense that the term gained international currency. It began circulating, particularly in the British press, which covered the Vicksburg events and used it to refer to an intolerable form of extralegal justice that was part of US culture.[10] Its first occurrence in French, *loi de Lynch*, dates from 1837, and the expression subsequently gained considerable popularity.[11] At the end of the nineteenth century, French journalists and criminologists continued to view it as a "typically American phenomenon, luckily unheard of in Europe," "a law that reason and humanity condemn," and they remained reluctant to use the term to describe local incidents in which hostile mobs called for a criminal to be put to death.[12] The expression took on a defamatory connotation, coming to refer to a countermodel of justice in all the languages that have adopted it, whether Spanish (*linchamiento, lei de lynch*), Italian (*linciaggio*), Portuguese (*linchamento*), German (*lynchjustiz*), Russian (*sud Lincha*), or Japanese (*rinchi*).[13]

In the late nineteenth century, the meaning of the term changed in the United States. It came to represent racial violence against Black people in the South after the abolition of slavery. Widely documented photographically, lynching was denounced at home and abroad and criticized as an example of the deceits of US democracy. In the Soviet Union, especially in the early 1930s, condemnation of the practice spurred a national campaign demonstrating the barbarity of those who portrayed themselves as the voice of democracy:[14] "[The white man who calls himself 'an American'] will subject a black man who goes anywhere near a white woman to lynch law—that is to say, he'll tear off his arms and legs and roast him alive over a bonfire," wrote Vladimir Mayakovsky in his account of his travels in the United States.[15] In Japan, criticism of vigilantism in the United States increased after Congress passed a law in 1924 barring Asians from immigrating to the United States and increased further following the US stand against Japanese expansionism in Asia.[16] Having spread worldwide, the sinister legacy of Judge Lynch undermined the US claim to be the land of the free.[17]

The notoriety of Lynch law exceeds the scope of vigilante justice described in Chapter 1, although the two phenomena have obvious similarities. Proponents of such methods often choose the same targets: thieves, rapists, child abductors. They justify their actions using the same arguments: all decry the failings, remoteness, slowness, or leniency of the judiciary as an institution. And in publicly administering their punishments, they express a similar conception of popular sovereignty. However, as this chapter shows, lynching differs from vigilantism in three respects. First, it arouses all the more horror because it calls up visions of an angry mob, not a squad of volunteers on patrol. The specter of ochlocratic chaos, of a mobocracy[18] enshrining the rule of the populace, is never far off: the circulation of the term *lynching* in Europe echoes the terror inspired by "the power of crowds," "last sovereigns of the modern age."[19] Moreover, with Lynch law, the right to punish tends to be confused with the right to kill. As in the scene opening this chapter, not all lynching ends in homicide, but the murderous intention is always clear. Last, in response to the threat of division and dispossession, the punitive spectacle fully restores the social body in its integrity. The mise-en-scène sets a specific ceremonial designed for a large audience that is either physically present or that gazes at the event retrospectively through its visual traces in photographs and videos.

THE RELATIVE ANONYMITY OF THE MOB

In the collective conscience, Lynch law calls up the image of a volatile, murderous crowd in which anonymous participants, horrified by the crime they have heard about, gather spontaneously to punish the culprit. By circulating accounts that arouse disgust, rumor plays a crucial role in the formation of a lynch mob and the unfolding of the punitive act. The narrative it conveys processes information through stereotypes, generally racist, as was apparent in the reactivation in the greater Paris area in 2019 of the myth of the gypsy child thief, the first occurrences of which can be traced back to the fifteenth century. Borrowing from the lexical register of revelation and drawing on unofficial sources, the accusation is propagated most successfully through circles of acquaintanceship, creating a relational climate of confidentiality that bonds the community.[20] In his analysis of the slow killing of a young nobleman mistaken for a Prussian in the rural village of Hautefaye in southwestern France in 1870, Alain Corbin noted that the fairground was a place

38   CHAPTER 2

where isolated farmers would meet and could "experience the joys of their time-tested identity," "enjoy the pleasure of being together," and "relish in sharing rumors."[21] A century and a half later, in the greater Paris area, the viral circulation of news reports on social media electrified groups of young people taking part in punitive actions against "Romanians." The few first-hand accounts put online were supplemented by a torrent of secondhand testimony, including alarmist word-of-mouth reports, videos, and photos. Corbin's "joys of their time-tested identity" were also apparent: youngsters of Block 140 in Noisy-le-Sec, involved in a punitive raid on a Roma camp, named their Snapchat group 140 X Roumains (Block 140 against Romanians).[22] Rumors reinforce "social complicity"[23] by acknowledging the strangeness of an Other who cannot even be named.

The semantic field of explosion, eruption, and fire dominates the media analysis of lynching. Whether spark or trigger, rumors touch off the powder keg and ignite the fervor of the mob, who are swept away by a sense of appalling injustice. Yet popular justice is not necessarily all that spontaneous. It often follows a "familiar script,"[24] overturning the conventional distinction between routine vigilantism and impulsive lynching.[25] When the cry of "Thief!" rings out in a Nairobi slum—a scene that could take place anywhere—it has a performative effect: those present know how to decipher the alarm signal and draw conclusions from it. A crowd forms. Some grab the accused to extract a confession from him, heedless of his denials. They tie him up, start thrashing him, call for him to be burned alive, and if nothing interrupts this well-honed scenario, they instantly enact it.[26] The myth of the volatile mob is eroded in many contexts by indications that the punitive act was premeditated. Thus, some public lynchings that occurred in the US Deep South in the early twentieth century were formally announced by the press: "Florida to burn negro at the stake: Sex criminal seized from Brewton jail, will be mutilated, set afire in extra-legal revenge for deed";[27] "John Hartfield will be lynched by Ellisville mob at 5 o'clock this afternoon."[28] For John Hartfield's lynching, the newspaper reported that, owing to the governor's and the sheriff's inability to prevent an event likely to draw thousands of people, arrangements had been made with a delegation of citizens to ensure viewers' and residents' safety.

The organization of this punitive ritual generally relies on an elementary division of labor among the members of the crowd.[29] In the least spontaneous variants observed in the early twentieth-century United States, local notables took charge of organizing a lynching, negotiating the sequence of events with the sheriff or other local law enforcement representative, who promised to direct traffic when the audience arrived by automobile in large numbers. For the public execution of the victim, the event's organizers turned to footloose youngsters and people at the bottom of the social ladder (store clerks, café owners, unskilled workers, and day laborers), recruited "in pool rooms and bars." The executioners were spurred by a third group, the spectators, often somewhat older men and women, who clamored for the culprit to be punished.[30] Close scrutiny of the crowd reveals those who egg on and assist the executioners, those who gather around the vigilantes and share their aims but do not partake in the violence, and those who remain at the back, either because they feel less concerned about the issue or are too afraid to come near. Even the most timid spectators contribute to the scene by helping create an "attention space" converging toward the center, occupied by the most self-assured and determined lynchers, bursting with enthusiasm and a sense of initiative.[31] In a trial following the lynching of Roma in Île-de-France in 2019, one of the defendants, who was ultimately acquitted, defended himself by explaining that he had joined the troop because he supported the plan to punish the Roma, but he had not taken part in the punitive act himself:

> I ran into guys on the road who said they were looking for Romanians to stop them kidnapping children. . . . I knew they were looking for a fight, but I agreed with the principle of stopping Romanians from kidnapping children.[32]

Whereas vigilantes claim to be protecting a reference group that is not necessarily present when they neutralize an alleged thief, lynchers do their best to involve the crowd. The crowd transcends social class to embody the unshakable unity of an outraged community. "Should the residents . . . again suffer the aggression of antisocial elements, we will rise up as one man [*como un solo hombre*] and punish this act," a Bolivian proponent of summary justice declared in the mid-1990s.[33] This archetypal formula disregarded the preponderant role women played in meting out punishment, though, because it was often they who burned thieves alive in the barrios.[34] Such unanimity increases anonymity and complicates the task of law enforcement officials on the rare occasions when they look for culprits, because difficulty in pinpointing the violent few in the crowd guarantees the impunity of the instigators.[35] As well as disinhibiting executioners and audience, "the strategic use of anonymity"[36] also works in favor of investigators who can hide behind it to justify their inability to identify the lynchers.[37] A report by the Bolivian police offers an apt illustration of the benefits of anonymity, including for the authorities: "Clearly it was impossible to identify any individuals given the dangerous circumstances of the moment and besides that no one present, neither men nor women, would give out their names and what's more they shouted: 'We are all responsible.'"[38]

40   CHAPTER 2

One must nevertheless beware sweeping generalizations, because anonymity is always relative: the inquisitional eye the mob avoids is the eye of the state. Lynchers may well be convinced of their impunity, but they are aware of the objectionable nature of their deeds. They seek to shield themselves from prosecution but act openly in the eyes of the community. The supposedly anonymous crowd taking part in a lynching is often made up of individuals who live in the same village or the same neighborhood—a sphere of mutual acquaintance in which each person can observe the others' contribution to building the local moral order. Interpersonal ties in such circumstances are "as opaque to the authorities as they are indispensable to sustained collective action."[39] In this "intimate crowd,"[40] lynching gives rise to negotiation and brokering that sometimes lead to revisions of the initial script. In particular, righters of wrongs may readjust their decisions according to the victim's identity—or their interpretation of it.

The anthropologist Sarah-Jane Cooper-Knock recounts the story of Blessing, a young orphan who in 2010 makes a living by stealing to buy his daily dose of *whoonga*[41] in a Durban township in South Africa. His friend Sifiso is a drug addict who lives by sponging off his mother. Furious that her meagre possessions are disappearing, the mother accuses Blessing of leading her son astray. The accused is sound asleep when a dozen men break into his home, drag him out, and begin assaulting him. They take him to Sifiso's house, where Sifiso, his mother, and other residents continue beating him. Both of Blessing's legs are already broken by the time his aunts burst onto the scene. Sifiso's mother repeats to them her accusation, which she will later retract so as not to compromise her own son in the ongoing investigation.[42] In this instance of mob justice, the preexisting ties between protagonists are the basis of justice. The victim's membership in the community plays an essential role, because outsiders with no local support are dealt with much more severely. The role of the accused's household is also crucial: the parents of a thief are expected to punish their son and compensate his victims, or else they will be subjected to street justice themselves. The lyncher's profile is not neutral either: Sifiso beats up his childhood friend as a means of redeeming himself in the eyes of his community and "renegotiating [his] own place in the moral order."[43] However, in this community younger people think hard before taking active part in a lynching, because their social networks—via school and other associations—might overlap with those of the victims and leave them open to reprisals. As one of them explains,

> I just stand there and watch [street justice]. You know those people if they know you—and I am at that age [where] they know you—and let's say I am beating you then [they] are going to tell [their] friend that Sonto

was there, so they can . . . come to me you know. So I just stand far away and watch.[44]

Lynching gives expression to a variety of grievances. For the dominant group, it reasserts their subordination of others, and the dominated can invest it with a message to the authorities. The lynchings that took place in the late nineteenth century and the early twentieth century in the southern United States are emblematic of the first instance. They are a manifestation of urban White people's resentment and their concern with reasserting their supremacy at a time when Black people were being emancipated and threatening to compete with them and the traditional forms of authority—patriarchal dominance, religion, the plantation elite—were being undermined.[45] Lynching is not, however, the preserve of a dominant group fearing loss of status: recurrent in the poor areas of certain large cities, it is a weapon for the oppressed as well, who are also concerned about the evolution of their status in societies subjected to the shock of liberalization in recent decades. Branded as the fetish of neoliberal experiments in self-help and responsible citizenship, the "community" temporarily coheres in the radical assertion of its right to punish. In fact, no collective act better affirms popular sovereignty than the "ceremonial of public punishment" contesting the state's claim to monopolize the "right of the sword."[46]

In the mid-1990s, a mother, her seventeen-year-old daughter, and her eighteen-year-old son traveled to a barrio on the outskirts of Cochabamba, Bolivia, to collect a debt. While they were waiting, Monica, the daughter, killed time by visiting an unlocked home. She stole a radio–tape player, a jerrycan of gasoline, a small stove, and a few blankets. A neighbor saw what was happening and shouted out an alarm, which immediately prompted the local residents to come out and gather with shovels and stones. After beating the three thieves, they tied them to a utility pole, cut off their hair, doused them with gasoline, and threatened to set them on fire. Police officers rescued the accused at the last minute, but they, too, faced a hail of stones. When the police went back later to investigate, they were greeted by the law of silence and were threatened with the same treatment as the offenders if they pursued an investigation.

According to the anthropologist Daniel Goldstein, this lynching aimed to dissuade thieves while sending a "clarion call" to the authorities.[47] In this "form of public protest" against institutions deemed incapable of ensuring their citizens' security, the victims are scapegoats who pay for "much larger social evils."[48] In defying the police by the brutality of their methods, lynchers subscribe to "a perverse form of community empowerment"[49] and convey demands in the name of poor and marginalized populations abandoned by the state. They render justice to reassert values they feel are threatened and to emphasize their rights, particularly the minimal provision of security.[50] The authorities discredit these outbursts of violence, ascribing them to the savagery of the poor. They also invoke the barbarism of customary justice applied within indigenous populations, which the latter refute, emphasizing that lynchings are a relatively recent phenomenon. However, the negative image of the neighborhood or the community that recurrent lynchings convey does not entirely displease its residents. In the Bolivian barrio where the incidents occurred, many women admitted that they didn't mind if their barrio had a bad reputation, whether or not they were actively involved in the punishments. They felt that if its residents were described as savages, delinquents would think twice before venturing there and would go elsewhere to commit their crimes.[51] These interpretations of lynching have the merit of integrating them into everyday subaltern politics. They are, however, overfunctionalist and tend to downplay the transgressive aspect of the punitive act: whatever the justifications offered, lynching is a sovereign act of violence that involves appropriating the right to kill for oneself and one's group.

THE RIGHT TO KILL

On February 23, 2020, Ahmaud Arbery was jogging in the streets of Brunswick, Georgia, when he crossed paths with Gregory McMichael, his son Travis, and their neighbor and friend William Bryan. Believing that the twenty-five-year-old African American was responsible for a series of robberies in their neighborhood, these three White vigilantes, armed with a shotgun and a Magnum .357, followed him in their two cars and intercepted him. During the ensuing altercation between Arbery and Travis McMichael, several shots were fired before the young African American collapsed. Arriving on the scene, law enforcement officials took a statement from Gregory McMichael, a sixty-four-year-old former police officer and retired investigator for the district attorney's office. He swore he had previously seen Arbery roaming the neighborhood and claimed that he'd seen him snooping around a house under construction before deciding to intervene; last, he stated that the young African American had tried to grab his son's weapon and that he was then obliged to defend him. None of the three would-be lawmen were further investigated by the police until a video of the incident taken by Bryan was posted on the Internet in May and went viral, leading to the arrest of the trio, only days before the George Floyd affair relaunched the Black Lives Matter movement. This apparently run-of-the-mill racist murder was labeled a "lynching" by the victim's father and by civil rights activists, Atlanta's mayor, a former Republican governor, and the then Democratic presidential candidate Joe Biden. Although no mob was present, White people had once again assumed the right to kill a man because he was Black.

Lynching has no legal existence and, though similar to other forms of collective violence—rioting, pogroms, vendetta, honor crime, hate crime, and so on—resists definition. It tends to thrive in violent contexts—armed conflict, regime crises, social upheaval—in which recourse to murder becomes commonplace and where the most common form of justice involves settling scores on one's own. Executions of Black people in the southern United States at the beginning of the twentieth century took place in a conflictual environment, where they were also targets of murder and beatings that cannot be called lynching, despite obvious similarities.[52] The waters are also muddied when the event is embedded in violent acts that transcend it. The boundary that separates a lynching from a pogrom appears particularly porous from this standpoint. As mentioned previously, the term was used by a lawyer to describe the series of attacks against the Roma in the Île-de-France region in 2019. The usual distinction between a pogrom, which targets persons for their membership of a hated community, and lynching, which aims to punish the perpetrators of a crime, does not always stand up to examination. In fact, the permeability of these practices is plain to see—for instance, in postcommunist Romania, where Roma are accused of every crime in the book. In 1993, after a fight between different communities in Hădăreni, Transylvania, in which a Romanian man died, Roma men accused of harassing village girls sought shelter in a house that was set on fire by their Romanian and Hungarian attackers. Attempting to escape the flames, three of them were caught and lynched. Thirteen houses burned down, prompting the Roma community to leave the village.[53] The connection between personal vengeance and collective punishment was already clear in the southern United States at the beginning of the twentieth century, where an incident officially recorded as a lynching might be accompanied by "other deaths by shooting during a manhunt, in reprisal" and could degenerate into "a riot or general racial attack."[54] In 1922, after the hanging of three Black men accused of rape, a climate of "White terror" descended on Kirven, Texas, and lasted for nearly a month: "All the Black people within a five-mile radius were hunted down and sometimes shot," several corpses were found, and "a pogrom atmosphere reigned over all of east Texas."[55]

Activists were keen to establish a definition of lynching to counter the vagueness of the notion and the dearth of related legislation. In the United States, such efforts were bound up with advocacy against racial discrimination. From the standpoint of civil rights activists, a consensual definition was crucial for identifying the incidents and producing the statistics they needed to draw attention to their fight. Lynching had to be dissociated from other forms of collective violence. This gave rise to endless quibbles: must the victim have necessarily been killed for the use of the term to be appropriate? Can it be used if the victim is already dead when hanged in public? Should a Black man accused of rape and killed by the police under the pressure of the mob be counted in the statistics? When lynchers act as a group, how many participants does it take to consider it a lynch mob? To put an end to these ongoing quarrels, the main organizations involved in the fight against lynchings met in 1940 at the Tuskegee Institute, a private university devoted to educating Black students. The National Association for the Advancement of Colored People (NAACP), the Association of Southern Women for the Prevention of Lynching, and the International Labor Defense finally agreed to a restrictive formulation: for a lynching to have occurred, a court must find that a person was murdered by a group of at least three people acting "in service to justice, race, or tradition."[56] This formulation was little more than window dressing and did not actually yield any progress—few people used it and activists reverted to their own definitions. Eighty years later, the terminology battle that ensued following Ahmaud Arbery's murder in Brunswick, Georgia, showed that the debate was far from settled.

The right to kill that lynchers appropriate is not entirely arbitrary; it punishes a crime, sanctions violation of a social norm, or carries out revenge. Although Lynch law may be underpinned by a radical critique of the judicial process, it nonetheless involves a notion of legality. By claiming to act according to "the people's will," lynchers are convinced they are "upholding the law and not violating it."[57] When one of the people, quoted earlier, attacking Roma in the Paris area wrote that he was going to "do the pigs' job, but . . . do it differently," he implied that violence would soon be unleashed while expressing his support for a certain conception of punishment. Criminal proceedings are replaced by impromptu action orchestrated by "their majesties the mob"[58] and carried out by volunteers who dispense with formalities. The rules applied are sometimes rather convoluted: in 1939, in Walhalla, South Carolina, the crowd that gathered around a prison to seize a detainee waited until their number reached one hundred before attacking, deeming this number enough to justify their action.[59] The fundamental elements of a judicial proceeding are indeed present—an accusation is formulated, evidence is produced, a verdict is declared, and a sentence is handed down—but because the practice involves the presumption of guilt, it is heavily biased in favor of the prosecution, leaving no room for the defense, no opportunity to hear the accused's point of view, and no possibility of appeal. Confessions are obtained through torture; the self-appointed judges impose their views on the basis of their personal authority rather than their assessment of the lawfulness of the acts being judged, and the impromptu jurors are in league with the prosecution. In this travesty of justice, it is passion that presides over the trial.[60]

As can be seen in Fritz Lang's *Fury* (1936), John Ford's *Young Mr. Lincoln* (1939), and Arthur Penn's *The Chase* (1966), the imagery of lynching is rife with mobs storming a police station or a prison to seize an alleged thief, rapist, or child kidnapper and put him to death. The challenge posed by the mob to the police is likely to turn into physical confrontation. This classic representation reflects actual events observed in two distinct moments in the lynching sequence. The first is when the mob grabs a detainee, as in Hollywood movies. In February 2008, in Chimoio, Mozambique, a mob of angry residents stormed a police station where twelve suspected criminals had been jailed the day before. The arrests were not enough to reassure the vigilantes, who believed the police would be too lenient with thieves suspected of using witchcraft to carry out their evil deeds. When events turned violent, six people died, including one police officer, the police station was partially destroyed, and several vehicles were damaged.[61] Confrontation with the police can also arise when law enforcement officials turn up at the site of the lynching to remove the victim, dead or alive. This is what occurred in the supermarket parking lot in one of the scenes described in the first pages of this chapter, in which police intervention sparked a violent reaction from a gang beating up a Roma man.

But the image of sovereign popular justice, in which the mob confronts law enforcement officials, is also a cliché, because in many situations the police explicitly or tacitly endorse the punishment out of like-mindedness or self-interest. Whether it is direct organizational assistance, tacit agreement, or an opportune absence, local police support is decisive. In some cases, law enforcement officials encourage residents to administer justice themselves, condoning the extralegal exercise of the right to punish and even inciting the vigilantes. In May 2008, in a barrio of Chimoio, a police officer in charge of a thief who had narrowly escaped being burned was reluctant to take him to hospital and chided his lynchers: "Why did you not burn him? You should end these things here."[62]

Beyond police support, vigilantes are more generally eager to obtain the assent of authorities likely to greenlight their punishment, as can be seen in two cases of *keroyokan*, or mob justice, in Indonesia. In the village of Gambut, in southern Kalimantan, an aging notable married a young woman who cheated on him with a man from outside the village. Neighbors noticed the wife's comings and goings, and Mat, the nephew of the wronged husband, soon discovered the lovers' secret meeting place. Over the next three weeks, without saying a word to his uncle, Mat consulted with members of his family, the neighbors, the wife's parents, the local police, religious leaders, and the

46   CHAPTER 2

village headman to secure their approval before serving justice. With Mat leading, a group of some twenty people dragged the lover out of his hiding place, beat him, paraded him through the streets, and let him know he was no longer welcome in the village. He was then turned over to the police, who released him soon after.

Fate was not as kind to Shaiful, burned alive in 2003 at age twenty-one in Indramayu, a village in northwest Java. The unemployed young man lived with his sister Mariah, who felt shame at his multiple petty thefts in the neighborhood. In exasperation, she went to Osman—a schoolmate of Shaiful's who had a job in a nearby city—and begged him to talk sense into her brother. Returning to his native village, Osman lectured Shaiful and urged him to fall in line. When Mariah contacted him again some time later to report that her brother had tried to steal a neighbor's bicycle, Osman again returned to the village and consulted with the family, the village headman, and religious leaders. All believed that Shaiful deserved to be punished. Fortified by this collective decision, Osman collected press clippings about local popular justice and opted to administer the punishment he considered most appropriate: death by fire. Six people went to the home of Shaiful, who confessed. After forcing him to repent before God and his sister, who was watching from afar, Osman threw a match on the gasoline-soaked clothing of his childhood friend.[63]

Studied by the political analyst Bridget Welsh, these lynchings were the result of a complex interplay of guarantees, in which the right to kill depended on collective endorsement. The approval of religious leaders is all the more valued because it authorizes transgression of positive law by referring to divine justice. By indicating their concern for finding the most appropriate punishment, Mat and Osman also intended to be acknowledged as legitimate punishers. Mat took over his uncle's business after the uncle relocated with his wife following his rival's thrashing. Osman, for his part, became an accomplished moral entrepreneur, taking part in the punishments of five alleged culprits.[64]

The support or passivity of religious authorities toward lynchings occurs in other contexts. Until the 1910s and 1920s, most southern churches in the United States avoided taking a stance on the issue. More evangelical leaders spoke out against lynching in later decades but still "largely assented to the worst of white southern racial views," showing understanding for these acts.[65] In postrevolutionary Mexico, the role of local priests in igniting the sentiments of churchgoers and provoking lynchings was framed as a political issue: according to the government press, such barbaric acts resulted from the opposition of the highest ranks of the Church to "the implementation of socialist education . . . and the defanaticization of the masses." This political interpretation did not absolve the priests from responsibility, however, and they were held up as "a moral compass that helped delineate the boundaries between acceptable and unacceptable behaviors, norms, and ideologies."[66]

The punishments inflicted by lynch mobs are often terribly cruel. Lynching can be likened to an "aggravated form of capital punishment," an inherently excessive public execution aiming to bring about the victim's death and, beyond that, "the debasement of the person and the desecration of his body."[67] Such spectacular, collective forms of punishment are clearly at odds with accepted theories about penal evolution and the civilizing process—especially those of Foucault, Durkheim, and Elias, for whom violent public punishment started to decline in modern Western societies from the late eighteenth century onward. Contrary to these assumptions, the lasting global appeal of lynching attests to an enduring trend that has largely escaped the attention of historians of punishment: the persistence of a "self-consciously uncivilized penal conduct,"[68] which existed in tension with long-term trends toward penal modernization.

In the most extreme cases found in the United States, the "crime of lese majesty"[69] allegedly perpetrated against the White community justifies stripping the victim, shaving him, and mutilating and torturing him until he breathes his last. Among the methods used to put someone to death, purification by fire seems to be preferred by contemporary lynchers in Asia, Latin America, and Africa. In Mali, "article 320 of the accelerated street code of procedure"—320 CFA francs being the price of a liter of gasoline and a box of matches—refers to a common method of popular justice applied to thieves. In Kenya, in the Korogocho slum of Nairobi, thieves are lynched by fire in a place nicknamed Golgotha, referring to the methods of torture administered there.[70] In Indonesia, Osman's decision to subject Shaiful to death by fire reflects the belief that the sufferings inflicted on the guilty linger in the hereafter.[71] Such religious symbolism, interpretations, and justifications also infused the punitive rituals of lynch mobs in the US Bible Belt,[72] which re-created "divine judgment on earth" and enacted the damnation that was undoubtedly awaiting Black criminals after death.[73] They were also invoked by Catholic mobs and vigilantes targeting Protestants, socialist teachers, and individuals accused of blasphemy in postrevolutionary Mexico.[74]

THE SPECTER OF DISPOSSESSION

Even though women are not spared, especially when accused of witchcraft, and men in the community are occasionally punished for their crimes, the archetypal victim of lynching is usually a man seen as strange, and often a stranger. Victims may belong to a different ethnic group or come from a distant place, they may be physically different or look disturbing in some way, but in every case they are punished for what they are: Black, a vagabond, a migrant, an albino, a homosexual, someone possessed or mentally ill. Abnormal and inherently suspect, "it is not so much his act as his life that is relevant in characterizing him."[75] As many examples in this chapter show, the absence of guarantors seals the victim's fate because no one recognizes him or intercedes on his behalf. Hostility toward vagrants and foreigners is also rooted in the suspicion of disloyalty aroused by their mobility. In Indonesia, for instance, in the years following the fall of General Suharto, the fury of "wild mobs" (*massa diamuk*) descended on people with no territorial attachment, who escaped the moral and bureaucratic framework of sedentary citizenship—those "floating individuals who are . . . sometimes this and sometimes that, sometimes here, sometimes there."[76]

Lurking behind lynching is the specter of dispossession. When the cry of "Thief!" rings out in working-class neighborhoods, it resonates with the shared experience of alienation, evoking a state of extreme vulnerability in which people's meager possessions—not only their property but also their flesh and the flesh of their flesh—are constantly in danger of being taken away from them.[77] The image of the thief who stole children, discussed earlier in the context of Roma lynching attempts in the Paris area in March 2019, is prominent in this anxiety-inducing imagery. Rooted historically in medieval representations—Jews were accused of stealing children to take their blood for ritual purposes, whereas the Roma were suspected of abducting them to raise as their own—this representation has taken hold today worldwide, from France to Mozambique and from India to Mexico. Rumors of child kidnappings for organ trafficking are fueled by conspiracy theories about international predatory networks.[78] The lynching of two traveling salesmen in the state of Hidalgo, Mexico, in the late 1990s resulted from a rumor circulating that "the men weren't salesmen at all but foot soldiers in a Texas-based ring of child kidnappers who not only trafficked in organs but had a liver or two in the cab of their truck, for which they were said to receive the awesome sum of $1,500 . . . apiece."[79] The child kidnapper is stealthy and motorized: to perpetrate his hideous crime, he travels in a small truck or van in which he can easily hide his prey. In an echo of the rumors that spread throughout the greater Paris area in 2019, residents of a shantytown in Timbaúba, in northeast Brazil, justified their dread of organ thieves by describing "large blue and yellow vans driven by Americans, sometimes by Japanese agents, who were said to be scouring poor neighborhoods in search of stray youngsters."[80]

The child snatcher is sometimes conflated with the wizard or the witch, another classic target for lynchers. Nightmarish figures par excellence, these specialists in the occult throughout the ages have embodied the collective fears of the moment. The etiology of sorcery provides a simple answer to unexplained individual and collective woes. In contemporary societies facing a sudden rise in precarity and inequality, especially after neoliberal reforms, the hostility these hated figures inspire also reflects concerns over the sources and distribution of wealth. The fight against witchcraft asserts an ideal of redistributive justice and a moral vision of success, and young men, often on the front lines, find in such campaigns an opportunity to settle accounts with a gerontocracy they accuse of depriving them of a future.[81] These fears and aspirations were manifest in the events that occurred in 2009 in Beira, Mozambique's second-largest city. Hostility had been mounting for several months against Boss Candrinho, a wealthy businessman known for his ostentatious spending habits. The rapid and mysterious increase in his prosperity aroused suspicions of witchcraft, and the rumor was that he kidnapped children to harness their life force and sell their body parts for a profit. When the police finally decided to bring him in, a crowd gathered around the station where he was being held, with the intention of seizing him. "Here in the prison he is just going to disappear," one female participant explained. The vigilantes were unable to achieve their goal, but the confrontation with the police descended into a riot.[82]

People suspected of witchcraft who fall into the hands of a mob are particularly unfortunate, because they often receive the cruelest punishment. This was the case in rural nineteenth-century Russia where, unlike other victims of peasant justice, women suspected of witchcraft were not merely humiliated by a charivari in the village streets but burned alive.[83] In Indonesia, during the turmoil that followed the resignation of Suharto in 1998, alleged sorcerers, witches, and so-called ninjas were tortured at greater length than other targets of *keroyokan* before being put to death, as happened to Saprudin, a man in his forties accused of black magic. Exasperated by his incessant comings and goings and the stench coming from his house, his neighbor Hussin issued the accusation and then, once he was assured of the local authorities' support, took charge of his execution. After stabbing him repeatedly with a parang, the mob decapitated him to release the evil spirit that inhabited him and then began a game of soccer using his head as a ball. Children who had complained that Saprudin had confiscated their ball when it bounced into his yard were invited to join in.[84] The punishment applied here blended elements of restitutive justice—the offense to the children had to be redressed—and cathartic exorcism.

The anxiety of dispossession associated with suspicions of witchcraft is reflected just as crudely in the moral panic caused by "sex thieves" in West Africa. According to the anthropologist Julien Bonhomme, some fifty lynchings were reported in nearly twenty countries, mainly in West Africa during the 1990s and the next decade.[85] The presumed victims were young men less than thirty years old and children who, in broad daylight and in crowded, congested places (markets, shared taxis), suddenly and publicly complained that their genitals had disappeared or shrunk following physical contact with a suspicious stranger, often foreign to the local community and simply passing through. Here the accusation was not based on a rumor but on the lived experience of physical contact that instantly aroused "the crowd's solidarity regarding the stolen genitals."[86] While the victim was lying on the ground or ran away, the alleged perpetrator was summarily executed. The purported thieves' focus on genitals reflected their desire to convert the life-giving potential of these organs into material wealth and political power, echoing the accusations leveled against Boss Candrinho in Mozambique. Often associated with the abduction or murder of children, the sex thief forces the community to face the specter of its own demise: whether "through its young or its genital organs, it is the group's very posterity that is under threat." This moral panic falls within a more general register of existential worries: "Last year, it was the story of disappearing penises and breasts. . . . This year, child killers are the ones hitting the headlines."[87]

The madman concludes this list of strange men exposed to the rough justice of vindictive crowds. In India in the late 2010s, people suffering from psychiatric disorders were prone to accusations of abducting children and featured prominently among the victims of lynch mobs. But it is with the bizarre case of Alextime that the fusion of the outsider and the deranged reached its peak. Born in 1975 in the Moscow area, Alexei "Alextime" Makeev achieved a degree of fame in his country by posting videos on YouTube in which he gave free rein to his paranoia. Convinced he was being targeted by a vast "terrorist" plot, he would bump into people—of all ages—who happened to be in his way and insult them while constantly filming. In one of his best-known videos, he encountered an old woman on a snowy path and deliberately knocked her down; he later explained that the way the woman looked at him and her attitude left no doubt about her belligerent intentions. Between 2013 and 2015, at a time when extreme content was proliferating on the Russian Internet—Occupy Pedophilia was at the height of its popularity—Alextime met with some success among fans of gratuitous violence and in neo-Nazi circles, by boasting on YouTube, like Tesak, of his fondness for knife fights and swastikas. Growing indignation at his shenanigans prompted Alextime to move to Mexico, where he became a scuba diving instructor. He continued posting similar videos, but this time in a country that was not his. *"Fucking mierdas!" "Morir, mierda, morir!"* and "Piece of shit!" became the favorite expressions of his YouTube channel followers, who delighted in his nonsense talk from afar. Looking like a disheveled hulk with disturbing eyes, camera in hand and driver's license hung around his neck, he would hurl insults at the Mexicans he met on the street, knock over women and children, and film his neighbors from his balcony while shouting obscenities at them. *"Fucking mierdas!"* On May 20, 2017, the neighbors had had enough: they assembled in front of the house of the man everyone knew as Lord Nazi Ruso, insulted him, and threw stones at him. A police car arrived on the scene but did not stay long. Its departure was taken as a signal for the lynching to begin: the emboldened neighbors broke down the door and burst into the house, where Alextime had taken refuge on his balcony. Alextime stabbed one of the attackers to death before collapsing under the hail of stones and blows. He was bloody and in a coma when the police finally intervened.[88] Sentenced in 2019 to thirty-seven years in prison for murder,[89] he embodies the hostile, lawless foreigner, threatening the community's survival, despite many voices in Russia reminding Mexican authorities of his psychiatric history. Alextime's aggressive, disturbing videos are now mirrored by the spectacle of his own lynching, filmed in extenso, posted on social media, and widely commented on.

DELIGHT IN PUNISHMENT

More than two centuries after his death, the ghost of Judge Lynch continues to haunt the United States, as illustrated by the excerpt of a report published in *Time* magazine in 2000 regarding the catalog for the exhibition *Without Sanctuary*:[90]

> By the time lynching exploded, photography had become a well-organized profession and a mass-market plaything. Even the Nazis did not stoop to selling souvenirs of Auschwitz, but lynching scenes became a burgeoning subdepartment of the postcard industry. By 1908, the trade had grown so large that the U.S. Postmaster General banned the cards from the mails. As bad as the pictures of the victims are, those of the faces of the crowd are worse.... You hear their voices in the inscriptions that appear on the backs of some of the postcards—words more unnerving, in their sleepy innocence, than curses: "This is the Barbecue we had last night my picture is to the left with a cross over it your son Joe." *Without Sanctuary* is a great and terrible book. It's an album of peacetime atrocities, during which hundreds of Kodaks clicked.[91]

Touring major cities in the United States, the exhibition prompted US society to engage with its past by placing it before an irrefutable and damning source: postcards depicting scenes of lynchings at the beginning of the twentieth century. Depending on the venue and city, the exhibit showed between forty and one hundred photographs with the names of the victims, nearly all Black. The postcards bore witness to the gruesome staging of tortured bodies, bringing the scene back to life: even in death, the victims remain "without sanctuary." Presented with considerable tact, sobriety, and ample warnings, the exhibition was meant as an educational tool, bringing the audience face to face with rituals of racial violence.

Although boredom may affect vigilantes in their everyday activities, lynching is experienced as exciting, sensational entertainment. The performance of popular justice has troubled activists and observers since the beginning of the twentieth century, when investigative journalism was developing quickly. The reformist muckrakers who immersed themselves in the mire of US cities, denouncing injustice and corruption, also investigated lynchings. Known for his perceptive writing about race relations in the United States, Ray Stannard Baker described one of these lynchings in *McClure's Magazine* in 1905. He observed a mob made up of young men ages sixteen to twenty surrounded by "more respectable citizens" that was soon joined by "idle boys" coming out of the local saloons, and he lamented that the "best citizens," despite their scorn for the populace, "turn[ed] over the law and the government to the criminal or irresponsible classes" and therefore avoided getting their hands dirty.[92] Baker noted soberly that the spectacle continued beyond the moment of the murder. The hanged victim's body was exhibited until the next morning: "His head was shockingly crooked to one side, his ragged clothing, cut for souvenirs, exposed in places his bare body: he dripped blood." Lynching continued to entertain passersby, couples pushing a baby carriage, men joking: "A dead n—— is a good n——."[93] Everyone wanted to view the corpse, and the development of photography in the late nineteenth century provided the opportunity to experience the event by proxy.

The market for lynching images found its way into the postcard industry in the United States at the turn of the century. When public executions were scheduled and announced in the press the day before, "hundreds of Kodaks clicked all morning at the scene."[94] Professional photographers set up their portable printing studios so that the spectators could instantly purchase a souvenir of the event. The postcards were sent by mail to friends and relatives, sometimes with a witty remark on the back. More ominously, these cards were also addressed to African American public personalities and civil rights activists as a warning and a sign of impunity on the part of White supremacists.[95]

The success of this "burgeoning subdepartment of the postcard industry" prompted the postal service in 1908 to prohibit sending "obscene" matter inciting murder—with mitigated success.[96] Other images of lynching circulated: pictures taken by professional photographers or snapshots by amateurs, who could easily acquire film cameras as of the 1890s. In a picture of the lynching of Leo Frank—a Jew who oversaw a small factory in the state of Georgia and was accused of murder in 1915—one of the men posing next to the hanged man is holding a camera. This new visual culture has contributed to a framing of lynching, for both perpetrators and their victims. In testimony left by a rare survivor of a lynching, James Cameron described his suffering in photographic terms.[97] As a deathly silence fell over the mob, he saw himself transported to the center of a darkroom:

> No one moved or spoke a word. I stood there in the midst of thousands of people, and as I looked at the mob around me I thought I was in a room, a large room where a photographer had strips of film negatives hanging from the walls to dry. . . . A brief eternity passed as I stood there as if hypnotized.
> Then the roomful of negatives disappeared and I found myself looking into the faces of people who had been flat images a moment ago.[98]

On lynching postcards, the faces in the crowd display the solemn or, conversely, delighted expressions of ordinary folk confident of their racial superiority. Clearly convinced of being within their rights, the spectators do not seem disturbed in the least. In fact, the circulation of these images indicates that, far from hiding their involvement in the lynching, the participants boasted about it and sought recognition from it. Like the lengths of cord sold for three to four dollars apiece,[99] the scraps of clothing, hair, and even the victim's fingers[100] that the audience vied for, the photographs of lynchings were souvenirs and trophies that "demonstrative extremists" went crazy over[101] and were intended to be exhibited, commented on, and valued.[102]

In the southern United States, ritual lynching drew inspiration from the spectacle of public executions, which, in contrast to the rest of the country, remained in practice there until the early twentieth century. In these official punitive rituals, the condemned individual was paraded through the center of the town to the scaffold. The mob gathered along the route, shouting at the victim and noisily accompanying the procession. The crowd grew even more excited when the gallows, erected on a platform so that it could be seen from afar, came into view. The accused's confession hastened the execution. These public killings sometimes drew thousands of onlookers who made a picnic out of the event and brought back souvenirs.[103]

In its propensity to represent the fight between good and evil, the spectacle involved in lynching was also a form of "political theater"[104] in which popular sovereignty was enacted. Emboldened by liquor, spectators applauded, booed, shouted, egged on others, and took pictures. All their senses were alert: in addition to what they could see, they could hear the accusations, the encouragements, the victims' confessions, their death rattles; they could smell the burning flesh.[105] Far from being mere consumers of this cruel entertainment, they were actively involved and sometimes even took part in the execution. In 1911 in Livermore, Kentucky, Will Potter, accused of shooting a White man, was executed on the stage of the local opera house, where the city marshal had hidden him in a dressing room. After forcing entry into the building and overpowering the law enforcement authorities, some fifty men seized the suspect and tied him on the stage. According to some accounts, admission tickets were sold, allowing spectators who had brought guns to take shots at the victim.[106] Two years later in Paris, Texas, ten thousand people attended the execution of Henry Smith, a Black man accused of raping and killing Myrtle Vance, the three-year-old daughter of a former police officer. Trains arriving in the city were jam-packed, and businesses were closed for the occasion. A tall scaffold on which the word "Justice" was painted was erected so that the scene could be viewed from a distance. Local photographers set up their equipment to get the best angle. Henry Smith was tortured for nearly an hour, including by members of the Vance family, before being burned alive. Many photographs of the crowd and the scaffold were available. One photographer printed them in his studio and sold them for fifty cents apiece. Another offered souvenir albums. A few years later, a civil rights activist came across some of these images in the streets of Seattle, presented along with audio recordings simulating Smith's dying moment to entertain passersby for a few cents.[107] The development of the stereoscope provided another means of exploiting the images to reproduce the crime and its punishment, and the cinema of attractions gave viewers the very first films of execution and lynching.[108]

Lynching photographs were not only a medium for the unabashed assertion of White supremacy but also played a key role in civil rights activism. These images, reprinted in publications put out by antilynching organizations and printed in the African American press, began to turn the tide of racism in the United States while feeding criticism of US hegemony abroad.[109] They precipitated the end of punitive spectacles after World War II. Like the horrific photographs of the body of Emmett Till, the adolescent slayed in Mississippi in 1955 for allegedly having tried to attack a White woman, such spectacles began to appear as indefensible as they were anachronistic.

Political and social upheavals brought about changes in visual sensibilities, determining what could be photographed and put on public display. As the civil rights movement progressed and African American veterans returned from World War II, protests against lynching got louder.[110] The decline of the most spectacular forms of lynching paved the way for a critical engagement with the past, which inspired several generations of artists and activists, culminating in the *Without Sanctuary* exhibit. Two decades later, the Emmett Till Antilynching Act, signed into law in March 2022, made lynching a federal hate crime, punishable by up to thirty years in prison. Named for the young martyr, the law pays tribute to him and also confirms the transformative power of photography.

Lynching attempts are often unfinished, interrupted by the arrival of the police. Sometimes they resemble a simulacra of violence, staged to draw the authorities' attention. In the barrios of Cochabamba, Bolivia, in the mid-1990s, local residents mastered the art of bluffing: "On Monday morning, four persons were almost lynched by infuriated residents of Cerro San Miguel. . . . The residents threatened to kill the detainees, to burn them and hang them, but instead they doused them in cold water, cut off their hair and hit them . . . until finally police officials were able to convince them to turn over the suspects."[111] In another instance, vigilantes waited seven hours to enact a murderous plan. Only when the police arrived on the scene did they pretend to go through with it. The parody reached new heights when a group of residents burned effigies of the offenders (*antisociales*) and demanded stronger police presence in their neighborhood.[112]

As a form of communication, lynching has taken on a new dimension with the advances in digital technology. Social media is a major soundboard for self-appointed rule enforcers and their emotional outbursts, and it is now the main vehicle for staging punitive spectacles. The wave of WhatsApp lynchings that swept through India in the late 2010s is emblematic of this: distinct from cow vigilantism (see Chapter 1), these lynchings act out a well-known scenario according to which suspicions of child abduction and organ removal end in the killing of the alleged culprits. It is a classic complaint sung to a familiar tune: "There are reports that 500 people disguised as beggars are traveling from Bihar to Jharkhand. Whoever they come across is killed, and the kidney and liver are removed. Six–seven people have been arrested. After interrogation they revealed that they are about 500, so please forward this message to all family members."[113] Unlike cow protectors, who primarily attack Muslims,[114] defenders of children express more general resentment toward the Other—not only Muslims but also Dalits, Christians, migrant workers, the mentally ill, and so on.[115] The targets are usually poor males, but the middle class is not spared, and one in five victims is a woman. One hundred twenty-four lynchings killed at least forty-eight persons between January 2017 and October 2019. They occurred most often in remote villages, in states that are not necessarily the most affected by child abduction.[116]

The mobile messaging application WhatsApp had 200 million users in India in July 2018.[117] The app plays the now commonplace dual role of social media in the lynching sequence described at the beginning of this chapter: it disseminates both the rumors that lead to the punitive act and the spectacle of popular justice. A study conducted by two researchers from the London School of Economics found that videos are shared without necessarily being viewed, solely on the basis of trust in the sender.[118] The images circulating sometimes come from very far away: the bodies of children from which organs were supposedly removed, leading to the lynching of five persons in Dhule (Maharashtra), were actually photographed in Syria in 2013, and some shots of the killing of a rapist in 2015 in the state of Nagaland came from Pelileo Grande, Ecuador, and dated from 2006.[119]

The Indian government accused WhatsApp of having provoked the wave of lynchings in May–July 2018 and urged the company to take action to prevent the spread of provocative rumors.[120] In 2019, the message service announced measures to help its users verify information they receive and report suspicious content. The campaign for responsible use of the social media platform had the slogan "Share joy, not rumors."[121] The company also committed to invest in research to stem fake news, restrict video sharing capabilities, and teach young people how to detect false information. The increase in lynchings drove an upswing in fact-checking: some websites urge Internet users not to be gullible, and the magazine *India Today* verifies images behind rumors and divides them into three categories according to their degree of untruth: "half true," "mostly false," and "false."[122]

WhatsApp's publicizing of punitive spectacles is the modern version of US lynching postcards. Several observers have noticed the similarity—one of them even refers to the exhibition *Without Sanctuary*[123]—pointing out that, in both cases, people are having "the best fun."[124] One of these journalists refers to a chilling photo of the lynching of an alleged rapist in Dimapur, Nagaland, that caused outrage in 2015. The victim, Syed Farid Khan, is naked, bound, and disfigured: his face is so bloody that none of his features can be made out. The "attention space" here is not solely the adults and children surrounding the dead man but also the cell phones everyone is holding up. In this moment of bubbling excitement, some of the attackers do not conceal their mirth, and one delighted spectator points at the tortured corpse. Even more than the victim's swollen face, it is the torturers' jubilation that makes the image so unbearable. The forest of cell phones adds to the feeling of unease, indicating an even broader audience and guaranteeing the reproducibility of the event.[125]

Syed Farid Khan sold used cars and car parts at a market in Dimapur. This thirty-five-year-old Muslim from the state of Assam, married to a Naga woman and father of their child, was accused of having raped a Naga student a few days earlier. The pair were identified by CCTV cameras in a hotel where they spent a few hours and seemed inebriated, despite the consumption of alcohol being theoretically banned in Nagaland. The student filed a complaint on February 25, 2015, probably at the behest of Khan's wife, and since then tensions in the town had been running high, and all public gatherings of more than five persons had been banned. That did not prevent the crowd from assembling on March 5 to take Khan out of his cell. Rumors made him out to be a Bangladeshi spy or an illegal immigrant, both archetypal figures of otherness in northeast India. Between four thousand and ten thousand people forced their way into the Dimapur central prison in midafternoon. Using a former detainee's familiarity with the premises, the crowd hauled Syed Farid Khan out of jail, bound him, and thrashed him. He was then hitched to a motorcycle and dragged for seven kilometers to the center of Dimapur, while being stoned en route. He died along the way.

When the police intervened to retrieve his body, which had been put on display in the town, they were greeted with a hail of stones. The clashes were so violent that one student who had taken part in the lynching was killed, fifty police officers were wounded, and around ten police cars were set alight. The police opened fire and charged with lathi. The mob then headed toward the market where the accused had worked, torching houses and shops run by non-Nagas, especially Bengalis. To quell the rioting, a curfew was imposed for several days; schools, markets, and government offices were closed and relations between the states of Nagaland and Assam deteriorated.[126] The slain man's family spoke out to say that the deceased, son of a soldier, was in no way a "Bangladeshi infiltrator" but on the contrary "from a family of patriots."[127] As in the Latin American cases discussed previously, Nagas had to defend themselves against a stereotype portraying them as a primitive, xenophobic community steeped in a culture of violence masquerading as "customary justice."[128] The Indian press attributed the lynching to widespread exasperation about rape cases, court inaction, hostility toward Bangladeshi illegal immigrants, and bitter struggles between regional political forces.[129]

With this gruesome incident, twenty-first-century vigilante justice has found its iconic image: a victim surrounded by spectators immortalizing the scene with their cell phones. Already heightened by nakedness, the vulnerability of the tortured body is further magnified by the electronic eyes trained on it without the slightest sensitivity to its suffering. This dehumanizing view

58   CHAPTER 2

is in no way specific to India: WhatsApp lynching, and app-led lynching more generally, has been noted elsewhere in Asia—Bangladesh, Sri Lanka, Myanmar[130]—and in Mexico, where similar photos show two alleged child kidnappers burned alive beneath the impassive gaze of dozens of cell phones.[131]

––––––

The importance of interpersonal ties and the transactions running through them, as revealed by studies of lynching, is far from the cliché of the anonymous, uncontrollable mob. Codified, organized, and even planned, lynching is an act that follows a certain routine, a punitive ritual that takes place according to a scenario with a basic plot and a cast to fill the roles.[132] The right of life and death that lynchers appropriate requires prior consensus among the offended community, which is essential to maintaining the murderers' anonymity. Participation in the punitive act is a public secret within the community that, barring rare exceptions, produces images but not witnesses, relics but not archives, reputations but neither memoirs nor confessions.

As acknowledged by the victims' lawyers in trials following attacks on Roma in the Paris area in 2019, even when the facts are judged, the defendants represent a minute segment of the lynchers and are far from the most violent. Lynchers go unpunished as a rule. The most controversial images, even those showing the lynchers' cruelty or cowardice, are focused on the victim and say little about the perpetrators. Despite its viral spread and scandalous content, the photograph showing Syed Farid Khan's tormentors in the act of openly lynching him did not lead to any of them being prosecuted. The killers' impunity helps erase any trace of them, as one of the critics of the *Without Sanctuary* exhibit points out:

> Why do we learn the names of the dead in those images and not the names of the living? Why do we learn very little about the people who participated in the tortures, took the photographs, and sent the postcards. . . . Without Sanctuary's focus on blacks as victims rather than whites as murderers, torturers, or at best spectators . . . produces an updated version of that old segregating story.[133]

By seeking primarily to rehabilitate the victims, the indictment of lynching almost never involves the lynchers. As proud to punish as they may be, the latter avoid boasting of their exploits beyond their sphere of acquaintance. Protected by relative anonymity, they view their deeds as an act of protest. By taking part in a punitive ritual that reflects their own conception of penalty, lynchers defy the authorities, assert the preeminence of an unwritten law over official criminal procedure, and threaten to subvert the political order. In so doing, they anticipate the possibility of an insurrectionary extralegal justice that is not just a criticism of the failings of the state but an outright attack on its institutions.

3 COP KILLERS

Here's the police ID of the officer we killed, cut up like a dog, like a pig, when he was sleeping off the booze on duty.

ALEKSANDR SLADKIKH, a Primorsky Partisan (2010)[1]

JUNE 2010 IN KIROVSKY, a small town in Russia's far eastern province of Primorsky Krai, near the Chinese border. The zinc roofs of the *izbas* and the asphalt of the narrow road almost disappear in the landscape of conifers and flowing grass. In this bucolic setting, so typical of the Russian countryside in late spring, the procession of dozens of young men in tracksuits seems out of place. Their short hair, inscrutable faces, and athletic appearance give them an intimidating, martial air at odds with the multicolored floral bouquets they carry. At the procession's head, a young man barely adult, his black shirt open over his chest, holds the framed portrait of his friend Andrey Sukhorada, age twenty-two, whom he is accompanying to his last abode. The image of the dead man's pale, youthful face is placed on the rudimentary wooden cross that marks his grave. This modest temporary tomb will later be replaced by a granite gravestone decorated with the same portrait and a *kolovrat*—a symbol of the sun, strength, and time in Slavic mythology, much favored by Russia's neo-pagan extreme right.[2] Andrey was the leader of the Primorsky Partisans, a gang of young diehards who had been in the news for several weeks because of their many attacks on the local police. When the special forces finally cornered him, Andrey killed himself.

The gang's first attack had taken place four months earlier in the regional capital Vladivostok. That night, three members of the gang were sitting in Andrey's car in a discotheque parking lot when the police turned up for a routine identity check. When the two officers told them to get out of their vehicle to ensure they were not armed, one of the young men fired, killing one officer, injuring the other and taking his gun. By May, the group was on the run and on the offensive, carrying out more and more operations. After a series of thefts, they set fire to an unoccupied police station and, two days later, attacked another, where they stabbed the officer on duty and tried to behead him. They then returned to their lair in the taiga, where they twice ambushed police vehicles and attacked them with machine guns. The hunt to catch them made national headlines. Federal authorities sent reinforcements to flush out the men, now locally known as partisans for their use of guns and art of vanishing into the forest to escape the police. Eventually, two gang members turned themselves in, and law enforcement made an assault on their den in Ussuriysk. Andrey and another rebel committed suicide and the remaining two surrendered.[3] Banners and graffiti in support of the six patriots, who had boldly stood up to a loathed and largely discredited police force, then began appearing all over Russia, declaring "Glory to the Primorsky Partisans" and "We will never forget what you did." The scale of this popular support caught the government and media by surprise, and over the following weeks they strove to show that the Primorsky Partisans were not righteous heroes but heinous criminals who had threatened the social order.

———

A lot of people hate the police, but not many act on their feelings. Although rappers have advocated attacks on the police,[4] the cop killer is largely a figure of fantasy. Murders of police officers generally occur during criminal actions that go awry. They are not premeditated and their main aim is to enable the perpetrators to escape arrest and prosecution. When they are planned, attacks on law enforcement officers tend to be the work of solitary snipers, such as the series of murders in the United States in 2014–2016, involving African Americans seeking to avenge acts of police brutality against their community. Aside from armed conflict, in which deadly attacks against law enforcement agencies are meant to demoralize and divide them,[5] coordinated attacks against the police are the exception rather than the rule. Offensives against the police are primarily destabilization tactics, in which the aim is to intimidate law enforcement officers rather than kill people. This is true of the campaigns to dox police officers that developed in the 2010s and that exploit the publicity opportunities offered by social media.

The Primorsky Partisans took their hatred of the uniform to a new level. In their quest for recognition, they sought to shed the image of mere criminals, justifying their actions with political arguments intended to appeal to a specific audience and promote support for the group. In discrediting the police and revealing the intrinsic vulnerability of officers, they sought to raise awareness and be emulated. They portrayed their desire for vengeance

62   CHAPTER 3

as part of a project to overthrow the established authority and power re-lations. So it is hardly surprising that these murderers of police drew on the imaginary of insurrection and revolution, with its lurking specter of civil war.

THE PRIMORSKY PARTISANS' CHALLENGE

The Primorsky Partisans, while claiming their attacks had political signifi-cance, seemed to have developed their ideas on the hoof and after the initial murder of the police officer in Vladivostok, when the gang was already a target for law enforcement. Although their improvised, homespun argu-ments were a practical response to the urgency of the situation, they were also rooted in the lived experience of these young men and echoed the wide-spread hostility toward the police in Russia at that time. The group's most pol-ished effort at justification was an "interview" filmed when they had come to the end of the line and were surrounded by police.[6] This twelve-minute video (made public after the events) shows four of the partisans in camouflage gear or stripped to the waist, holding guns, and clearly exhausted but calm. The virility, confidence, and determination of these young men—described as "Slav-looking, tall, fine-featured, fit and blond"[7]—added to their image as romantic heroes. The interview focuses on Andrey and Aleksandr Kovtun and was filmed without journalists or questions. It offers a distillation of vigilante ideas, portraying the police as the symptom and cause of broader social pathologies, and conveys a challenge, an accusation, and a call to all Russians of good will. The challenge is commensurate with the transgres-sion committed and resembles a declaration of war. The group's crimes were "premeditated," were "planned," and are claimed with pride. Watched by his brothers-in-arms, Andrey is all bravado and boast: "We attacked a police car and wounded two of the passengers. We also killed a cop and wounded another, we took his gun off him [*smiles*]. The cop we shot dead with a bullet to the back of the neck was calling for assistance, he was shouting 'Help!' It was funny . . . [*laughter*]." The hubris of these insurgents is palpable in the evident pleasure their crime gives them. They are all swagger as they recall their position as underdogs in a clearly unequal power relation: "We made life difficult for the local police. . . . They had to call for reinforcements: three hundred Omon,[8] two helicopters, but they still couldn't catch us, we ran rings around them. Even their dogs couldn't catch us." They taunt the police by emphasizing how young and how few they are and how poorly equipped:

You put on your bullet-proof vests and your helmets, you grabbed your automatic weapons. . . . Who [did you think you were going to fight]?

COP KILLERS 63

All we had was one assault rifle and small-bore hunting rifles. . . . It's ridiculous! You're shit. . . . If we had the same weapons as you and five hundred trained guys, we'd smash you, there'd be nothing you could do, your army and your powerful empire would be powerless. You can't even handle six twenty-year-old guys.[9]

The vigilantes' euphoria reaches its height when, in an act of defiance, one of these blowhards points his gun at the screen. Even the likelihood of capture cannot dampen his enthusiasm: "We'll fight you to the end, until you kill us or we defeat you. . . . Well, you're almost certainly going to kill us [*laughter*]." As Andrey says, the inevitable prospect of defeat cannot reduce their satisfaction with the battles they have fought. "We've already won. . . . We've overcome the fear and cowardice that we had inside and that you can never overcome."

The complaints leveled at the police by these young men are undisputed. The vigilantes accuse the police of "incompetence," "inconsistency," and "stupidity": "You can't even defend yourselves." In their eyes, their attacks on police stations reveal the depths to which law enforcement has sunk: they endlessly repeat that, when they broke into a safe, "there was nothing interesting in there, just vodka." Their criticisms become more vitriolic when they portray the police as boundlessly cynical brutes: "You only know how to torture alcoholics and junkies in your stations, scare people, put pressure on families. . . . Your methods are revolting." "You only know how to terrorize your people, who are defenseless, resigned, and used to humiliation." Andrey also calls the police "Evsiukov's gang," referring to a tragic event that occurred in Moscow in 2009, when a drunken police officer with no apparent motive killed two people and wounded seven others in cold blood. This gratuitous violence was caught on the security cameras of the supermarket where most of the events happened. It aroused a strong reaction across Russia and was instrumental in portraying the police as a public menace.[10] Another accusation sees the police as "pure bandits," "bandits in law,"[11] who use their position to amass wealth:

What else can we call you? It's you that controls the drug trade, prostitution. . . . It's you looting the forest. Everyone knows this, but people are scared of you because you've got enough power to do it, you can cover yourselves, clear yourselves of responsibility, you know all your predatory laws.[12]

The vitriol directed at the police is more than simply criticism of individual monsters who use their prerogatives to enrich themselves and indulge their sadistic tendencies. It has a much broader target, because the police are also identified as the guardians of a political regime that is fundamentally unjust. "You protect those in power against ordinary people." In this depiction of the social order, the police enslave the population by guaranteeing impunity to the elites while protecting their own interests. The organic link between the elites and the police reflects the pure power relations through which the partisans seem to read the social order: "You can't lock up the civil servants who steal billions because you're afraid of them, unlike the ordinary people you're not scared of." The vigilantes call for vengeance against an institution whose role is to maintain the oppression of a people deprived of any future:

> You don't do anything for ordinary people. You rob them, you kill them, you rape them. . . . You put people in prison for ridiculous amounts of money, [all those who have] stolen something because they had no other choice. Unemployment in the country, alcoholism, prostitution. . . . You've already locked up all the men; half the young people sleep in prison. Have you ever wondered why they went and stole something? Because there's no normal work, because there's nothing in this country. That's why they went and stole.[13]

Alcohol has a prominent place in the partisans' indictment. They see it as a symptom of a degraded society, cynically promoted by rulers to stifle any popular desire to rebel. Alcohol and the police are portrayed as two of the main pillars of political domination in Russia: "Your powerful empire called the Russian Federation is kept in place by alcoholism, fear, and cowardice. One day it will collapse, and you will go down with it."

So the police are targeted for two main reasons: they are riddled with corruption, and they protect those responsible for the overall state of chaos. By murdering police officers, the vigilantes are also explicitly targeting representatives of the government: "Our rifles are shooting at your constitution [*laughter*]. . . . We're already hitting your emblems [*laughter*]." They are waging war against the Leviathan that is the Russian government. Rejecting "the power of the Russian Federation in its totality," the rebels compare themselves to another contemporary figure of insurrection against the Russian authorities and hail "all those who have been part of the resistance in the North Caucasus, all good, worthy, and decent people." Coming from Andrey, these words may seem surprising, and they generated a debate to which we return later. The vigilantes saw themselves as both precursors and prophets: in the interview video they predict the collapse of the state, which they seek to actively provoke. "This country is sliding toward the cliff edge and we will help it go down sooner with our murders and our chaos." To implement this prophecy, the partisans call on Russians of good will, who cannot fail to support them: "The people will be on our side because justice is on our side." So they see themselves as an enlightened avant-garde with a mission to awaken the masses through propaganda by deed:

> To ordinary people we would like to say, open your eyes, look around you, look at these atrocities, look at yourselves. Our women sell themselves for money, all the young people smoke; finding a fifteen-year-old girl who's still a virgin is now impossible. The country is a den of vice, the society is rotten. How can you not fight? Where are the normal people? Look around you. Everyone drinks and screws around. It's disgusting.[14]

Once Russians "get a grip," "stop enduring these humiliations," "take up arms and do something good for the people as a whole" to "save their souls before it's too late," the prophecy will be fulfilled: "And those who have opened their eyes will grab an automatic rifle, will shoot and kill or help us in some other way to destroy that world. The world those degenerates live in."[15]

THE HUNT FOR "WEREWOLVES WITH A BADGE"

The Primorsky Partisans emerged in a very particular local and national context. At the time of the events, they were young men ages eighteen to twenty-three who had grown up in the Russian rural heartlands known as the *glubinka*—in this case a backwater of ten thousand in Russia's Far East. Kirovsky is an ordinary town three hundred kilometers from Vladivostok. The alma mater of the future partisans was the Patriot, a military and patriotic club[16] on the main square, overlooking the statue of Sergei Kirov, a Soviet Bolshevik leader. In this youth club the gang learned how to handle guns, defend themselves, and survive in the surrounding taiga, which they knew like the backs of their hands.

A slogan painted on the small spectator stand at the sports grounds reads "The school of patriotism is the school of courage." In the vicinity of the main square stand a church, a café, a pool hall, and a Chinese-owned supermarket and, on Lenin Avenue, the police station so reviled by the local youth. For adolescents struggling in school, local job prospects are limited to a canning factory, where Andrey worked for a while,[17] and a factory bottling mineral water. Otherwise, the only jobs in town are growing and selling drugs or smuggling wood, mostly to China. These illegal activities prosper, locals believe, only because they are carried out with police complicity.[18]

With the exception of Aleksandr Kovtun, all the partisans were raised in disadvantaged neighborhoods by families who left them to their own devices.

They quickly lost interest in school and planned military careers. Meanwhile, they found refuge in the taiga. Its forest was their playground and their inspiration; it made them who they were, as individuals and as comrades. Since childhood they had gone there to hunt, fish, collect pine nuts, and camp. Later, under the aegis of the Patriot club, they did military training in the forest in two-week courses in which the older ones wore uniforms and handled assault rifles. Sometimes they went deep into the forest to camp for several days. This was entirely unremarkable in Primorsky Krai, where hunters for pheasant, duck, badger, deer, bear, and even tiger are legion. Aleksandr Kovtun was the gang's most hardened member. Many photographs show him in combat gear, rifle in hand, smiling with his trophies. In Kirovsky, they say that at the age of thirteen or fourteen, when he was a scout for a hunting expedition, he came on a bear hiding behind a tree trunk, blocking his way. It rushed at him, but he kept a cool head, loaded his rifle, and killed it without fuss.[19] Although this story may be apocryphal, it shows that from childhood the future partisans had skills that would prove crucial when they were on the run: they knew how to hunt, how to handle hunting rifles, and how to find their way around and hide in the taiga and on the many rivers that run through it. At one point, they were reportedly seen in a boat belonging to the father of one of them, moving silently downriver in camouflage gear to evade the police. Similarly, when they shot up police vehicles with machine guns, they stayed under cover and then disappeared into the forest.

Logically enough, the enthusiasm of these young men for hunting and survivalism went hand in hand with a fit and healthy lifestyle, also promoted by Tesak and the Russian vigilantes of the 2010s (see Chapter 1). Many accounts note that they were the only youth of their generation to abstain from alcohol, cigarettes, and drugs. They enjoyed combat sports, especially kickboxing, which they practiced at a professional level. According to the Patriot club founder and Afghan war veteran Yuri Ivachko, two of them were "real warriors, hard men with balls. Looking at them you could see they were built for prowess."[20] In fact, Ivachko recommended one of them for military service in the GRU's prestigious *spetsnaz* (special forces).[21] The young conscript was accepted, but he ultimately deserted. However, the intensive practice of combat sports did not turn these boys into models of virtue. They got into a lot of fights and used the skills they had learned at the military and patriotic club. This attracted the attention of the police, in both their home town and the region's larger cities of Ussuriysk and Vladivostok. Seeking to lend their violent impulses political meaning, from adolescence onward these hoodlums placed their martial skills at the service of radical ideologies hostile to the Vladimir Putin regime.

In 2003, sixteen-year-old Andrey ran away from his difficult childhood in Primorsky Krai[22] in the company of his twelve-year-old sister. They took the train to Moscow, a nine-thousand-kilometer journey. Their idea was to join the National Bolshevik Party, headed by the writer Eduard Limonov, which appealed to them with its promises of insurrection and attracted young revolutionaries of all stripes.[23] They found shelter in the party activists' Bunker,[24] and Andrey took part in publicity stunts, such as occupying the offices of the pro-Putin United Russia Party in March 2004, where he handcuffed himself alongside other activists, clearly delighted to attract the attention of journalists.[25] He was arrested and placed in a detention center for minors but was soon sent back to Primorsky Krai. Former party activists remember him as clearly "on the right," a "nationalist patriot."[26] Once back in Primorsky Krai, he began hanging out with neo-Nazi skinheads and was involved in racist attacks on Chinese and Korean nationals in 2006 and 2007. At least two other future partisans were wanted for xenophobic crimes at the same time, seeming to have embarked on criminal careers.[27] Photographs easily accessible on the Internet show Andrey wearing a helmet with an iron cross, giving the Nazi salute, and displaying the SS *totenkopf* tattooed on his heart, leaving no doubt as to his political affiliations.[28] Other photographs taken around 2007–2008 show him posing in combat fatigues and boots with his Kirovsky friends, all with fresh faces and shaved heads.[29] However, when the gang took up arms against the police in 2010, their support for neo-Nazi ideas was less explicitly stated. In their "last interview," they make few allusions to a racist vision of the social order but use vocabulary with anarchist connotations—"we don't give a fuck about your laws"—and express respect for the jihadists of the North Caucasus and their determination to fight Russian authorities. In a photograph revealed later during the trial, Andrey poses with another partisan in front of graffiti for "Aryan jihad," a succinct key to understanding a composite ideological world shaped by insurrectional fantasies.[30] The Primorsky Partisans targeted law enforcement officers first and foremost because they had scores to settle. Several of these young men bore the traces of traumatic experiences with the police. Aleksandr was arrested at a post-soccer-match fight and tortured at a police station to make him admit responsibility for a murder that it seems he did not commit. His spine was damaged by the blows he received, preventing him from following the army career he had planned. According to his brother, "Something inside him broke at that time."[31] At his trial Aleksandr said he was motivated solely by the desire for revenge for what the Kirovsky police had done to him. Meanwhile, Andrey was having repeated altercations with the police. One story about him often comes up: on his way to a fight with a rival gang involved in

68   CHAPTER 3

poppy production, he fell into the hands of Kirovsky police officers working with the traffickers, who took him to a deserted spot and gave him a severe beating. The father of a third partisan was apparently killed by the police in unclear circumstances. Last, the gang's youngest member, age eighteen at the time, had a brother murdered while in police custody and was himself beaten up by the police just before he went into the forest with Andrey and his companions.[32]

Late in the first decade of the 2000s, this personal resentment and desire for revenge against police officers echoed a unanimous and vitriolic indictment of the Russian police force at the national level. Loathing of the police was at its height, fueled by decades of complaints and revitalized by recurrent and chilling scandals. Back at the end of the Soviet period and in the early years of democratic transition, the indifference, incompetence, and venality of law enforcement had been frequently criticized. As crime rose in the 1990s, the police were perceived as incapable, underequipped, poorly trained, and ultimately concerned only with enhancing their abysmal salary. This image changed in the late 1990s, when the first reports emerged of routine torture in Russian police stations.[33] In the next few years, growing criticism of the police culminated with the figure of the *oboroten v pogonakh* (werewolf with epaulets), a new variation on the theme of the corrupt and brutal police officer, which has become a lasting element of Russian imaginary and echoes the words of the Primorsky Partisan vigilantes.

This image of a uniformed monster—which appears as a "crooked policeman" in other countries[34]—was rooted in a major scandal revealed in 2003 by Alexander Khinshtein, a muckraker specializing in sensitive investigations and a representative of the pro-Putin party United Russia, concerning corruption in the antidrug section of the prestigious Moscow police department. Khinshtein revealed that officers, who had received several bonuses and medals for their exemplary work, in fact led a double life. Instead of fulfilling their duties, they faked statistics and fabricated dossiers, pinning blame for selling and dealing drugs on homeless and marginalized people, thereby freeing up time for their real stock in trade: extorting money from the businesses and shops in their area.[35] This iconic scandal illustrates both the duplicity of the werewolves in the police and the damaging influence of the requirement for quantified results for police work.[36] Pressure from superiors to improve crime solution rates had particularly harmful effects and explains why officers in the Primorsky Krai police stations brutalized idle youths who fell into their hands to extract murder confessions and "tortur[ed] alcoholics and junkies," to use the words of the partisans themselves.[37] The police torture, well documented by human rights groups, included the "little elephant," which suffocates victims by placing a hermetically sealed gas mask over their faces while beating them. Two of the partisans were said to have suffered this treatment.[38]

The image of the police was profoundly damaged by revelation of their methods, as shown by the very clear results of surveys carried out in the first years of the 2000s on perceptions of the police in Russian society.[39] The dominant view, as relayed in the "last interview of the Primorsky Partisans," was that the police favored the powerful and its own interests, being indifferent to the fate of those it policed and quick to brutalize those it caught. Perceptions that the Russian police were a danger to the public rose further following the shootings carried out by the officer Evsiukov in Moscow in 2009. From then on, the threat no longer applied solely to certain social groups (disenfranchised youth and illegal immigrants) but could potentially affect anyone.

Police bashing became so ubiquitous that even the ruling elite came to publicly accuse the force. Vladimir Putin and Dmitri Medvedev often made vitriolic speeches about the police,[40] complaining that "citizens cross the street when they see a uniform."[41] This unanimity was accompanied by the ever-growing specter of denunciation, enhanced by the rise of new information technologies at the onset of the twenty-first century.[42] In 2009, a police officer named Aleksei Dymovsky posted an irrefutable accusation on YouTube, launching a wave of similar videos addressed to the president and denouncing from within the corruption permeating the force.[43] In addition to this internal criticism, the police became a target for pop singers,[44] performance artists,[45] and activists of every stripe. For more radical groups—for example, in anarchist circles—these public indictments of the force were not enough. On February 20, 2009, a video posted online by the "combatant group 'Popular Reprisals'" showed militants throwing Molotov cocktails in a police parking lot. The group claimed to have destroyed two vehicles and called for a fight "against the power and despotism of the police, the special services, and bureaucracy."[46] However, in all this cacophony of denunciation, the extreme right proved far more determined than other political persuasions to include the murder of police officers in their repertoire of actions.

One far right group, the Combat Organization of Russian Nationalists (Boyevaya Organizatsiya Russkikh Natsionalistov; BORN), took up direct action in December 2008. At first, punitive expeditions targeted foreigners, seen as "social parasites . . . parading in Porsche Cayennes." They also went after antifascist activists and human rights groups, as demonstrated by the widely reported murder of the lawyer Stanislav Markelov and the journalist Anastasia Baburova in Moscow's city center in 2009. Although BORN did not physically attack police officers, it criticized them without restraint and, on one occasion in August 2009, claimed responsibility for bombing a Moscow branch of the Russian prosecutor's office—the *prokuratura*—causing material damage. Following this attack, BORN put out a press release stating that this action was intended to be "demonstrative" and had deliberately avoided causing deaths, because most of the staff working there were "Slavs." "We do not want to spill the blood of our brothers, we do not want to kill Russians, however loathsome they may be, but we know that Russian nationalist prisoners are tortured during interrogation, and that people with Slav family names and faces are mutilated and killed." Faced with the "replacement of the Russian people in their own country by colored migrants" and "repression by police and *prokuratura* punishers in uniform," "BORN militants are determined to wage war until Rus[47] is entirely liberated from the yoke of traitors to the Nation and accomplices of the colored occupiers." With this in view, the attack on the *prokuratura* was merely a "warning." BORN's hostility to public servants in general was displayed in December 2008, when they threw the decapitated head "of an occupier from Central Asia" into the courtyard of a local council building. This "surprise" was presented as a warning, "because there is no worse enemy than a traitor in power who sells his Russian roots. Civil servants, if you do not start kicking out the Blacks [people from Central Asia and the Caucasus], we will avenge their crimes by targeting you. And then it will be your heads that roll." In another press release claiming responsibility for a racist crime, the organization denied that magistrates, or "flunkeys of the regime," had the right to "judge [our comrades]" and called for recruits: "Get hold of guns, steal them from the cops. Hunt down those responsible for committing crimes against Rus' and punish them without mercy."[48]

Despite fundamental differences—notably the explicit assertion of a racist vision of the social order—the militant language of BORN recalls that of the Primorsky vigilantes. They defy the "punishers in uniform," refer to "partisan tactics," and through their actions, call on Russians who are "not indifferent" to take up arms to overthrow the established regime. There are two reasons why the murder of police officers was not ruled out by violent far right activists. The activism of the Movement Against Illegal Immigration[49] and the growing importance of the annual Russian march since 2005,[50] backed up by interethnic clashes in Kondopoga in 2006,[51] showed that the far right was gaining momentum. Its most diehard militants were no longer afraid to spill blood. On August 21, 2006, a bomb exploded at Moscow's Cherkizovsky Market, where people from Central Asia and the Caucasus worked, and caused thirteen deaths. Two years later, nationalist militants were convicted for the attack. As revealed by organizations that monitor the activities of xenophobic skinhead groups, after about 2005 the number of racist crimes observed in Russia was the highest since the dissolution of the Soviet Union.[52]

In 2010, the thirteen members of the National Socialist Society North were found guilty of twenty-seven murders of foreign nationals—Africans, Asians, Caucasians—committed from January 2008 until their arrest the following July. This competitive increase in murders and attacks, filmed and posted without objection on social media, was linked to internal struggles within the Russian far right at that time.[53]

Would-be murderers were also inspired and emboldened by the actions of Islamists who, in the same period, were attacking Russian security forces in the republics of the North Caucasus, especially Dagestan. Although it may at first seem paradoxical, these examples appealed to observers on the Russian far right. In a book judged extremist by the courts and banned,[54] Aleksandr Litoy and Ilia Falkovsky show that neo-Nazi groups took a close interest in the methods used by jihadists to undermine law enforcement. In particular, they followed posts on websites such as Kavkaz-Tsentr,[55] also judged extremist by the courts.[56] Ideological affinities between radical Islam and the far right, "in solidarity against their common enemy, liberal society and the western world,"[57] were noted before 2010. The Primorsky Partisans constantly referred to the fighters of the North Caucasus, in both their language and their actions and gestures. Several photographs taken shortly before their arrest show the young neo-Nazis posing with index fingers pointing to the sky. In an earlier video, two members of the gang parody a video they found on the Kavkaz-Tsentr site, in which two Islamist fighters—Yasin Rasulov and Murad Lakhiyalov—drive through the streets of Dagestan's capital Makhachkala with automatic weapons, hunting for police officers. Driving around Vladivostok, the future partisans copy the North Caucasian accent and punctate their trip with sudden cries of "Allahu Akbar."[58] Originally seen as a nasty joke, this video was later taken more seriously. Once behind bars, Aleksandr Kovtun and another Primorsky Partisan converted to Islam, observing that they shared the Muslims' concern for the poor and their aversion to alcohol, drugs, and sexual depravity.

ROBIN HOODS WITH DIRTY HANDS

The attacks by the Primorsky Partisans were deliberately provocative, and Russian society was divided in its opinion of them. They had barely surrendered when the tributes and demonstrations of support began. Graffiti honoring the "heroes" appeared in cities far beyond Primorsky Krai, and pages on them proliferated on the Internet. In cities where ultranationalist groups merged with soccer fans—Moscow, Saint Petersburg, and Oryol—banners declaring the glory of the partisans appeared in the stands.[59] On July 7, 2010, Vladimir Zhirinovsky, leader of the Liberal Democratic Party of Russia, caused a scandal by defending the young rebels in the Duma, saying their

72   CHAPTER 3

desire for vengeance against the police was legitimate and expressing outrage that they had been called "bandits."[60] The romantic dimension of the challenge to the regime made by these young men, certain of both defeat and the legitimacy of their fight, inspired budding poets on social media:

A sheaf on the tomb of the Primorsky insurgents

> *In memory of those who fell for Rus'*
> *Alexandr Sladkikh and Andrey Sukhorada.*[61]
> . . .
> *Heroes of the white, Russian Intifada,*
> *Fire in your eyes, faith in your hearts,*
> *You went to your death, driving back every boundary.*
> . . .
> *Casting yourselves into the twilight of the land of Mordor,*
> *You threw down the gauntlet to cowardly power*
> *And, leaving us your example, you departed.*[62]

The glorification of the Primorsky Partisans was not confined to graffiti, banners, and dithyrambic verse. As soon as their capture was announced, copycat attacks were reported in different parts of the country. On the day the gang members were arrested in Ussuriysk, there were two attacks on police officers. In the Novgorod region, an armed attack on a traffic police patrol car seriously injured two officers. In the Urals, on the border between Sverdlovsk and Perm regions, assailants dressed in camouflage fatigues opened fire on the traffic police department, killing one officer. They wounded two others who were barricaded in their building, set their car alight, stole a Kalashnikov and a pistol, and hid in the forest before committing further offenses.[63] Other radical Islamist assailants emerged in late July in Astrakhan, attacking police officers three times and killing two of them. Following their second attack, they were described as partisans in the press.[64]

In Oryol, a city on Russia's western border, the deeds of the Primorsky Partisans found their strongest echoes in the summer of 2010. A neo-Nazi group known as The Pyromaniacs had been making its presence increasingly felt since 2009. The group formed around an officer and sports teacher at the Academy of the Federal Security Service of Russia who trained agents for a Russian secret service—the Federal Protective Service. This gang of academy students and other young men had already perpetrated several racist attacks and tried to set alight the headquarters of both the police and the *prokuratura* with Molotov cocktails, without much success. After the arrest of the Primorsky Partisans they became notorious, mounting more spectacular operations and putting out a statement similar to BORN's at the end of July. It was addressed to the "Russian citizen who, one day, felt the bitterness of oppression . . . , who carries protest in his heart, but lacks the necessary courage and will to carry out actions that will put pressure on the machine of tyranny and genocide." This message, signed "NS/WP center"[65] and accompanied by "revolutionary greetings," was equivalent to a declaration of war. "We have raised the banner of open insurrection in the city." With this text the group sought to raise two "issues." The first was that of the "moral decadence" of the young, who had been rendered "puny" and "impotent" by alcohol and replaced by "foreign scum, lecherous animals who profane the bodies of Russian girls" and who will produce "genetically sick children, . . . incapable of serving their country." The "second issue" discussed the faults of the police, using language similar to that of the Primorsky Partisans:

> Are you not sick and tired of living in a country where police stations are the realm of the most blatant arbitrary power, where so-called officers deal out their own justice, where scumbags use sadistic methods without the training or skills to investigate a case as required by the Code of Criminal Procedure? Are you not sick and tired of living, knowing that tomorrow, maybe, your son will be accused of a murder he didn't commit, just because a fat cop couldn't be bothered to look for the real murderers? Aren't you sick and tired of living in a country where, instead of catching drug dealers and closing the dives that bring about the moral destruction of society, as soon as these animals in uniform get the smallest degree of power, they use their authority only in the service of their own maniacal interests?[66]

There is some irony in this criticism of police arbitrariness emanating from self-proclaimed avengers. What deserves to be underlined, however, is that this gang was led by an intelligence officer and formed within a prestigious institution, giving them cover to transport and store explosives and to run a training camp in the forest. These characteristics may explain the relative leniency with which the court treated them in 2012. In addition to the attacks on police buildings, they were accused of having murdered an Armenian national and wounded one of his compatriots in April 2010 and then injuring four people in a bomb attack on a café used by Caucasians few months later. The judge did not take into account any aggravating circumstances or extremist leanings.[67] In court, the defendants swaggered in the dock, holding up pieces of paper: "The terrorists are in Dagestan," "God is with us," and "For your freedom and ours."[68] When the verdict was announced and proved less harsh than the prosecutor had asked for, the room exploded with joy and "took on a party feel," despite cries of indignation from the victim's family.

The lawyers spoke of a "great victory for the defense," and some of the accused said that for them the day of the verdict was like a "second birthday."[69]

Tributes to the Primorsky Partisans and the copycat actions they inspired fueled debates that were at their height when the trial of the surviving members of the gang opened in 2012.[70] They had supporters in Russian society and detractors. Competing narratives positively or negatively assessed the fighters' moral qualities, their integrity, their relative independence, and the legitimacy of their claim to act on behalf of the people. At stake in these debates was their description as heroes: praise for their bravery was countered by criticisms of the survivors' cowardice during their trial; the celebration of their revolutionary sincerity by observations on their cynicism and the triviality of their criminal actions; their autonomous organization of armed struggle by suspicions of hidden links to individuals or groups who were manipulating them;[71] and their claim to act in the name of the Russians by accusations of treason.

In early June 2010, the unexpected popularity of the young vigilantes and their image as partisans caused embarrassment and indignation among the police, who set about developing their own communication strategy about them. At first this involved denying the group the status of vigilantes and presenting them as ordinary criminals. Contrary to the image the young rebels sought to convey, for the police they were nothing like social bandits[72]—"Robin Hoods" (*Robin Gudy*), as they were often described—avenging the Russian people for injustices they had suffered. As reflected in a Russian newspaper headline, they were not bighearted outlaws but cruel murderers: the so-called Robin Hoods were "up to their elbows in blood."[73]

The police emphasized that the young men had committed other crimes in the course of their deadly operations and while on the run. They were said to have burgled houses looking for guns and money, beaten and robbed a person, and tied up a taxi driver to steal her car. During the hunt for their hideouts in the taiga, the police said that, in addition to guns and extremist literature, they had found items stolen in burglaries. So in this narrative, the police were not the group's only victims. This argument was reinforced later, during the judicial investigation, when the group was accused of killing four people in 2009, targeting individuals suspected of being involved in drug trafficking. This new accusation, which added considerable weight to the case against them, diluted the murder of police officers in more ordinary crimes. It also shed new light on the group's motivations in attacking police officers: according to public prosecutors, the young extremists turned on law enforcers to steal their guns and use them to settle scores with local drug dealers. The judicial investigation did not rule out the idea that, far from being vigilantes at war with drugs, the accused had themselves been traffickers who wanted to eliminate their rivals. In the vocabulary of law enforcement, the so-called partisans were bandits in the derogatory sense. They had banded into a gang and deserved to be known as the Primorsky gang or even the Primorsky Partisans gang, but nothing else.

The second main discrediting tactic of the authorities consisted of denying these young people the label partisans. This popular designation emerged in late May to early June 2010, when the group was carrying out numerous attacks and evading the police. With its positive connotations, *partisans* reflects the support that the young enemies of the police received from the society around them. In the post-Soviet imagination, *partisan* is still associated with heroic exploits and synonymous with legitimate resistance to oppression. It expresses admiration for the tactics of the young vigilantes, notably their ability to melt into the taiga. Reacting against this description, in late May the local media used "forest brothers" (*lesnye bratia*), which has more negative connotations. In its strict historical sense, it refers to the combatants who fought against the Soviet Union in the Baltic countries in 1941 and after the end of World War II, but in current usage it is more neutral, associated with a type of combatant who merges with his natural surroundings. During the trial, the investigation committee challenged the use of the term *partisan*, emphasizing the group's support for national-socialist ideas. At the trial the most compromising photographs of Andrey, showing him posing as a neo-Nazi, were added to the case file to undermine his credibility. Partisans or Nazis, either way, the debates adopted categories taken from the Soviet past, reproducing the antagonisms of the Great Patriotic War, to borrow the relevant Russian terminology for World War II. The struggle over epithets combined with arguments over whether the partisans were patriots or traitors. Although their image as true Russian guys defending their nation against evil had earned them a solid base of sympathy, the revelations that two of them had converted to Islam muddied the waters and fueled suspicions.

The debates around the Primorsky Krai police killers surfaced again in the 2010s, when they provided the inspiration for many other punitive actions against law enforcement by ultranationalists and Islamists.[74] The partisans left a sulfurous legacy that was revived whenever the police announced that they had foiled a plot targeting state interests,[75] a young man attacked the police, or an artist created a stir. In 2016, the provocative performance artist Petr Pavlensky received the Human Rights Foundation's Václav Havel Prize for his work.[76] When he said that he was giving the prize money to the lawyers for the Primorsky Partisans, who were "real fighters for justice" and "brothers in arms in the struggle against police terror," the foundation revoked his prize on the grounds that the Havel Prize could not be used to support acts of violence against the police.[77] However, in February 2023, when Aleksandr

76   CHAPTER 3

Kovtun died on the battlefront in Ukraine, after striking a deal with the private military company Wagner in the hope of being released from jail, he seemed to have faded from memory. His burial in a Muslim cemetery in Primorye, under the name Saifullah, went almost unnoticed, in stark contrast to the crowd that had accompanied his friend Andrey Sukhorada to his final resting place thirteen years before.[78]

––––––

How does the Primorsky Partisans case fit into a discussion of vigilante justice? The vigilance committees and lynch mobs of previous chapters had no lack of loudmouths proclaiming their aversion to the police and, however much vigilantes may prioritize the punishment of deviants and offenders, they inevitably become involved in more or less violent confrontations with law enforcement, whom they accuse of laxity, incompetence, or corruption. They may challenge or set upon officers deployed on the site of a lynching to disperse the crowd or recover the body. On rare occasions, police officers themselves may become the target of lynch mobs. This happened in Mexico City in 2004, when three officers of the Policía Federal Preventiva, who had been accused of trying to kidnap children on their way to school, were violently beaten and set alight by hundreds of people, as a result of which two of them died.[79]

Premeditated attacks on law enforcement officers are extremely rare outside a context of civil war—or in postconflict situations where police officers are being targeted as a reprisal for their past involvement in repressive operations, as was the case of the Karachi police in the 2000s, when the Muttahida Qaumi Movement settled its accounts by methodically eliminating the officers involved in the "clean-up campaigns" of the preceding decade.[80] Police officers were also lynched in postrevolutionary Mexico. These lynchings, however, were not prompted by past involvement in repression but by the "people's disapproval of their abusive practices as well as their handling of certain criminal or illicit conduct", which were "regarded as legitimate in certain neighbourhoods and communities."[81]

The simple threat of carrying out such an attack is enough to trigger a violent reaction, as can be seen when moral entrepreneurs (conservative politicians, police representatives. and so on) express outrage at the words of a pop song and call for it to be censored. In Moscow in late August 2010, shortly after the arrest of the Primorsky Partisans, the electro-punk band Barto performed a protest song: "I'm ready. And you, are you ready to set fire to a cop car tonight?" The band was interviewed by the police to see whether the song was extremist, but the case was closed a few months later. The most intense controversy of this kind arose in the United States, around the 1992 song "Cop Killer." The song was written by the rapper Ice-T and recorded with Body Count, a band combining rap with heavy metal. It was released by Warner Brothers shortly after the beating of Rodney King by Los Angeles Police Department officers, caught on video by an amateur cameraman. Written in the first person, the song expresses a desire for revenge that also found echoes in riots in Los Angeles's South Central neighborhood when the officers responsible were acquitted. The moral crusade against the song involved not only law enforcement unions and parents' groups but also President George Bush and Vice President Dan Quayle, who both expressed their outrage. Despite Ice-T's efforts to explain himself[82] and the many voices raised in his defense, recalling that other songs in US history with a similar message had not met with the same reaction, the scandal hurt the artist's career. Faced with a possible boycott, Warner and the artist parted company, and the album was reissued without the song.[83]

The spectrum of tactics for settling scores with the police ranges from vindictive language to actual murder. Policing the police first involves documenting abuse or violence they may commit. Since the surveillance of the police carried out by the Black Panthers in Oakland in the late 1960s, cop watching has become widespread.[84] In many sites of struggle, journalists, lawyers, academics, and activists are alert to abuses and remind misbehaving officers of the law.[85] In France, the anti-speciesist activist known as Marie ACAB-Land[86] infiltrated the private Facebook page of the group TN Rabiot Police Officiel, where officers were posting racist, sexist, and homophobic messages and calls for murder.[87] The screenshots that she posted on her own Facebook page made her the enemy of police across France. Their hostility was reinforced by other accusations that she had stalked officers in the Paris region before putting their personal data on social media. In December 2019, following complaints from officers that she had caused them psychological damage, the woman the press called the cop hunter was imprisoned for two months.[88] Her pugnacity and skirmishes with the justice system earned her a great deal of support from anarchist and antifascist groups.[89] Graffiti hailing the courage of "Marie ACAB-Land the best of us all" appeared in Paris on the route of a demonstration against pension reform on December 17, 2019.[90] Without actually naming this "anti-cop militant," Gérald Darmanin, the minister of the Interior, exaggerated the importance of her case during the parliamentary debate on article 24 of the global security law, which aimed to ban the malicious distribution of images of police officers.[91]

Hacking to attack law enforcement officers includes doxing campaigns on the fringes of various protest movements. In October 2019 in Chile, two hackers launched a Pacoleaks website[92] giving access to the personal data—names, addresses, phone numbers—of 21,000 carabineros responsible for law enforcement during social protests. In an explanatory note, they said this would "arm Chileans" to avenge those killed by the police since the uprising began.[93] In Hong Kong in the same year, hostility toward police officers, regarded as "dogs," led to the launch of a "doxx-a-cop" Telegram channel, which had over 240,000 subscribers. More or less daily, the channel published the personal data of police officers, including their addresses, phone numbers, social media accounts, the names of their family members, and even photographs and extracts from private conversations.[94]

Although the extreme actions of the Primorsky Partisans were highly unusual, the cop killers making headlines in the United States in the 2010s shared some of their attributes. Although some came from White supremacist groups, as demonstrated by the murder of two police officers in Des Moines in 2016, it was during Black Lives Matter protests that the greatest number of attacks occurred. In New York in 2014, Ismaaiyl Abdullah Brinsley killed two officers in their car to avenge Black victims of police brutality. In Dallas in July 2016, Micah Xavier Johnson fired on police officers lining a march in memory of Alton Sterling and Philando Castile, two African Americans killed by police a few days previously. This Dallas attack had the most casualties, with five dead and nine wounded. A few days later in Baton Rouge, Gavin Eugene Long murdered three police officers and wounded three others to avenge the death of Alton Sterling, who had been killed there in early July.

These attacks by African Americans in the mid-2010s have many similarities with the incidents that occurred in Russia's Far East: The attacks were motivated by a desire for vengeance and to discredit the police. In New York, shortly before his murders, Brinsley posted a justification on Instagram: "They take one of ours, let's take two of theirs."[95] As in Primorsky Krai, the chosen targets were vulnerable and tactically easy to reach. The officers in New York were on duty in their car; those in Dallas were policing a demonstration and were shot from the top of a building. Beyond the officers themselves, it was the routine presence of the government in the public space that was targeted. However, we should note an important particularity of the US murders: in both Baton Rouge and Dallas, the murderers were veterans, former soldiers who regarded the police—or at least the "bad cops,"[96] in Long's words—as an enemy to be cut down. These self-proclaimed avengers portray themselves as being on a mission to defend their community, which is a victim of racism. Micah Xavier Johnson denounced the lynchings and other acts of violence perpetrated against Black people in the history of the United States. As indicated by Long, referring to the "people that are behind him,"[97] these vigilantes believed they had a popular mandate that gave them the right to kill. Their statements took the form of letters and short messages on social media.[98] They saw themselves as martyrs and used revolutionary rhetoric to justify their actions. Their choice to commit murder was based on the observation that the peaceful Black Lives Matter demonstrations had no effect on racism in the United States. As in Russia, the events in Dallas and Baton Rouge were a source of inspiration for others. In the following days, several attacks on police officers by African Americans were seen across the United States.

Ultimately, the case of the Primorsky Partisans reflects a kind of monstrous hybridization, the distorted combination of two registers of rough justice. Murderers of police officers are neither a vigilance committee nor a people's court, but they do perhaps reveal the missing link between vigilantism and revolutionary justice. Like other vigilantes, they subscribe to an inverted vision of the social world in which they see themselves as liberators who take on authorities they regard as "bandits in law." But in attacking the police, and the state more broadly, they also open up new horizons. In using the language of insurrection and emancipation, and portraying themselves as an enlightened avant-garde with a consciousness-raising role, they cease to stand for the defense of the established order and instead embark on a project of radical social transformation.

4 POPULAR JUSTICE, REVOLUTIONARY JUSTICE

> Justice must be done by the people, but not the outdated, archaic justice handed down to us in the form of alms by the bourgeoisie. The people must give themselves . . . laws that protect their work and condemn their oppressors. . . . The enemies of the people must be judged by a new [form of] justice: popular justice.
>
> PRESS RELEASE BY M-19, announcing the kidnapping of the Colombian labor union leader José Raquel Mercado, accused of having betrayed the working class (1976)[1]

IN THE EARLY 1970S THE KOT LAKHPAT industrial zone in Lahore was gripped by the revolutionary fervor that had seized much of Pakistan. The 1968–1969 mobilization of students and workers against Pakistan's first military government, followed in 1971 by the rise to power of Zulfikar Ali Butto, promising "bread, clothing and shelter" for all, convinced the laboring classes that the *mazdoor kisan raj* (workers' and peasants' rule) was imminent. When their factory shift was over, workers in Lahore would venture into the city's upmarket districts, identifying the mansions they would live in after the revolution.[2] Social unrest became more violent, and Bhutto himself was quick to criticize the excesses of the proletariat, threatening to counter "the strength of the street" with "the strength of the state."[3] This period of widespread turbulence saw the resurgence of paid anti-labor union gangs.[4] After acquiring a reputation for insubordination that made them unwelcome in the factory environment, some workers decided to turn their backs on it altogether to form gangs whose main activity—ironically—became the suppression of worker unrest on behalf of the bosses.[5] Khushi Muhammad Dogar was one of these mercenaries. A former employee of Packages Limited, he maintained close links with the "yellow unions"[6] in Kot Lakhpat, offered his services to settle struggles over territory and workplace conflicts, extorted money from shopkeepers, and terrorized the inhabitants of the working-class neighborhood of Qainchi, where he had his *dera* (lair). However, his rise was interrupted by another Packages employee, who was also gaining authority in Lahore's working-class districts. Abdur Rehman was a solidly built trade unionist in his thirties, prone to back up his arguments with his fists—"confrontation was his cup of tea," as his biographer put it[7]—and similar in many ways to the gangster Dogar, the difference being that he took the workers' side. Like many young people from his village, in a region that provided a great bulk of the recruits for the Pakistani army, Rehman originally planned to follow in his father's footsteps with a career in the military, before trading his uniform for a worker's overalls. In 1966, age twenty-two and armed with a bachelor of arts degree, he joined Packages, a packaging company founded ten years previously as part of a joint venture by Pakistani group Wazir Ali and the Swedish company Akerlund and Rausing. Packages was a highly successful company, a beacon of industrial capitalism in Lahore, open to managerial innovation and providing its 2,500 employees with attractive pay and working conditions. The business was headed by Babar Ali and Wajid Ali, brothers born into the propertied class and used to wielding almost feudal authority,[8] who bore a deep aversion to labor unions. This hostility was not enough to discourage Abdur Rehman. Despite management's attempts at intimidation—including the threat to undermine his virility by shaving off his mustache[9]—Rehman managed to unseat the company union and establish his own independent union as the legally recognized representative of Packages employees. The sixty-five-day strike he organized in 1969 enhanced his reputation for intransigence, and his fame spread to the surrounding countryside, where he took part in numerous meetings to mobilize the small peasantry against the landowners. As well as embodying a resolutely combative Pakistani unionism, not linked to partisan organizations, Rehman was also a charismatic dispenser of justice. The workers of Kot Lakhpat compared the office where he received visitors to a *kacheri*, a Hindi and Urdu term for a magistrate's office or court. In the years 1972–1974, people flocked in to complain of domestic violence, workplace harassment, the greed of usurers, and financial swindles. Rehman recorded the complaints and expeditiously dispensed justice, always to the benefit of the underdog. As noted by a fellow traveler of the workers' movement and former university professor in Lahore, "Instead of taking their grievances to the police station or turning to the *chaudhry* [notables] for help, complainants knocked on the door of the court of Abdur Rehman, where they were given justice without delay."[10] As his authority became established, Rehman grew bolder and demanded compensation for the victims of road accidents and police brutality, backed up

82   CHAPTER 4

by his working-class supporters—"Everywhere he went he took the 3000 workers of Packages with him," remembers the company's former head of production[11]—and drawing on the protest tools of the labor movement to implement his sentences. On several occasions he set up a *gherao* (encirclement, siege), a tactic of workers' struggles that became widespread in the industrial areas of Pakistan in the late 1960s, where factory exits were blocked to imprison managers and bosses. Rehman used this tactic in one of the most famous episodes of his vigilante career, triggered by the death of a *chai wallah* (tea seller). This elderly Pashtun ran a small stand near the Lahore General Hospital, led prayers in a local mosque, and was very popular with the workers of Kot Lakhpat. The official version of his death stated that he had died of an ulcer, but the state of the body cast doubt on this story. The old man had clearly been savagely tortured and murdered by the police, perhaps for being late in paying the protection tax imposed on street hawkers. Outraged by yet another manifestation of police brutality, Rehman and his companions refused to allow this crime to go unpunished. They blocked the area's major roads, surrounded the local police station, and demanded the payment of 10,000 rupees in compensation, which they obtained. They then set off for the tribal marches of the Pakistan-Afghanistan border, where they handed over the money to the dead man's family.[12]

Also high on the list of requests for justice addressed to Rehman—the self-styled "true Bhutto"—was policing the gangsters who carried out the bosses' dirty work and extorted money from shopkeepers.[13] When Qainchi residents called on him to do something about Dogar's abuses, Rehman gathered his supporters and went to teach the kingpin a lesson. It was common at the time for union men and bosses' enforcers to be armed and to use fists, knives, and even guns, but this time it seems Rehman went too far. Not content with a simple beating, his men, with his approval, apparently tortured Dogar with cigarette burns.[14] This workers' vigilantism sealed Rehman's fate. A few weeks later, on April 30, 1974, on his return from a visit to Pakistan's Labor Department, the champion of the proletariat was brutally murdered by Dogar and his henchmen—Rehman was riddled with bullets and also repeatedly slashed with a knife and a machete. Although the identities of those who ordered the carnage remained shadowy, the magistrates charged with investigating Rehman's murder highlighted the responsibility of reformist unionists, sidelined by this charismatic leader who had captivated the working class.[15] They also decried the partiality and "serious irregularities" apparent in the police investigation.[16] The police routinely supported local crime bosses, monetized the reporting of crimes by citizens, and extorted money from shopkeepers, street hawkers, and migrant workers, so they had every reason for revenge against a workers' leader who had presumed to keep them in line and deprive them of their clientele.[17]

———

Though brief, Rehman's vigilante career is a reminder that the propertied classes and the guardians of established order are not the only ones to assert their right to punish in defense of their plans for society. In its own way, every revolution claims to make justice accessible to the people. Revolutionaries plan to build a radically different world,[18] leading to social justice and a new juridical order in the service and, indeed, the hands of the oppressed. There is a crucial nuance here: providing justice in the name of the people and giving the people the power to punish relate to quite different conceptions of the law and the organization of the justice and penal systems. The insurgent movements of the twentieth century endlessly wrestled with this tension inherent in revolutionary justice. In an essay published in 1920, Mao Zedong praised the dictatorship of the proletariat, under which "politics and law are no longer the sole property of officials dressed in mandarin robes, but of workers and peasants. . . . They will make laws according to their convictions."[19] A few years later, after spending time in rural areas of Yunnan plagued by violent land conflicts, the young revolutionary noticeably modified his position on the transformative potential of the law. Written in 1927, *Report on an Investigation of the Peasant Movement in Hunan* enabled Mao to systematize his juridical thinking, which had been profoundly influenced by the spectacle of peasant vigilantism.[20] The excesses perpetrated by the Yunnan peasantry against their oppressors—ranging from parading victims through the streets to summary execution—are hailed in this early piece as expressions of righteous anger, overturning relations of oppression:

> At the slightest provocation they make arrests, crown the arrested with tall paper hats, and parade them through the villages, saying, "You dirty landlords, now you know who we are!" Doing whatever they like and turning everything upside down, they have created a kind of terror in the countryside.[21]

Even the worst eruptions of violence have their reasons, because "the peasants are clear-sighted . . . and very seldom has the punishment exceeded the crime."[22] All of Maoist revolutionary ideology is already there, in its idealization of peasant uprisings and its understanding of the law as an instrument in the class struggle, ruling out the establishment of predetermined legal limits to revolutionary violence.[23] The tension between revolutionary law and liberation of popular anger would later influence Maoist China's experiments with the justice system.[24] To differing degrees, it can also be seen in all movements that aspire to revolutionize society by radically transforming the judicial apparatus—or by eliminating it altogether.

Drawing on the pioneering work of Mario Aguilera Peña on Colombia's "insurgent order,"[25] we here approach revolutionary justice as a descriptive category, without assuming it will depart in practice from the bourgeois law and justice system. Understood in this way, the notion covers judicial arrangements established by emancipation movements in the context of struggles claiming to radically transform people's livelihoods.[26] The popular dimension of this revolutionary justice is harder to identify empirically. Even though it may sometimes be manifested in public trials, it reflects an ideal rather than directly observable norms and practices. A plan for alternative justice, with its quest for institutions and principle of "political elucidation,"[27] does not emerge fully formed from the inventive minds of professional revolutionaries. It is also strongly influenced by repertoires of authority wielded by de facto rulers[28] embedded in working-class life, including local crime bosses who settle disputes in their area, major landowners with feudal airs, and village councils that punish deviants. There is nothing progressive— quite the opposite in fact—about these authority figures who appropriate the right to punish and sometimes even kill with complete impunity.[29] However, as we see later, in the imagination of Lahore's proletariat, it was these ordinary penal repertoires that were manifested in Rehman's rough justice rather than some hypothetical revolutionary model. The appropriation of the function of justice by the working classes for the immediate ends of security and dignity relates to the "revolution in the revolution" described by James Scott.[30]

Subject to purposeful misunderstandings, creative appropriations, and criticisms from all sides leveled at its summary nature or the adventurism of its promoters, popular justice emerges more as a matter of controversy than as a set of stable practices. Embodying an ambition to "take justice away from the state and ring it into being 'through the people's will,'"[31] it triggers a debate around sources of validation for judicial authorities and the degree of formalization necessary to the administration of justice.[32] This is not simply a question of form: behind arguments over the composition of juries, procedural rules, and who is responsible for carrying out sentences, it relates to the possible existence of judicial actions that neither replicate state justice nor legalize score settling and lynching.[33] This is the fine line that must be trod by revolutionary justice with popular pretensions, which oscillates between two strategies: on the one hand, the grand symbolic act, which is favored by groups with no social or territorial base, and on the other,

THE JUDICIAL ARM OF THE REVOLUTIONARIES

On May 29, 1970, around 1:30 p.m., all of Argentina's radio stations interrupted their programs with a news flash announcing the kidnapping of General Pedro Eugenio Aramburu. Radio Rivadavia told its listeners that "the ex-President left his home this morning, shortly after 9, escorted by two men dressed in military uniform. Since then there has been no news of the general. Informed sources have raised the possibility that he was kidnapped by a commando group."[34]

As tension was rising across the country, a Gladiator pickup truck made a four-hour drive to Timote, a small town in Argentina's Buenos Aires Province, carefully avoiding police checkpoints. Inside, the general sat in silence, hidden behind bales of straw, and guarded by young Peronist militants who had disguised themselves as soldiers to kidnap him in broad daylight from his home in the center of the capital. The general's fate was already sealed. When the operation was first mooted, it was decided that Aramburu would expiate his crimes before the court of the people. Having brought down Juan Peron and suppressed opposition movements, the general was a symbol of de-Peronization. And as the profaner of Evita's tomb and prime mover behind the disappearance of her embalmed corpse—the "mystic body of the national movement" in the eyes of the Peronists[35]—the young revolutionaries also regarded Aramburu as the embodiment of "antipeople politics."[36]

Arriving at the La Celma cottage in Timote around 6 p.m., the kidnappers took their prisoner to a bedroom, sat him on a bed, and put him on trial. The proceedings were recorded, which caused a few problems, as one of those present remembered: "It was slow and tiring, because we didn't want to intimidate him or put pressure on him, and he used that to play for time, always answering 'I don't know,' 'I don't remember,' and so on."[37] As soon as the recording was paused, the general became more talkative. He clearly understood that he was living his final hours and was not afraid to confide in his jailers, but he stubbornly refused to go along with this mock trial in the service of Peronist propaganda. The mismatch is apparent in the account published four years later by the Montoneros, the politico-military organization for which this kidnapping was the founding act.[38] The three comrades simultaneously acting as prosecutor, judge, and executioner wanted to retain the appearance of a judicial procedure. Charges were leveled: the general was accused of executing General Juan José Valle and his companions during the uprising of June 9, 1956,[39] and then of mounting a further military coup. The trial continued the next day. This time the accused was charged with having exhumed and hidden the corpse of Eva Peron and then disposing of it. At this point Aramburu insisted that the recording be stopped, after which he confessed to his judges that the "workers' standard-bearer," as the Montoneros called her, had been reburied with a fake identity in a cemetery in Rome. This was untrue, because, after a macabre and murderous journey, the mummy was finally buried in Milan.[40] A few hours later, the three young men told their prisoner they were going to deliberate. The verdict was delivered at daybreak: the general was condemned to death and would be executed within the next half hour. He was taken to the cellar and shot in the chest with a 9 mm bullet, followed by a coup de grace with a Colt 45. The kidnappers would have preferred a firing squad but had to abandon the idea for lack of space in the cellar.[41]

Four years later, two of the kidnappers, Mario Firmenich and Norma Arrostito, published a detailed account of the event, unique in its depiction of the years of lead[42] and the enthusiasm for a particular idea of justice among the young revolutionaries of the day. The narrative uses the tropes of detective stories and classical tragedy to emphasize the mythical aspect of an event that was designed to shock and that has gone down in the annals of Argentina's revolutionary struggles as the Aramburazo.[43] It confirms that vengeance was the main impetus, elevated by its symbolic and instructive dimensions into an exemplary punishment rather than a simple settling of scores. In the minds of the Montoneros, "vengeance underpins the world: instead of sowing disorder it reestablishes order. Vengeance is an act of social education, and at the same time it restores justice."[44] The urge for vengeance was not specific to Peronist militants. Many other Latin American insurgents of the 1970s repeatedly referred to the "avenging arm" of revolutionary justice, mercilessly felling its enemies. This rhetoric has a particular presence in the prose of the Trotskyists of the Ejército Revolucionario del Pueblo, another Argentinian guerrilla group founded in the 1970s:

> Faced with this blind savagery, the Argentinian people demand and require punishment and a response. Interpreting the workers' feelings . . . , the [Ejército Revolucionario del Pueblo] has decided to carry out reprisals against the enemy army's criminal authority. . . . The avenging arm of the people's guerrilla movement rises up against the enemy's savagery. Every time that arm strikes, our people enthusiastically approve the measures of revolutionary justice.[45]

Two years later, a press release from the Colombian group M-19, published following the kidnapping of the unionist José Raquel Mercado (who was held for a month before being executed on April 19, 1976), uses similar rhetoric:

From today, the bosses will find no rest in their palatial residences, comfortable offices, or peaceful vacation resorts. They will not escape the avenging arm of the people.[46]

This rhetoric around justice reflects the rejection of the bourgeois law and legal system by these movements, who proclaim the arrival of a new sovereign power ruling in the name of the people.[47] Their revolutionary justice, supposedly hailed by the people, did not seek to democratize the power to punish but aimed to educate the masses and reveal them to themselves.[48] In Timote the Montoneros supposedly demonstrated "that beyond the traps, legal nitpicking, and regulations oppressing the workers, there was a path to the true justice, which is born of the will of a people."[49] So, without entirely departing from the trial format, the justice delivered in the name of this abstract entity was intentionally direct and swift. The trials undertaken by insurgent groups followed the accusatory model, eschewing such encumbrances as defense rights, the distinction between judge and prosecution, and criteria of admissibility for questions and evidence. The proceedings were based on a presumption of guilt and favored shortcuts to a conclusion known in advance, thereby reflecting the summary justice meted out by vigilantes of every stripe.[50] With a very few exceptions—such as the case of the president of the Uruguayan national electricity company, Ulysses Pereyra Reverbel, who was freed after being held for four days in August 1968[51]— this swift justice had no time for acquittal and favored capital punishment. And although the verdicts were given the greatest possible publicity, and the harshness of the sentences made an impression, the trials themselves were held behind closed doors, away from prying eyes.

The summary nature of these judicial proceedings was heightened by the clandestine lives of those conducting them. Combatants were always on the move, which encouraged them to resort to execution because that freed them from the need to take prisoners with them. Although some groups occasionally locked up their opponents in "people's prisons," the lack of a physical base where institutions could be established made imprisonment and community service more difficult. The harshness and speed demanded by revolutionary justice is thus not reducible to an ideological project; it also reflects tactical adjustments to power relations that oblige militant organizations to be constantly on the run.

FROM SUMMARY JUSTICE TO SETTLING ORDINARY DISORDER

The wild rush forward by a segment of the radical Left during the years of lead vividly illustrates the spiral of self-destruction that faces social struggles

88   CHAPTER 4

when they go underground. As it went into hiding, the revolutionary avant-garde was condemned to autarky, and the avenging arm of popular justice often came down on its own most fervent zealots. In Argentina the Montoneros' combination of avenging fervor and flagellatory Thomism[52] wreaked havoc in the movement's ranks, notably among those militants accused of physical and mental weakness under torture.[53] Purges of the weak, deviant, and renegade culminated in the self-annihilation of the United Red Army of Japan (Rengō Sekigun) in the confined space of a mountain chalet in Gunma prefecture where, in February 1972, ten of the twenty-nine participants at a training camp perished after what were often self-inflicted abuses, and two more were executed for attempting to desert. This unusually violent purge, reflecting a radical approach to "self-criticism" (sōkatsu) and somatic proofs of commitment that were characteristic of the organization,[54] contributed to the almost total disappearance of the far left, and indeed the Left as a whole, from the national political landscape. This traumatic episode—which only fringe artists, some of whom were fellow travelers of the radical Left in the 1960s, had dared describe in their works[55]—has been abundantly revisited in the twenty-first century in many works of historiography and autobiographical accounts, most of them exploring the same burning question: How could such lynchings—in the Japanese sense of uncontrolled and gratuitous violence—erupt among comrades?[56]

Nothing, however, is inevitable about the spontaneous combustion of revolutionary justice. In consolidating their authority over a particular population and territory, the most highly organized militant groups tend to reorient, as Abdur Rehman did, their justice-dealing intentions toward settling everyday disputes (such as territorial and neighbor disputes and domestic violence) and suppressing delinquency. In Colombia, the first penal code drawn up by an insurgent group—the 1952 Laws of the Llano—thus sought to punish "those who steal, rob, are vagabonds, spy, betray, and foster disorder."[57] In some guerrilla groups, a Marxist approach to social justice coexists with the promotion of public order, as, for example, in a 2012 press release from the central committee of the Communist Party of the Philippines–Marxist Leninist to mark the forty-third anniversary of founding of the New People's Army:

> The broad masses of the people strongly demand the arrest, trial and punishment of landowners with blood debts, all the human rights violators, the plunderers, ringleaders of criminal syndicates in drugs, human trafficking and cattle-rustling.[58]

The maintenance of public order often combines with the imposition of morality. Generally speaking, as Eric Hobsbawm observed in the late 1960s, "revolution is puritan."[59] Throughout its history, the radical Left has tended to promote a "revolutionary moralism"[60] that contrasts with the hedonism and depravity of bourgeois society. The first to be affected by these rules are the combatants themselves: within armed groups, the regulation of sexuality and conjugality is a matter of internal discipline and a means of differentiation from civilian populations.[61] Differentiation is enforced by punishing transgressors and may involve heterodox solutions to the "sex problem"[62] or the imposition of asceticism reminiscent of the "warrior communism" described by Max Weber, in which "the existence of the warrior is the perfect counterpart to the existence of the monk," notably through its members' renunciation of all family ties.[63] Moral policing sometimes extends to civilian populations when armed groups infiltrate civilians' private lives, harshly suppressing illegitimate relationships, domestic violence, and incest. The imposition of morality by the Nepalese Maoist guerrillas of the 1990s was exemplary in this regard and was in keeping with the monarchy's attempts to regulate the behavior of the population in all its aspects.[64] The Colombian guerrilla group Ejército Popular de Liberación went even further in punishing adultery and those who abandoned their family responsibilities, and it sentenced to death those who committed incest.[65]

Armed groups that see their role as emancipatory do not always take on a policing role. When it comes to dealing with common criminals, some prefer to hide behind vigilantes. In Northern Ireland, the Catholic population recognized that the Irish Republican Army (IRA) was behind the organization Direct Action Against Drugs, which emerged in 1994 and murdered ten drug dealers.[66] On the other side of the wall, the Protestant paramilitaries punished political crimes (such as exchanging information or collaboration with the enemy or using the organization's name for personal gain) as vigorously as everyday criminality (such as drug dealing or pedophilia), which they extended to cover antisocial behavior (such as disturbing the peace at night, lack of respect for elderly people, and dumping garbage in the street).[67]

The punishments set in place by consolidated revolutionary justice—provided by insurgent groups having a solid social or territorial base but not fully established through the seizure of power—reflect its intent to defend the public and moral order. During the consolidation phase, revolutionary justice may treat politically charged offenses more severely while being open to financial penalties for less serious transgressions. Describing common criminals as "antipeople," the IRA imposed fines and payments for damages in its sentencing hierarchy, and the sums demanded tended to reflect the solvency of the guilty rather than the gravity of the offense. The Protestant paramilitaries took a similar approach.[68]

90 CHAPTER 4

Imposing fines on delinquents has also been a favorite of Colombian insurgents. In 1957, the communist guerrillas in the Tolima region adopted a
legal code that set fines for different categories of offense, from the illicit
use of firearms to disturbing the peace and infringing its family code.[69] Over
the following decade, fines were commonly imposed in areas under their
control.[70] The Fuerzas Armadas Revolucionarias de Colombia (FARC) developed out of this peasant self-defense movement and also regulated society
in its strongholds in the center and south of the country. It imprisoned and
banished and even carried out summary executions, but the most frequent
punishments were fines, property seizures, and community service or forced
labor (cleaning streets, painting buildings, repairing public benches, road
building, and so on).

The idea that revolutionary organizations favor definitive punishments
(banishment and executions) therefore needs nuance, along the lines adopted by Anne Simonin in relation to the French revolutionary tribunal of
1793.[71] The few available studies, such as that from the International Commission of Jurists on the justice system of the Nepalese Maoists, confirm that
some revolutionary organizations may adopt a more conciliatory approach
than their assertions of radicalism might suggest. The Maoist judges in Nepal
tended to be less harsh than those employed by the state. Executions were recorded during the People's War of 1996–2006[72]—although the juridical code of
the *maobadi*[73] made no reference to capital punishment—but criminal trials
seldom led to a sentence of more than five years in prison. In fact, where
sentencing was concerned, *maobadi* justice systematically used public humiliation and, in the most serious cases, forced labor.[74] In civil cases, judges
tended to seek compromise, which did not rule out all use of force (for example, when no consensus could be reached in a land dispute, threatening both
parties with confiscation of the land).[75]

This arbitrage between the will to punish and the search for mediation
evolves with the circumstances. The Marxist guerrillas in Colombia tempered their punitive ardor as popular discontent increased and paramilitary
groups gained momentum. This is particularly clear in the FARC's consolidation of its justice system during the ceasefire of 1998,[76] which created a
vast demilitarized zone in the south of the country. In this area the size of
Switzerland and with a population of 1.5 million, the FARC's claim to govern
met with strong resistance from the inhabitants.[77] The group's administration of justice, which was central to its project for a new society, did not
escape criticism. Its aspiration to regulate and above all cleanse society
sometimes took an exceptionally brutal form—for example, at Vista Hermosa in the Meta Department, where the FARC required every inhabitant
age twelve or older to take an HIV test. Some of those found to be positive

were subsequently deported or even executed.[78] These abuses tarnished the group's image, even among its habitual supporters. However, the abuses do not seem to have undermined the FARC in its role of dispensing justice and maintaining order.

For all its excesses and arbitrariness, rebel justice sometimes had a "calming role"—for instance, by providing an alternative to mob justice.[79] Moreover, in its strongholds in the country's central and southern regions, which had been profoundly destabilized by the drug trade, the FARC's actions led to a noticeable decline in levels of violence and the regularization of illicit activities (such as coca cultivation and trading, timber trafficking, and occupation of land in forest reserves). This regulation of the illicit economy was accompanied by social progress, such as the establishment of a minimum price for coca and the end of appalling practices such as paying workers in *bazuco*, a highly addictive cocaine derivative similar to crack. Stamping out this kind of enslavement earned the FARC popular support, and its authority was consolidated by the traffickers' compliance with the rules it had imposed.[80]

The FARC's justice also owed its relative popularity to the possibilities for improvement that it offered offenders.[81] As with the IRA in Northern Ireland, the harshest penalties were inflicted only after a series of warnings had been given, and the refusal of transgressors to mend their ways, rather than the nature of the transgression itself, led to banishment or, in incorrigible cases, to "skinning."[82] Even crimes that the guerrillas considered most serious (cattle theft, rape, murder, or spying for the army or paramilitaries) were usually punished by forced exile rather than death. Although this insurgent justice had a reputation for inflexibility, it offered the poorest offenders an opportunity to pay their fines in installments.[83]

THE TEMPTATION TO NORMALIZE

Revolutionary justice emerges in zones of unrest when insurgents seeking to seize power at the national level attempt to govern the local population. It offers juridical services that are fairer and less costly than those of the official courts, for the benefit of the greatest possible number. In Colombia, for example, the plan to establish "people's courts" emerged during the "first guerrilla conference" of 1952, at the same time as the call for a justice system that was "effective and free of charge."[84] Unlike the "countertrials" staged by European left-wing movements since the 1930s, which were essentially symbolic,[85] the aim here was to address actual requests for assistance by people on the ground—particularly, but not solely, the poorest. This counteroffer of justice involved codifying juridical standards, organizing a justice system, and less commonly, professionalizing judges—in other words, steps toward

92   CHAPTER 4

an institutionalization destined to remain incomplete and liable to irregularity and improvisation.

This kind of rationalization relativizes the contrast between a justice with revolutionary ambitions and bourgeois legality. As noted by Michael Taussig in relation to the Laws of the Llano and the codes of conduct that followed them, these texts show the influence of a "legal mentality" with its origins in the state and apparent in the reasoning, language, and penal categories they adopt.[86] The writers of these codes used state justice as their model, and this is hardly surprising given the role played by some activist lawyers—such as José Alvear Restrepo (1913–1953), one of the main authors of the Laws of the Llano—in developing this body of law.[87] Similarly, in Nepal, in the last years of the People's War, the *maobadi* redoubled efforts to appear as the country's de facto rulers, codified the law, and set up their own judiciary. In 2003, they adopted a code of justice drawn up by Khim Lal Devkota, an eminent member of the Maoist party who was also a senior advocate. This code was largely based on the *Muluki Ain* (literally, "national code"), which combined the civil and penal codes and had been adopted by King Mahendra in 1963. The judicial system set in place by the insurgents reproduced the tripartite structure of its official counterpart, with district courts (which became "people's courts" under the Maoists), appeal courts, and a supreme court (renamed the Court of Final Instance).

The mimicry of forms sometimes goes hand in hand with overlapping institutions. This "interlegality," to borrow a notion favored by advocates of legal pluralism,[88] can be seen in even the most informal experiments in alternative justice. Although Abdur Rehman's workers' court carried out some sentences, it sometimes also brought in the police and factory owners to oblige them to enforce the law. Like many vigilantes, Rehman adopted a relationship of ascending subsidiarity in relation to the state, appropriating the right to punish some offenses while recognizing the government as the supreme arbiter of social conflict. After punishing the gangster boss Dogar, Rehman handed him over to the police with a crowd of workers present as witnesses.[89]

The dynamics of armed conflict in revolutionary civil wars do not in themselves prevent these circulations of both litigants and legal files. The delivery of justice by the FARC in Colombia, which culminated in demilitarization from 1998 to 2002, was closely linked to the regulatory role of the Juntas de Acción Communal (JAC), the communal action councils set up by the government in the late 1950s as an interface with local populations. These organizations, which were widely infiltrated by the FARC in the areas under its influence, dictated the norms of collective living and set the amount of fines for offenses. In the first decade of the 2000s, overwhelmed by ordinary cases (such as disputed land boundaries, damage caused by livestock, and weights and measures disputes), the FARC delegated part of this role to the conciliation committees within the JAC. Only when a committee failed to settle a case was one of the interested parties allowed to *llevar arriba* ("take [the case] to the top," or in other words, to the FARC), after obtaining a certificate from the committee confirming that mediation had failed. This arrangement enabled the FARC to offer its own arbitration as the last resort of justice, without being burdened with the business of settling everyday disputes.[90] And when this subsidiarity arrangement was not enough to unclog the complaints offices opened by the FARC in places under their control, they sometimes moved their unofficial courts to the "mountain," giving a literal meaning to the phrase *llevar arriba*.[91]

Developments in the justice system of the Nepalese Maoist movement over the course of the People's War reveal similar examples of interlocking provision. The Maoist judges were nonprofessionals, chosen for their loyalty to the party. They had at least a rudimentary knowledge of state law and were known in the village community where they officiated and from which they usually came. They were appointed by the local cadres of the Communist Party of Nepal (Maoist) and received a minimum of legal training—one or two days at most. In principle their appointment had to be approved (with a nod or raised hand) by an assembly of the local population. These judges had considerable discretionary power, in accordance with the doctrine of revolutionary legality inherited from Soviet law, which, as described by Andrey Vyshinsky, a prosecutor of the Great Terror, in 1932, "requires flexible, and so-to-speak, free-spirited (which is not to say, arbitrary) relationship with law. Not the letter of the law, not legal chicanery, not blind formal obeisance to the law, but a creative relationship to law."[92]

This doctrine was popularized by Nepal's progressive elites beginning in the 1950s[93] and influenced the code drawn up by the Maoists in 2003. It was a legal mentality that encouraged judges to apply "prevailing laws . . . creatively in the context of wartime and the nature of the crime" while giving precedence to "real justice" over "legal justice."[94] However, we should not overestimate the practical repercussions of the code, which was drawn up late in the conflict and had little effect on the way that the Maoists dispensed justice in real life.[95] The *maobadi* judges were largely unfamiliar with socialist legal doctrine and preferred to base their opinions on natural law[96] or common sense,[97] to signify their break with positive law, although this break was far from complete. Some judges appointed to people's courts sought precedents for their cases in the district courts or supreme court before giving a judgment that might ultimately be transferred to the jurisdiction of the state for validation.[98] Meanwhile, as in Colombia, plaintiffs whose cases had

94   CHAPTER 4

been dismissed by the state courts could have them tried by rebel justice.[99] Between 1998 and 2002, residents of urban centers far from the demilitarized zone, like Bogotá and Cali, traveled to the FARC's strongholds to submit their complaints to the guerrillas.[100] However, to unburden themselves from a heavy load of cases, the FARC sometimes advised plaintiffs to turn to state courts, especially for the adjudication of family disputes.

Some supporters of revolutionary justice regularized their procedures and defended themselves against accusations that they dispensed summary justice. In Colombia, the consolidation of the FARC justice system after the ceasefire of 1998 was accompanied by noteworthy efforts to strengthen investigative work (zone commanders heard witnesses, sites in the dispute were inspected, and evidence was collected, possibly with support from a team of investigators), even if the verdict was still decided during the first inspection and at best within a week.[101] The IRA, accused of extracting forced confessions, began to make audio recordings of its interrogations and sometimes used extracts from CCTV surveillance in its judicial investigations.[102] It also established appeals procedures, particularly for supposed spies sentenced to death, who were able to take their case to the adjutant general and present evidence to prove their innocence.

These procedural elements were introduced primarily in response to criticisms from the local society and sometimes also in an attempt to conform to international human rights standards. In the early 1990s, the Communist Party of the Philippines–Marxist Leninist, whose New People's Army (NPA) had been fighting a guerrilla war since the late 1960s, committed to respecting the principles of international humanitarian law and the Geneva Convention in its *Hukumang Bayan* (people's courts), which operated in the provinces, districts, municipalities, and barrios. This formalist concern is illustrated by the following case, recorded by the young cadre in charge of the investigation, Renato Santos.

In August 2004, a female minor was abducted in the Visayan Islands by a farmer known for his drug addiction and membership in a street gang. He repeatedly raped her over several days. The victim's family went to the police, but to no avail. The suspect was not even interviewed. The resulting outcry reached the ears of the insurgents, who decided to open their own investigation. According to the investigator, the suspect was notified of his rights during his arrest, before being made to sign a statement under oath, confirming his consent to the judicial process. While awaiting his trial, the young man was imprisoned in an NPA jail. He was judged by a jury of nine— three party members, three members of its armed branch, and three local sympathizers. A day was spent hearing the witnesses for the defense and prosecution, and the deliberation took a further half day. By a verdict of five

POPULAR JUSTICE, REVOLUTIONARY JUSTICE   95

against four, the accused was judged guilty of rape and condemned to death. In accordance with the movement's established mediation procedures, the victim was given the opportunity to pardon her attacker, which she vigorously refused to do, saying she would prefer to see him die "several times." In contravention of the group's procedural rules,[103] at no time did the accused have access to a lawyer. According to the investigator, he "chose" not to appeal. Because the sentence was death, the jury should have consulted the movement's supreme court for advice and approval, but the local guerrilla cadres decided that this was not necessary. The execution took place behind closed doors, after which the body was left in a public place, with a letter claiming the action in the name of the NPA.

This story, collected from Santos by the researcher Teresa Jopson, reveals that some revolutionary organizations do attempt—in however desultory a fashion—to follow international law.[104] As we see in the next section, the efforts they make—to codify legal rules, bureaucratize judiciaries, and adhere to due process—are rarely enough to gain the support of international organizations and supporters of human rights. They are also hindered by the tendency of revolutionary justice to make exceptions to its own rules. Irregularities include procedural flaws and the random nature of punishments, which are seldom made to fit the crime in any systematic way. In areas under FARC control, for example, only a few infractions led to a specific type of punishment. The others were punished in different ways, and the manner in which punishments were enforced was never predictable. During his field study in the Serranía de la Macarena in the first years of the 2000s, the anthropologist Nicolás Espinosa Menéndez noted that some people sentenced to death by the FARC were indeed executed, but others were forced into exile, still others managed to get their sentences commuted to fines, and some even obtained absolution following interventions by community groups.[105]

Apart from the most institutionalized organizations—such as the Liberation Tigers of Tamil Eelam guerrillas, who opened their own law facility to train magistrates in 1992 and greatly expanded their judicial system after the 2002 ceasefire[106]—revolutionary justice usually remains an amateur affair, subject to conflicting norms and arbitrary decisions. We are a long way from a rational legal paradigm, which as Max Weber shows, is notable for its regularity, based on the empirical "validity" of its "juridical principle"—in other words, the actual capacity of its laws to regulate individual behavior and to guarantee that social actors can access legal aid that is free of arbitrariness or lordly grace.[107] However, divergences from this ideal may not in themselves discredit the justice system in the eyes of the people, because irregularities are always relative and the population is comparing this system not to an ideal model but to a flawed system of state justice. In addition, unlike

96   CHAPTER 4

professional magistrates, the insurgents who are invested with the power to judge are generally seen as people of integrity. This seems to be the view of Don Vincente, a coca grower interviewed by Espinosa Menéndez in the early years of the 2000s, at a time when his village had no officiating judge:

> Even if we had a judge today, we would still seek out the guerrillas every time, because, whereas the guerrillas settle your problem in the blink of an eye, someone only has to go to the judge with a bribe and the other guy gets taxed. You don't get that with the guerrillas, they don't tax anyone. They just follow the law.[108]

The suggestion that the guerrillas are more legalistic than professional magistrates is not without irony, particularly coming from a coca producer and part-time fuel trafficker. But it shows that, in some circumstances, groups engaged in armed struggle can take on the role of ultimate decision-makers. In replicating the administrative and judicial bodies of the state, they also transcend them, ascending to the head of the hierarchy of jurisdictions, because the scope of insurgent justice is not confined to everyday civil and penal cases but extends to disputes relating to the illicit economy. Such hierarchies are unstable and depend on the capacity of militant organizations to ensure respect for their verdicts and on whether revolutionary justice is accepted and adopted by populations. The main blind spot of this justice is the participation of those on the receiving end. In what conditions and at what cost is its popular mission achieved?

THE BATTLEGROUND OF POPULAR JUSTICE

In December 1967, when China's Cultural Revolution was in full sway, the authorities in the province of Guangxi published a communiqué calling on the population to show restraint in expressing their anger against the class enemy: "Mass organizations should not randomly arrest, beat, or kill. All the current detainees should be released immediately."[109] To discredit vigilante activities of this kind, the new term *luanda luansha*, "indiscriminate beatings and killings," appeared in public discourse. Formed from the character 乱 (*luan*), which can signify "arbitrary" or "chaotic" when referring to illegal acts, the phrase emphasizes the subversive weight of such practices.[110] It also reveals the internal tension between two different conceptions of the justice system within Maoist China's political and judicial apparatus: a participative, flexible model in which the codification of laws, the professionalization of judges, and the rationalization of legal procedures ran counter to the ideal of popular justice and a more bureaucratic model, drawing on Soviet law and

POPULAR JUSTICE, REVOLUTIONARY JUSTICE   97

promoted by the party's more conservative members, such as Liu Shaoqi.[111] In the first decades of the regime, these two conflicting conceptions were held in an unstable equilibrium. With the advent of the Cultural Revolution, the Maoist ideology of living law (reflecting the first conception of punishment) seems to have come to the fore, but the debate was not closed and the excesses inherent in this model continued to encounter resistance.

Disagreements around popular justice continued within the regime that had become its standard bearer while largely escaping the attention of Maoist China's supporters beyond its borders. On the contrary, as the Cultural Revolution went on, a fringe of the global revolutionary left enthusiastically supported the project to replace bourgeois law with a justice seen as the avenging arm of the people in struggle and embodied by the revolutionary avant-garde. The project itself was not new: during the Spanish Civil War, the anarchists had experimented with a class justice that covered everything from professional disputes to family matters. The mission of the Oficina Jurídica de Barcelona, founded by the lawyer Eduardo Barriobero, was to "incorporate the spirit of the people into the administration of justice [and] open a path for a new legality."[112] Although the Oficina Jurídica de Barcelona was soon dismantled and Barriobero prosecuted, in subsequent years other popular courts emerged in Republican-controlled zones.[113] However, these historical antecedents were eclipsed by the experiments of Maoist China, which became the model for all panegyrists of popular justice after 1968. The militants of the Gauche prolétarienne in France, for example, dreamed of a counterjustice that would find inspiration, legitimacy, and a transgressive power of excess in the people's legitimate anger. The Gauche prolétarienne gave free rein to its vigilante fantasies in the Bruay-en-Artois affair, relaying calls for the lynching of the notary Pierre Leroy, who was suspected of murdering a young woman called Brigitte Dewèvre. In its first issue of May 1, 1972, *La Cause du peuple* praised lynching as a tool of class vengeance, overturning the stigma attached to it in bourgeois and progressive circles:

YES, WE ARE BARBARIC
"He must be made to suffer bit by bit!" "They should give him to us, we will cut him up piece by piece with a razor!" "I will tie him to the back of my car and drive through the streets of Bruay at sixty miles an hour!" "He needs his balls cut off!"
How many other punishments do the miners and their families imagine? Are these words barbaric? Yes, they are, but to understand them you have to have suffered 120 years of exploitation in the mines. In every family, from father to son, grandfather to grandson, it's been nothing but tears, sweat, and blood. Murder transformed into fate, silicosis transformed

98   CHAPTER 4

into asthma. Everyone has a brother, father, or family member who has been murdered or mutilated.[114]

The French Maoists' enthusiasm for popular justice caused a dilemma for left-wing intellectuals of the day. This can clearly be seen in the positions publicly adopted by Jean-Paul Sartre. His participation in the great countertrials of the time (the Russell tribunal of 1966 on war crimes in Vietnam, the popular tribunal of 1970 in Lens, where he acted as prosecutor) made Sartre a promoter of law as a political weapon. But his rapprochement with the Maoists did not stop him denouncing the calls for lynching put out by *La Cause du peuple.* In the publication's following issue, he concurs that the bourgeois Leroy deserves "the people's legitimate hatred . . . for his *social* activities" but certainly not for an untried crime. Reaffirming his belief that the law must remain independent of historical processes,[115] Sartre defends the presumption of innocence. Although this principle is an integral part of bourgeois justice, in his view it constitutes a "popular victory of the French Revolution." And lynching, he adds, "is far too shady a practice (look at the lynchings in the United States), often too influenced by reactionary ideology for it to become a regular punishment of popular justice."[116]

Michel Foucault also joined the debate with the "Maos." His critique was not aimed at the right-wing echoes in their ideas of justice but at their insistence on reintroducing an intermediary between the masses and their enemies under cover of establishing authentic popular justice. In a dialogue with the leaders of the Gauche prolétarienne (which was a banned organization at the time), Foucault identified another tension in these alternative justice projects, which was their continued attachment to the "bourgeois judicial state apparatus" of which the courts were "the visible, symbolic form."[117] Was this self-proclaimed justice of the people seeking to "break" or simply "bend" the staff of justice?

In a still-famous exchange between Foucault and Benny Lévy (as Victor), the latter states, "At the first stage of the ideological revolution I'm in favor of looting, I'm in favour of 'excesses.' The stick must be bent in the other direction, and the world cannot be turned upside down without breaking eggs." To which Foucault replies, "Above all it is essential that the stick be broken."[118] In other words, don't settle for adopting targets of repression different from those of bourgeois justice, do away with the penal system itself. In seeking to be popular, revolutionary justice thus appears incompatible with the use of courts that embody the fiction of a "neutral body between the people and their enemies" and that also have the potential to reestablish a state apparatus and class oppression. However, Foucault did acknowledge that the conditions for the "elucidation" of an authentically popular justice had yet to be "invented."[119]

This critique, which is typical of the antiauthoritarian struggles of the time, is sometimes shared by practitioners of popular justice themselves. Looking back from his Milan prison at the abduction of Christian Democracy leader Aldo Moro, Mario Moretti—who acted as prosecutor in the popular court that passed judgment on Moro and then executed him—went so far as to deny that the exercise was a trial. Lamenting that the group had used a "very poor, almost forced terminology that merely aped bourgeois courts," the former Red Brigade leader added that he and his comrades were "never capable of conducting a trial."[120]

The debates around the conditions for implementing popular justice were not confined to intellectuals and small groups using shock tactics to make a splash. Armed movements on a mission to seize power also engaged with these issues in a concrete way, looking at how the laboring classes could participate effectively in judicial action, beyond their incantatory role as a point of reference. The positions adopted on this issue by insurgent groups were seldom definitive. The Colombian guerrilla group Ejército de Liberación Nacional was always less well integrated into local society than the FARC or the Ejército Popular de Liberación. They applied their rigorous penal approach to both combatants and the civilian population and usually distanced the peasant masses from their judicial actions. However, there were some exceptions to this rule—for example, in the Opón region, where in the late 1960s the peasants were encouraged to pass judgment in murder cases.[121] The FARC, meanwhile, sometimes put the fate of rapists and murderers to a vote, although they did not do so systematically. Questions around popular participation extended to how cases were referred to the revolutionary courts. In most cases denunciation (or the provision of "information," in the terminology current within insurgent movements[122]) was the simplest way to access this form of justice. Far from taking offense, some guerrilla groups saw it as the mark of trust with the masses. Into the late 1990s, the FARC tended to give more credit to the word of an informant than to that of the accused, because they regarded merely speaking to the group as evidence of good faith.[123] In an interview published in 1994, the FARC leader Manuel Marulanda Vélez, alias "Tirofijo" (Good Shot), asserted that the punishment of delinquents was a response to a social demand, expressed in written requests, for the FARC's protection against lowlifes "who steal cows and chickens" or "won't allow girls to go out alone." According to Tirofijo, the FARC studied each of these requests and proceeded "entirely logically to cleanse harmful individuals."[124]

These operations of social cleansing (or *limpiezas*—see Chapter 5) opened the way to score settling. The instrumentalization of popular justice in private disputes is not specific to the context of armed struggle, as can be seen from

100   CHAPTER 4

the requests addressed to Abdur Rehman by local shopkeepers in the Qainchi neighborhood. However, it becomes a more serious risk in civil wars, when the state can no longer guarantee the security of transactions and respect for property rights, leading inevitably to the proliferation of family, trade, and property disputes. Concerned to defend their position as impartial arbiter, which they must maintain to have their judgments accepted, some armed groups, such as the Taliban in Afghanistan, try to remain above the fray by making their judicial activities as objective as possible.[125] In tandem with the risks of private appropriation, popular justice projects tend to be diffracted through abuses and judicial microenterprises. In his ethnography of the everyday revolutionary justice of the FARC, Espinosa Menéndez provides a striking illustration of these detours. An elementary school teacher was infuriated by the mess left in his school after parties held by the pupils' parents and put up a sign saying that those leaving trash in the building would be fined 15,000 pesos. This angered the parents, who quickly complained to the local guerrilla commander. He ordered the offending sign to be taken down at once and used the opportunity to remind people that the authority to impose fines was his alone.

Disputes around the practical implementation of an authentically popular form of justice are not played out solely between the masses and revolutionaries, sometimes mediated through the third party of a court. They also involve politicians and legal specialists who criticize revolutionary justice as a subterfuge and promote their own ideas of legality. Critiques of this kind emerge in the national political landscape in support of the state's monopoly on the power to punish or to promote an alternative, more considered conception of political and social change. They discredit popular justice experiments by presenting them as cover for criminal intent or new forms of tyranny. Proletarian avengers are not immune to this classic critique of vigilantes of every stripe, which aims to undermine their legitimacy by revealing their hidden vices and authoritarianism.

In the early 1970s, when the more conservative section of the Pakistan People's Party and part of the Pakistani Left were denouncing Abdur Rehman's "adventurism," the reformist trade unions were accusing him of being a vulgar *goonda* (thug).[126] These accusations were not unfounded: as we have seen, at this time in Pakistan, levels of physical violence in social struggles and interunion rivalries were rising sharply, and every side in the conflicts hired coercion specialists. Abdur Rehman surrounded himself with armed bodyguards, his vigilante practices were similar to those of the city's gangster bosses, and his court of justice reinvented the masculine social space of the *dera*. In urban settings, these institutions halfway "between a reception salon and a den of thieves" ranged from workers' boarding houses to less salubrious establishments run by the underworld.[127] Here gangsters offered their mediation services in different cases, slipping into a much older, more rural repertoire of authority. In the countryside, *deras* started out as places of refuge for those on the social fringes (bandits, drug addicts, and other deviants). They were owned by the landowning elite and gradually evolved into places where villagers could go to ask landowners for help, goodwill, or mediation. Rehman played on these cultural references and the ideas that they had engendered among the working classes as to how justice could be done, maintaining a confusion with their ambivalent authority figures. Like many other self-proclaimed avengers, he was caught in a mirror illusion in which dominators and dominated, bandits and vigilantes, and defenders of order and forces of disorder did not simply reflect each other in reverse but tended to become merged in a single ambiguous form, like the face of the sheriff superimposed over that of the desperado in Sam Peckinpah's 1973 film *Pat Garrett and Billy the Kid*. This confusion of roles gives vigilantes their power, investing them with an evocative force that draws on different registers of authority while transcending everyday categories of practice. Such blurring, however, also exposes them to accusations of imposture and duplicity.

As soon as revolutionary justice acquires a degree of external recognition, it is also exposed to the critical eye of the international guardians of juridical order, who downplay the ideological content of their critique with an emphasis on procedure. These critics are keen to demonstrate that the kangaroo courts run by insurgents are biased, that their judges are untrained in the law, that defense rights are not respected, and that military and judicial roles are not clearly separated within rebel groups.[128] For international jurists and human rights advocates, the penal systems of insurgent movements provide a mere "veneer of legality" for practices that are in fact forms of vigilantism, seen as arbitrary justice incarnate.[129] These criticisms from experts emerged in the first half of the 1990s in El Salvador, where the local United Nations mission contrasted due process with the law as laid down in areas controlled by the guerrillas of the Frente Farabundo Martí para la Liberación Nacional (Farabundo Martí Front for National Liberation).[130] The same arguments later reappeared in relation to armed groups in the Philippines and the parody of justice they were said to dispense by human rights advocates. In an accusation leveled against the NPA's popular courts, the assistant head of Human Rights Watch Asia wrote,

> By pretending that it is operating a real justice system, when in fact it is carrying out bloody vigilante justice, the NPA only adds to the misery of the Filipino people directly affected by the country's long internal armed conflict. If NPA leaders pride themselves on carrying forth the

102   CHAPTER 4

aspirations of the Filipino masses, they will stop holding sham trials and shooting people down in the streets.[131]

In this case, revolutionary justice equates to summary justice, and the accusation of vigilantism discredits both judicial practices and the overall political project of insurgents. Sham trials make the movements hard to defend. The recognition of liberation movements by global nongovernmental organizations and international organizations is conditional on their at least stated adherence to the liberal regime of rights that they fiercely denounce. The compromise these movements sometimes adopt is support for juridical pluralism, which places the positive justice of the state on an equal footing with revolutionary law. The Frente Farabundo Martí para la Liberación Nacional in El Salvador advocated international recognition for the coexistence of "insurgent legislation" and "government law" but argued that each side had the legitimacy to deliver justice according to its own rules.[132]

Procedural critiques are not the monopoly of international legal experts who, while invoking a universal ideal of justice, nevertheless ground their authority in the status of a "juridical spokesperson for state interests."[133] Similar critiques of a different form are found among the working classes in whose name revolutionary organizations claim to deliver justice. Some are angered by sham justice that supposedly serves the masses but in reality leads to the creation of new inequalities before the law, in the name of which new abuses are perpetrated. Here, however, criticisms sometimes take an affectionately ironic view of kids setting themselves up as guardians of the law. In Colombia, for example, a set of idiomatic phrases encapsulate the arbitrary nature of this swift justice (such as *fiscalia 45,* or "prosecutor 45," referring to the caliber of a pistol used by the guerrillas), its marginal status, and indeed its wildness (*la ley del monte* means "the law of the mountain") and at the same time its amateur, makeshift aspect that, despite all its faults, turns this kids' law (*la ley de los muchachos*) into a true local justice that is less intimidating than its state equivalent.[134]

———

The rejection of legal law and the aspiration for swift, cheap justice are certainly not the monopoly of reactionary elites. They have been an integral part of the social and political struggles conducted by many liberation movements since the start of the twentieth century. In Europe and particularly in Latin America, these demands reached their peak in the 1970s, which saw the rise of criticisms of the penal and prison systems among left-wing intellectuals and the emergence of new, armed nationalist and revolutionary movements determined to restore justice to the people. Although, in general, these judicial intentions and the armed movements that promoted them subsequently faded, they did not entirely disappear, and the same ideal of justice continued to inspire revolutionary experiments, as can be seen in the establishment of people's courts in the areas of Nepal under Maoist guerrilla control during the People's War of 1996–2006. At the same time, more minor policing operations have been observable, such as during the COVID-19 pandemic. In Colombia, for example, armed groups enforced health safety measures with increasing brutality. Between March and August 2020, thirty people were killed for having violated their lockdown conditions.[135] And although some community leaders were glad of the assistance to make up for deficiencies in government provision,[136] more critical voices denounced the sham of health policing used as a cover for extortion and score settling.

Away from situations of civil war, the implementation of revolutionary justice programs rarely progresses beyond shock tactics intended to raise awareness by puncturing the myth that the dominant classes are untouchable. This justice then becomes an extension of propaganda by deed and is confined to proclaiming an alternative to bourgeois justice without any real means to reach its ends. If judicial acts are to be more than simply provocation, the militants promoting them must be rooted to some extent in a society and a place; they need a stronghold that can support their delivery of revolutionary justice. For armed groups in control of a locality, whether independently of the state or concomitantly with it, justice ceases to be the expression of an abstract ideal or a propaganda tool and becomes an imperative of social regulation in response to the failings of the state, to ward off the threat of chaos.

Once revolutionary justice becomes consolidated and acquires a role in the maintenance of order, defense of property, and security of licit and illicit transactions, the punitive fervor of insurgent movements is tempered in favor of justice that is less swift and more oriented toward arbitration. This also leads to the codification of laws, the construction of a justice system, and the professionalization of judges. Even if these rationalization efforts necessarily remain incomplete, some of those subject to irregular justice may acknowledge that it is relatively predictable and incontestably authoritative, due to the probity of the judges and the solid coercive apparatus on which their verdicts are based.

These efforts to establish popular justice show some general features of vigilantism, despite the gulf that separates them from the most reactionary forms. Above and beyond any ideological divergences, all share a radical critique of the justice system, the ambition to repair it through violence, and a determination to overturn the liberal regime of rights in order to restore sovereignty to the people. This convergence extends to the realm of morality, where a kind of revolutionary puritanism flourishes. Last, most popular justice movements share vigilantism's fundamental ambiguity with regard to the law and the judicial apparatus of the state. Revolutionary actors often remain in thrall to the legal mentality of the state, which influences their legal codes. Far from developing in independent spaces, revolutionary courts and state jurisdictions may interlock and complement each other, with accused and plaintiffs passing from one type to the other. For marginalized populations whose relations with state bureaucracy and its judicial apparatus have historically been distant, revolutionary justice can paradoxically foster their integration into the sphere of state sovereignty. In addition to being excellent doormen, facilitating access to what had hitherto seemed an impenetrable judicial system,[137] some insurgents are a powerful vector for the spread of state thinking in juridical and administrative matters, to the point of being assimilated to state authorities by some traditionally neglected populations.[138]

The break that revolutionary justice represents with both state jurisdictions and more conservative forms of vigilantism is primarily a reflection of revolutionaries' chosen definition of the people. Vigilantes, lynch mobs, and paramilitary groups usually claim to be defending decent people, who are economically and racially dominant. Revolutionaries lay down the law in the name of the laboring classes, battered women, and oppressed peoples. Whereas, for the former groups, vigilantism is a means of restoring the natural order, for revolutionaries it has a constitutive power. However, these intentions rarely survive the test of practical implementation, partly because revolutionaries tend to rein in their fervor as they become more embedded in society and partly because merchants and landowners may take control of revolutionary justice to defend their own economic interests.[139]

Whatever the order it promises to usher in, rough justice always involves excess. Although attempts by self-proclaimed avengers to deliver justice in the name—or even into the hands—of the people seldom measure up to their radical project, they do foster transgressions and abuses. Amplified by state propaganda, these excesses then abet counterprojects to restore order, contrasting the revolutionary threat and popular disorder with the uninhibited violence of the state and its auxiliaries. The following two chapters enter these troubled waters of political domination to consider the vigilante practices of countersubversion actors and policing professionals and also how the state itself can take on a vigilante status when freed from the constraints of the law.

5 CLEANING UP SOCIETY

The cleaning hand has arrived. As of today, all the scum, the marijuana smokers, thieves, whores, and diseased consumers will be mowed down.

COLOMBIAN PAMPHLET ANNOUNCING THE ARRIVAL OF A *LIMPIEZA* GROUP IN A CENTRAL NEIGHBORHOOD OF BOGOTÁ (2015)[1]

THIS EVENING, AS ON EVERY SATURDAY NIGHT, María de los Angeles Iquira opened her doors around 7 p.m. Every weekend in Santa Viviana, up in Bogotá's working-class suburbs, La Gran Esquina hosted a young crowd that came to let rip in its bar and discotheque. The party was in full swing when, on the stroke of 11 p.m., six balaclava-clad men burst in, armed with pistols and a pump-action shotgun. They separated the men from the women and ordered the men to lie face down on the floor. One of the attackers walked along the rows of captives and yanked up their heads to see their faces. When this brutal identity check was over, the intruders left with seven of the young men. One resisted and was killed with a shot to the head. The other six vanished with their abductors into the night. In the hours that followed, four of the prisoners were summarily executed. Their bodies were found in the early hours in a ravine in the neighboring locality of Corinto III, in Soacha. After a brief reprieve, the other two were murdered a day later, on February 18, 2001.

The massacre was a matter of controversy from the outset. Rumors in the barrio portrayed it as a *limpieza social* (social cleansing) operation commissioned by a group of local shopkeepers, in which the Gran Esquina's owner was said to have played an active role. These suspicions were confirmed by the boasting of one of her accomplices, a craftsman by the name of Gil Roberto González Martínez, who, from the comfort of his workshop, bragged to anyone who would listen about his role in the operation. But this act of summary justice was not to everyone's approval, and one witness soon

106   CHAPTER 5

reported his words to the police who, in a highly unusual move, launched an investigation. Barely a week later, the three shopkeepers suspected of having overseen the operation and the two *sicarios* (killers) presumed responsible for the young men's deaths were arrested. This was the start of a judicial saga that saw local magistrates clash over the description of the events, the motives of those who commissioned them, and the identity of the victims.[2] As the twists and turns of this controversy reveal, not only the rational for social cleansing was in dispute but its very existence. For although the "ill named" practice of *limpieza social,* as the first judge in charge of the case described it,[3] had become widespread in Colombia's larger urban centers since the late 1970s, it had never had the status of a specific crime in the country's penal code.

The silence of the law only added to the mystery of the *limpiezas* and the confusion they sowed. The punishments were carried out in a gray area between social prophylaxis, financial accumulation, and political power. We draw on Christian Lund's work on "twilight institutions"—forms of authority at the intersection of the public and the private, simultaneously mimicking and opposing the state[4]—to see in this space of interaction a "twilight zone," where self-proclaimed dispensers of justice, narco-traffickers, and law and order professionals become indistinguishable in a shifting play of shadows. Under the cover of restoring order by purging society, the *limpieza* groups sowed discord, doubt, and terror. Their collusion with the business world, the state, and drug traffickers fueled an economy of generalized suspicion. Their frequent blunders meant even law-abiding people could not feel safe, and their repeated attacks on labor union leaders accelerated the disorganization of the laboring classes. Yet this disorder also proved productive. It integrated the residents in affected localities into the social network of paramilitarism and, through violence and terror, hastened their incorporation into the circuits of neoliberal capitalism.[5] This social prophylaxis was not specific to Colombia. It was present across the region and was spread throughout South America by supporters of economic liberalism who used authoritarian methods. Although revolutionary movements sometimes carried out cleansing operations, they were reactionary in origin and emerged within the state. Historically, they were linked to death squads whose mission was to defend the established order against the threat of subversion and the dregs of humanity.

Although social cleansing is distinguished by close ties to the state security apparatus, its protagonists' vehicular mobility, and the intensity of their purifying violence, it also has much in common with more ordinary modes of vigilantism. The radical yet cheap solutions to problems of insecurity that it offers, its blurring of categories, and its dialectics of secrecy and publicity, as well as its entrepreneurial dimension and complicity with the propertied elites, place it firmly within the same repressive repertoire.

THE GENEALOGY OF A VIOLENT SOCIAL PROPHYLAXIS

Nowhere outside Latin America has the vigilante ambition to clean up society through violence found such systematic expression on such a scale—or at least not until the election of Rodrigo Duterte as president of the Philippines in 2016 (see Chapter 6). This "art" of terror, with its rituals, language, and aesthetics,[6] was first formalized in Brazil. As early as the 1880s, a group calling itself the Mão Negra (Black Hand) went around killing people from marginalized groups in the region of Rio de Janeiro.[7] During the dictatorship of the Estado Novo, in the 1930s, an elite force, the Polícia Especial, became infamous for its extralegal methods (illegal detention, torture, summary executions, and so on) against political opponents of the regime and for its extrajudicial killings of vagrants (vadios), beggars, prostitutes, and thieves. In 1957, some Polícia Especial officers joined the Serviço de Diligências Especiais (SDE; Special Diligence Group), which is widely considered the beginning of later death squads.[8] The war against the poor that broke out in Rio de Janeiro with the help of this elite police force intensified during the military dictatorship of 1964–1985, which drew inspiration from the social hygiene movement that shaped the Brazilian elite's and the city's treatment of undesirable segments of the population.[9] Since the nineteenth century, the most conservative element of the elite, particularly in the business world, has been advocating "the 'sterilization' of the city and its spaces 'polluted' by the presence of poor people regarded as undesirable."[10] A similar conception of social order came to the fore in Colombia, which also has a long social hygiene tradition.[11] In both these Latin American countries, social issues had long been dealt with by institutions responsible for hygiene and public health,[12] reinforcing the idea that poverty stemmed from the moral failings of the lower classes, made worse by the tainted air of cities, rather than any failure of the collectivity as a whole.[13] Excluded in this way from the common humanity of citizens, the poor appeared as "a menace to the well-being of decent people."[14] This "obsession with disorder, defilement, and contamination"[15] provided the ideological underpinning for social cleansing and shaped its language, as we see later. This legacy of hygienist ideas and institutions—in Colombia the Ministry of Hygiene was not replaced by the Ministry of Health until 1953—combined with other ideological sources, including biblical and, to a lesser degree, revolutionary references. Whereas the biblical prophylactic discourses lambasted the unproductive by comparing them to a sterile tree that exhausts the soil while producing nothing, the

108   CHAPTER 5

revolutionary references attacked the parasites, that "dangerous superfluity that exists only as an excess," whom Lenin had earlier raised to the rank of "main enemies of socialism."[16]

In Brazil, the concrete manifestation of these social ideas initially involved avoidance strategies that saw the self-segregation of the rich and the expulsion of the poor. In the late 1950s, this program of social prophylaxis turned increasingly violent. Under pressure from Rio de Janeiro's trade associations, the federal police chief and army general Amaury Kruel set up the SDE and gave it carte blanche to cleanse the city. This task was entrusted to a seven-member group within the SDE, the Turma Volante Especial de Repressão aos Assaltos à Mão Armada (Special Flying Squad against Armed Assault), which was soon decried by local journalists as the Esquadrão da Morte (Death Squad)—referring to extermination groups operating both within and outside the law. The SDE was dissolved in 1960, following the death of an innocent bystander in a shootout. The same year a new group was formed to combat crime by the secretary of security of the state of Guanabara, Gustavo Borges. The group was headed by Milton Le Cocq de Oliveira, a veteran of the Polícia Especial, who recruited several members of his team from this elite force to do President Getulio Vargas's dirty work during the dictatorship of the Estado Novo.[17] In 1964, Milton Le Cocq was shot and killed by the notorious gangster known as Horse Face. His associates in the renovated death squad swore to get revenge and kill ten criminals for every dead police officer. They organized as the Scuderie Le Cocq—officially, a club supporting the families of police officers killed in action—and opened branches in the cities of Niteroi, Victoria, and São Paulo. Eager to publicize its actions, the group pinned a note on the bodies of its victims listing their alleged crimes ("I was a thief" or "I sold drugs"), which was often accompanied by the group's emblem (a skull and crossbones, with the initials E. M., for Esquadrão da Morte[18]). As the murders increased, from 1968 onward, the group recruited public relations officers, who used poetic names (Red Rose in Rio, White Lys in São Paulo) that contrasted with their macabre task: informing journalists of every new "ham" (tied up and strangled bodies of alleged criminals) ditched in a wood, beside a road, or in a garbage dump.[19] These public relations efforts meant that the activities of the death squad received extensive, broadly positive media coverage. Some newspapers also gave further visibility to the death squads by circulating their statements. In October 1968, *Última Hora* published a manifesto justifying the extrajudicial killings of "bandits" in the state of Rio:

> The voice of the Esquadrão da Morte to the people of Guanabara: many of our people have already fallen victim to robbers and bloodthirsty criminals. The people testify that these bandits do not respect children,

old people, ladies, and workers. They rob and kill without mercy. We have only one intent: to defend the families that live and work in this state. The distance between the judiciary and the police does not always allow an effective fight against crime and criminals. Thus, the only way [to be heard] is to speak their language: the law of the dog [i.e., the law of the strongest].[20]

Press coverage helped the death squads justify their actions and reach a larger audience, and the official cover provided to these executioners marked "the beginning of a new symbiosis between the 'informal' murder teams, long a fact of Brazilian life, and the modern centralized police apparatus."[21] This continuum of extralegal violence flourished under the military dictatorship in Rio and in other major Brazilian cities (notably São Paolo) but also outlived the dictatorship. In the mid-1980s, human rights organizations discovered the existence of a concerted campaign of abductions and murders perpetrated against the country's street children. The justification given for this violence was the effort to clean up the cities by eradicating the *malandros* (lowlifes), who were said to be bad for business, tourism, and public health. There was also a preventive dimension to the program, because it neutralized future criminals. For the anthropologists Nancy Scheper-Hughes and Daniel Hoffman, it was akin to "post-partum abortion," reflecting the relative nature of the right to life in a society riddled with discrimination.[22]

The extermination campaign was funded by small businesses and shopkeepers (*lojistas*) who contracted the services of vigilantes (*justiceiros*), hired killers, and police officers supplementing their salaries as capitalists' henchmen. Although some self-defined "exterminators" initially refused payment for their services, an industry gradually developed as the more highly regarded among them used their contacts in the police and the corporate world to set up private security companies. Respectability was not available to all, however, and the police targeted some vigilantes who succumbed to greed and lust for power and wealth.[23] All the same, nearly five thousand children and teenagers living on the street from 1988 to 1990 are thought to have been killed in Brazil's cities.[24] Most of the victims were Black—a racial bias that reflects both the structural aspects of poverty in the country and the prejudices of the dominant class concerning young Afro-Brazilians. Similar violence against street children and supposed criminals was identified in Guatemala in the late 1990s.[25] In Central America in the late 1990s, paramilitary groups emerged seeking to exterminate the *mareros* (members of street gangs), at least two hundred of whom were killed by death squads in Honduras in 1999 alone.[26]

In some areas of conflict in Latin America, *limpieza* operations transcended ideological divisions between far right death squads and far left guerrilla groups. In Colombia, the communist insurgents regularly carried out cleansing operations and sometimes joined forces with other groups in shared *limpiezas*.[27] In Peru in the early 1980s, the punitive expeditions by the Shining Path guerrillas were applauded by small farmers in Ayacucho. The guerrillas attacked the *shensi malvados*—literally, "bad squires"—a Maoist term in the Shining Path's revolutionary phraseology that usually referred to "enemies of the people" and extended to the bandits and cattle rustlers despised throughout the Andes. But when the *senderistas* (members of the Shining Path) tried to integrate into the everyday life of peasant communities, the guerrillas' violence against abusive husbands, drunkards, and supposed gay people hastened the divorce between the Maoist movement and villagers.[28]

Across the continent as a whole, however, the origins of social prophylaxis projects were reactionary, and this is reflected in their genealogy and supporters. In Colombia, some groups formed in the preceding decades to fight communist subversion, such as the Association of Middle Magdalena Ranchers and Farmers (Asociación Campesina de Ganaderos y Agricultores del Magdalena Medio), widened their targets. The main financial and political supporters of these groups were drug traffickers but also ranchers, large landowners, industrialists, and shopkeepers—in other words, the propertied classes and entrepreneurs who always back self-defense efforts—from Brazil to Mexico. Salvadoran entrepreneurs backed the training of the Sombra Negra, a death squad that emerged in San Miguel in 1994 to exterminate *mareros*,[29] and avocado and lime growers contributed to the mobilization of self-defense forces in Michoacán, Mexico, 2013–2015.[30] In Colombia, collusion between the death squads and wealthy elites was rooted in a long history of government by violence.[31] In the 1950s, the *pájaros, aplanchadores,* and *chulavitas*—armed gangs in the service of the conservative party and propertied elites[32]—established a reign of terror in the country's rural areas, where they hunted down liberal and communist activists, peasant leaders, and labor unionists. Indeed, it was during this "dirty war" against "subversion" that *cleansing* was used for the first time to signify an extermination as a prophylactic.[33] Not until the 1980s, however, did this terminology enter everyday language in Colombia, at a time when a new form of summary justice was taking shape.

LIMPIEZAS: SOCIAL CLEANSING IN COLOMBIA

On December 5, 1979, the city of Pereira, in Colombia's main coffee-producing area, launched Red Hands, an operation to end a supposed epidemic of thefts and burglaries. The city council's security committee planned to dye the hands and faces of *cacos* (thieves) with indelible red ink, to make finding them easier and to dissuade them from reoffending. The measure recalled the branding of enslaved people by landowners of the past, but it still fit with contemporary mores in the council's view. Elements of the local society, including the Catholic Church, opposed the dyeing, and it was suspended after a thief injured himself trying to remove the ink with hydrochloric acid. A mysterious group called the Black Hand then called for the murder of dozens of alleged criminals in the region.[34]

In 1980, murders of this kind began in Medellín and Bogotá and spread to the rest of the country in subsequent years. Although the available statistics tend to underestimate the phenomenon—mainly because the victims had cut ties with their families or their families feared reprisals if they reported the murders to the police or media—the most credible estimates suggest a spectacular rise in the number of deaths, from 62 in 1979 to 281 in 1988 and to 426 in 1992. After 1992, the number of murders fluctuated wildly, but the violence never entirely stopped. The Centro de Investigación y Educación Popular, reputed to have the most reliable database, estimates that nearly five thousand people were killed in *limpiezas* in Colombia in 1988–2013.[35] Some forty groups were estimated to be active in the country as a whole.[36] In the early 1980s the Colombian press used *death squads* and *cleansing operations* when describing events in Brazil and Argentina[37] before the phrase *limpieza social* became part of everyday vocabulary in the second half of the decade. Enforcer groups also adopted the language of cleansing, reflected in names such as the Magdalena Medio Limpieza Committee and the Cali Limpia.

The rise of this form of rough justice coincided with government pleas for citizen self-defense at a time when political life was dominated by the military. Alongside initiatives supported by the army to counter insurrections, some city councils tried to get the population involved in the fight against crime in their locality. One of the civilian leaders promoting citizen policing was Ricaurte Losada Valderrama, the government secretary in charge of security in Bogotá, who, in 1981, called on all Colombians to "become a kind of guardian of order [*vigilante del orden*]" to relieve the authorities of some of the burden.[38] At the same time, attempts by the civilian authorities to reform the justice system fueled a deep mistrust of official justice among conservatives. In 1980, partisans of strong-arm tactics criticized amendments to Colombia's penal code as yet another concession to criminals. Those in favor of social cleansing called for harsher sentences, partly because they believed that crimes were committed by born criminals. They thus were mouthpieces for a popular criminology according to which deviant behavior had its origins in the personalities of antisocial individuals, who could be identified by visible characteristics such as facial features and general appearance.[39]

Congestion in the judicial system discredited the official channels for resolving litigious disputes. Remaining undecided in 1982 were 1.4 million criminal cases and 1.7 million civil cases, and fewer than 3 percent of reported crimes and offenses led to a conviction.[40] The 1985 decree Unblocking the Justice System resulted in the release of thousands of prisoners jailed for petty crimes, which only strengthened concerns among conservatives. In Bogotá alone, 3,462 prisoners had their sentences remitted.[41] This policy fueled a moral panic, preparing the way for social cleansing in larger conurbations and some smaller Colombian towns—*limpieza* being mostly an urban phenomenon primarily targeting young men (there were few female victims). Unlike Brazil, where street children were most vulnerable to the *malandro* hunters,[42] Colombia's *limpieza* operations targeted a vast population of undesirables, mostly thieves but also sex workers, drug addicts, the mentally ill and street dwellers, *eros* (homeless people), *gamines* (street children), and ragmen.

The operations were sometimes carried out by amateur vigilantes determined to clean up their local area (such as the working-class districts of south Bogotá and the *comunas* of northeast Medellín). However, most *limpieza* groups consisted of violent specialists recruited from the police, paramilitary groups, and more rarely, guerrilla groups. As in Brazil, from the late 1970s to the mid-1980s in Colombia, social cleansing was dominated by (former) police officers. The Muerte a Secuestradores (Death to Kidnappers), created in 1981, marked a turning point. Established by the Medellín cartel after the abduction of Martha Nieves Ochoa,[43] this group—or rather, this constellation of very loosely coordinated initiatives—evolved into narco-paramilitarism, gradually expanding its targets from street dwellers and sex workers to progressives. In Cali too, left-wing militants and labor unionists were regarded as "guerrillas in civilian clothes" and regularly targeted by *limpieza* groups.[44]

The entanglement of social cleansing with the dirty war against communist subversion reflected a commercialization of violence rather than a coordinated strategy, thus it was subject to tactical turnarounds and porous and ill-defined groupings.[45] The entanglement accelerated during the presidency of Belisario Betancur (1982–1986), whose government entered peace negotiations with the FARC (Fuerzas Armadas Revolucionarias de Colombia). This worried both the traditional elites and the drug traffickers, who expanded into agriculture and agribusiness and who feared the negotiations would lead to reforms favoring the guerrillas and their sympathizers. The same concerns were shared by the army, which encouraged contacts between officers, regional elites, and fiercely anti-communist paramilitary groups.[46] This convergence fostered a confusion of genres: whereas the paramilitaries regarded communist activists and sympathizers as *desechables* (scum), they saw street dwellers, and particularly hawkers, as potential guerrilla informants.[47]

CLEANING UP SOCIETY   113

These shifting populations targeted by *limpieza* groups and the diverse crimes they were accused of singularize Colombian-style social cleansing. The main characteristic of the *limpiezas* is not their death toll—much lower than that of the war on children in Brazil—but the variability of their aims, in which the struggle against deviance and suppression of subversion overlap. They also reflect the ambivalent relationship between social cleansing and legality. Simultaneously invoking laws and moral prescriptions, the *limpieza* groups officiously punished both lawbreaking and practices that were not illegal but seen as deviant, such as homosexuality and prostitution. And while claiming to be defenders of the established order, they administered prohibited punishments, with a predilection for death sentences.

THE DIRTY WORK OF PUBLIC HEALTH

Working for the *paracos* (the Colombian paramilitaries), Luna says, "is a bit like being a hired killer, but you're part of a group." Luna knows what he is talking about: before joining the country's main paramilitary organization, Autodefensas Unidas de Colombia (United Self-Defense of Colombia) in the mid-1990s, this key informant for the anthropologist Aldo Civico operated as a *sicario* throughout the Urabá region. He admits that the *urbanos* (urban paramilitaries) do a dirty job but takes pride in his contribution to public hygiene:

> The guerrilla is the dirty thing, and then one goes to clean it up. One takes the broom to sweep the dirty and to leave everything clean. For something to be clean, there has to be someone who removes the garbage. The cleaning is done for guerrillas, gangs, thieves, and vicious people. I began cleaning in Urabá, killing a lot of people. . . . We also cleaned it up of those gays who were there; there were about three hundred, and we began to kill them. *Gamines* used to walk on the street gathering cardboard. We started killing all of these too, and the town was left clean and healthy.[48]

As a street hawker in a working-class neighborhood of Ciudad Bolívar, Rogelio is a casual participant in cleanups, in which he takes part only now and then. Nevertheless, when he was interviewed in 2012 by researchers from the Centro Nacional de Memoria Histórica in Bogotá, he described his involvement in *limpieza* activities with similar pride and righteous confidence:

> In Ciudad Bolívar we have a problem, which is thieves and vice. Drugs have really messed up people's lives, they only live for the *jíbaro* [petty

114   CHAPTER 5

dealer], and meanwhile he's filling his pockets. It's really unsafe here, if a kid takes out a banknote, he immediately has it snatched. That's why I join in with getting rid of them [*yo soy participe de bajarlos*], because the Bible says "Every tree that bears no fruit must be cut down." . . . I like working but if I'm given the chance to do justice with my own hands, I take it [*si me dan la justicia por mis manos yo la tomo*].[49]

As emphasized by these two quotations, the stigmatization of certain categories of people as useless and harmful is central to the justificatory framework of Colombian cleansers. For paramilitary groups connected to the far right, the removal of undesirables becomes merged with the counterinsurgency and the restoration of morality to society. Within less professionalized groups and for auxiliaries like Rogelio, the political component of these cleansing operations tends to lose importance. Despite their diverging ideology and professionalization, however, all these groups aim to eradicate *marginados* (marginalized urban populations not integrated in the industrial proletariat) and *delicuentes* (petty criminals, drug users, and other "deviants"). They reject coexistence with a set of people seen as useless, costly, damaging and contagious, and justify putting them to death in terms of society's right to protect itself and the imperative to be productive. Because those on the fringes of society are not useful, they have no justification to live. Moreover, their incorrigibility means any attempt to rehabilitate them is doomed to fail and will be a waste of public money.[50]

The search for cheap solutions to the problem of insecurity is as old as social cleansing itself. In Pereira, where Red Hands branding began in the late 1970s, the operation could be seen as a way of saving money on "prisons, guards, three meals a day, and walks in the sun."[51] At a time when unbridled liberalism was rife elsewhere in Latin America, in Colombia—where it did not fully develop until the late 1980s—the social groups funding the *limpieza* operations (industrialists, entrepreneurs, shopkeepers, and landowners) called the shots. The Toxicol-90 group, which was dominant in the city of Barrancabermeja in the early 1980s, compared itself in one press release to a company "whose name matches its aim, which is to promote healthier living."[52] The group's name was also linked to the hygienist tradition in Colombia and across the continent. In taking the name of a well-known insecticide, the group defined itself as a tool for eradicating vermin. Hygiene aside, the epidemiological approach of the *limpieza* groups echoes the political discourse of animalization that can be seen in all twentieth-century extermination projects.[53] The emergence of the term *desechables* in everyday language confirms the currency of these exterminatory ideas in Colombia, which went far beyond labeling marginalized groups as deviants. The word's widespread use was part of the popular representation of people who seemed socially and economically superfluous. One *limpieza* group of the 1980s declared itself to be dedicated to the eradication of the "dregs of humanity."[54]

Drugs, delinquency, and even a life of idleness are distilled in the broad notion of vice, which corrupts body and mind. The *desechables* are rotten (*podridos*) in the most literal sense of the word. Pamphlets announcing *limpieza* operations systematically refer to the sexually transmitted diseases that such people are assumed to carry, and the social hygiene implicit in their vocabulary of combat and purification is even more pronounced in relation to sex workers. These prophylactic ideas proved highly durable, as can be seen in the announcement of the imminent launch of a *limpieza* operation in Bosa (a neighborhood in Bogotá) circulating on social media in 2009:

> Today it's the turn of the filthy, putrid, AIDS-carrying whores. From now on you'll be giving AIDS only to the worms. All you whores who hang out in bars and dives, your days are numbered. You've given AIDS to [too] many people.[55]

Language of this kind was not confined to the killers: it was given currency by the media, in which victims were described as "depraved" and "deadbeats."[56] Without being quite so explicit, some judges also questioned whether the murdered young people really were victims, suggesting that their sins had caught up with them when they were shot by a rival gang. The law itself encouraged this kind of argument. Decree 2578 of December 8, 1976, authorized the arrest of suspects on the basis of their lifestyle or as a preventive measure, in situations that "suggest that offenses will be committed."[57]

However, in the view of Carlos Eduardo Rojas Jr., author of the first in-depth study on social cleansing in Colombia, the *limpiezas* were intended to not only eradicate a threat to the established order. More perniciously, by disciplining the inhabitants of working-class neighborhoods and expelling undesirables, *limpiezas* imposed a new social and moral order. After being tested on the socially marginalized, the behavioral standards promoted by the paramilitaries—starting with a curfew for young people—were then often extended to the entire population.[58] In 1987 the Amor por Medellín group circulated a leaflet advising "We recommend that decent people do not hang around in the street after midnight, because decent people have no business outside their homes at that time."[59] So for some paramilitary groups, social cleansing could establish and anchor their presence in a locality and build up a political clientele.[60] This strategy of territorial conquest distinguishes *limpieza* groups from other vigilantes, who can rely on their local roots.

116   CHAPTER 5

ROUGH JUSTICE AS ITINERANT SPECTACLE

"I was working in *limpieza* within a town. I remained there for eight months. They gave me a house for my ten comrades. We had cars and motorbikes."[61] This account by a paramilitary involved in *limpieza* operations in Antioquia, Colombia, over several years, recorded by Aldo Civico, indicates the degree to which social cleansing fundamentally differs from other forms of rough justice discussed in this book. With a few notable exceptions—such as digital vigilantes and some migrant hunters who patrol borders—self-proclaimed avengers tend to be rooted in a particular locality. The topography holds no secrets for them, and their embedding in local society makes it easier to identify troublemakers. We have seen that *limpieza* groups sometimes formed within a particular neighborhood; however, more usually, cleansing operations were carried out by external actors, brought in by prominent individuals or shopkeepers to protect their property. Whereas routine patrolling within a defined area is the modus operandi most favored by vigilantes, *limpieza* groups prefer lightning raids, in localities where their services are requested. Their mobility requires them to have deployment capabilities far exceeding those generally available to vigilante groups, let alone lynch mobs. *Limpieza* groups tend to drive around in SUVs (often with tinted windows and no license plates), on motorcycles, or in taxis stolen or hired for the occasion. Above and beyond their usefulness, these vehicles and their anonymization are part of the mechanical art of cleansing. Through a powerful effect of fetishization, they fuel ideas of brutality and furtiveness, also seen in other conflicts. For example, in Sri Lanka in the 1980s, mysterious white vans came to represent the threat of disappearance orchestrated by the Sinhalese intelligence services. This metonymic relationship is reflected in the term *white vanning*, referring to the abduction of members of the opposition, often followed by their death by torture.[62]

The blacklists of *limpieza* groups are another fetish feeding the culture of terror, which draws on theatricality and inspires fantastic representations. The lists of subversives and delinquents to be killed are drawn up in consultation with law enforcement officials and local residents, confirming the externality of the itinerant dispensers of justice. Whereas most vigilantes and lynch mobs use knowledge and skills acquired in a personal relationship with the local area—making them better able than the police to identify disruptive elements[63]—*limpieza* groups do not have this advantage. Blacklists bring legibility to the area to be cleansed. However, these artifacts are more than purely functional. They add a bureaucratic dimension to exterminations in the form of data collection, verification and compilation, and ultimately, operational processing, further blurring the boundaries between the official state and the parastate of the exterminators.[64] At the same time, the lists also fuel speculation and imitation, maintaining an aura of suspicion that reinforces the paramilitaries' hold over the society and allows masked avengers to settle scores with total impunity. In his ethnography of a small Colombian town dealing with a *limpieza* episode in 2001, Michael Taussig describes how, a year before the paramilitaries arrived, mysterious black-lists had appeared on local walls, featuring the names of delinquents from all social backgrounds, including the elite. Taussig observes that the locals reacted to this public unveiling of dirty linen with some jubilation, but he notes they were also perplexed by the anonymous lists, which mimicked paramilitary kill lists.[65]

The distribution of blacklists is a spectacular form of communication that owes its capacity to terrify both to the threats it conveys and to its implicit assertion of impunity. By publicizing their murderous intentions, the cleansers indicate that they are acting with the tacit agreement of the authorities, from whom it would be pointless to expect protection. The accusations of named individuals are reinforced with leaflets using offensive language against deviants and other vice-riddled delinquents, fueling the rumor of an imminent *limpieza* and calling on the population to submit to the cleansers' iron rule. Like Brazilian police death squads, the murderers also communicate with the locals by leaving notes on their victims, giving the reason for their execution.[66] Some groups claim their actions with a press release. In every case, the cleansers portray themselves as the strong arm of self-defense initiatives and popular justice, supported by the "decent citizens" of a town or a particular neighborhood.[67]

In urban centers, the most affected areas have been poor districts on the outskirts. Such areas had high concentrations of country people and peasant farmers displaced by armed conflicts who were struggling to find a place for themselves in the job market.[68] In the targeted localities and neighborhoods, most attacks were carried out in the street, but victims could also be struck down in places of pleasure and perdition, including discotheques like La Gran Esquina, bars, game rooms, and drug-consumption sites.[69] The bodies, which were left in isolated places but not hidden, were sometimes ostentatiously mutilated or dressed (thieves had their hands amputated, rapists were castrated, or homosexuals were adorned with fake pearl necklaces). Indeed they were intended to be found and to make an impression on passersby. The place was sometimes chosen for its symbolic importance, echoing the theme of filth that runs through all these vigilante practices. Thus, it was quite common for victims' bodies to be left in garbage dumps, literally reaffirming their status as waste. They were also degraded through mockery. The murderers of Luis Jairo Henao Arango, a young delinquent killed in October 1986, left his corpse under a sign saying "Garbage disposal prohibited."[70] Some groups also developed a signature to make them identifiable in what became over time a highly competitive field. The Terminator group, for example, marked its victims by executing them with three bullets to the head and chest.[71] Although such competitive branding strategies could lead to an upward spiral of horror, they also reflected the constraints of the penal code—a sign that, even as they took the law into their own hands, Colombian vigilantes remained indebted to prevailing legal norms.[72] To avoid being accused of massacre—in Colombian law the murder of three or more people—many exterminators thus murdered their victims one by one or dispersed groups of bodies.

LIMPIEZA SHADOW PLAYS

The Colombian cleansers exist in a world of subterfuge where the substance of people and things always seems elusive. In this upside-down world, appearances cannot be trusted. Thieves are often said to disguise themselves as down-and-outs, and cross-dressers are said to use their feminine appearance to commit crimes. These creatures of the night who haunt the darkest corners of the cities are also said to escape the vigilance of the police by frequently changing their name and appearance.[73]

The perpetrators of *limpiezas* more or less deliberately maintained this confusion. Although links between law enforcement and death squads are an open secret, the precise line between the state and its vigilante counterparts remains a matter of speculation. The exterminators muddy the waters, blurring the boundaries between the state and private justice by deflecting responsibility for their punitive actions or claiming them in the name of other groups. In this chaotic situation, clear facts and uncertainties are not mutually exclusive. Everyone knows that the police and the military are behind the *limpiezas*, but it is impossible to know the precise outlines and motives of the groups. The paramilitaries kill in the name of restoring social and ontological order but cross the line between crime and the law. The state plays a crucial role in maintaining this confusion by surreptitiously exploiting the terror it claims to combat.

In this regard the Colombian case recalls that of Spain, where the Grupos Antiterroristas de Liberación (GAL; Antiterrorist Liberation Groups)—a death squad established by Spanish intelligence officers—claimed the murders of twenty-six Basque separatist militants in France in 1983–1987.[74] The police officers involved in this murderous enterprise, which included a number of bloody blunders, played at being terrorists by organizing kidnappings, extorting money from French industrialists, and putting out press releases carrying an imitation of the seal used by the Basque separatist group ETA (Euskadi Ta Askatasuna). The sheer amateurism of these budding terrorists—the vice president of the Partido Popular political party described their activity as "bar terrorism"—made their entire enterprise look like a grotesque parody. In reality, the terrorism that these police officers were imitating was largely fantasy, overdetermined by images in film and literature. Yet this "disorganized mimesis"[75] generated real terror, promoted by a febrile state carried away by the fantasy of an omnipotent enemy and released from the straitjacket of the law. The Spanish state terrified Basque society with this deranged, unconstrained, and jubilatory violence that became an unstable, ungraspable, spectral presence that drew its strength from transgression.

In Colombia, for a long time the confusion of genres cut both ways. When the conservative militias emerged in the 1950s, they took to aping the police,[76] and the custodians of so-called legitimate violence sometimes merged with the armed gangs or imitated their methods. The police sometimes lent their uniforms to the *pájaros* before their attacks, and some officers would don sneakers and a *ruana* (a kind of poncho) to merge with the militiamen and take part in their punishments.[77] These mimetic practices reappeared with *limpieza* groups in the early 1980s. On both sides of the theoretical line between legality and illegality, the "theatrical, even childish nature of the deceit" was sometimes openly embraced.[78] As the risk of prosecution grew in the 1980s, police officers and soldiers involved in *limpiezas* took increasing care to wipe away their traces. However, their precautionary measures were not enough to dissolve suspicions of collusion among security forces, paramilitary groups, and vigilantes. On the contrary, by becoming invisible, these transactions created a space for rumor, which enhanced the impact of the violence. These shadow plays took sustenance from the lack of differentiation between the state and its vengeful counterparts and from the entanglement of capital and coercion. As we have seen, *limpieza* groups were often funded by actors both legal and illegal, including landowners, shopkeepers, industrialists, and drug traffickers. The nature of these links seems to have played an important role in the choice of targets. Groups with the closest links to the propertied classes seem to have prioritized problems affecting their activities (hindrance to trade, abduction, and cattle rustling in rural locations) and ignored street children or the mentally ill.[79] The punitive expedition to La Gran Esquina discotheque in Santa Viviana is emblematic of this kind of collusion, which saw some *limpieza* groups acting as corporate militias. Investigations by the media and the justice system revealed that this operation was commissioned by a group of local shopkeepers angered by a spate of robberies and burglaries. Gil Roberto González Martínez, alias "Carafea" (Ugly Face), acted as coordinator, and John Fredy Henao Orrego, a baker, gathered the shopkeepers, decided who would do what, and drew up the list of people to be killed. The conspirators, a group of around fifteen, held their meetings at his bakery. María de los Angeles Iquira was appointed treasurer for the operation and given the task of collecting the 650,000 pesos needed to recruit the *sicarios* (who charged very low fees).[80]

Collusion between economic interests, *limpieza* groups, and law enforcement reflected local configurations of power and wealth. But it was also impelled by a national conjuncture in which "armed neoliberalism" was on the rise.[81] Colombia was slower than its neighbors to adopt neoliberal reforms, in part because it was less indebted and thus preserved from structural adjustment plans and also because its financial elites (such as prominent industrialists) favored protectionist policies.[82] However, the late 1980s saw the emergence of new conglomerates that vigorously supported free trade ideology, in tandem with a handful of neoliberal economists. The intensification of conflict with drug traffickers and FARC guerrillas pushed the government of César Gaviria (1990–1994) to open up the economy to foreign investment in exchange for increased financial and military aid from the United States. Subsequent years saw a profound transformation of the Colombian economy, marked by deregulation of the labor market, privatization, suspension of subsidies for national businesses, lower levels of social assistance, and decline of public services.

These structural reforms were met with fierce resistance, to which the far right paramilitary groups responded with massive attacks on labor union activists, several thousand of whom have been murdered since the 1990s. This violence accelerated the dismantling of citizens' rights and the collapse of organizations working to defend and mobilize the working classes. It particularly affected unionists and workers in the banana[83] and oil[84] sectors and in big foreign companies. In the early years of the 2000s, the Castaño brothers' Autodefensas Unidas de Colombia maintained a strong paramilitary presence near the oil fields exploited by BP, the multinational oil and gas company, in the eastern province of Casanare and in the area around a coal mine owned by the US company Drummond in northeastern Colombia. Crucially, the group had bases near every Coca-Cola bottling plant, where unionists were subjected to a bloody intimidation campaign.[85]

Limpieza operations were an extension of this repression. Left-wing activists were included in the category of *desechables*[86] and targeted for their ideological beliefs and, like delinquents and deviants, for a perceived pathology that threatened the social fabric. As stated in a leaflet by the Hermandad Hitleriana de Pasto (Hitlerian Brotherhood of Pasto) and emailed to defenders of LGBTQ+ rights in that region in 2010, eliminating these polluting elements would strengthen society's health and restore the "natural order of things"—in other words, racial, sexual, and generational hierarchies.[87] The cleansers' tendency to violate their own laws—for example, by attacking healthy people and trafficking drugs, did not undermine their plans for social control. On the contrary, it was integral to the discretionary power they wielded.

The blunders and deviations from their own standards made by these moral entrepreneurs, and their suspected collusion with business and the government, engendered a general sense of insecurity among the working classes. Even if *limpieza* groups and paramilitaries did not always act in tandem, both were instrumental in establishing a paralyzing chaos—a state of sometimes arbitrary violence that "[sapped] the capacity of the working classes to take back control of their lives."[88] In fostering a state of disorganization, this chaos prepared poor workers for new forms of exploitation and control. Social cleansing thus opened the way for the reorganization of Colombian capitalism on bases that were more inegalitarian, insecure, and authoritarian.[89]

THE DIRTY LINEN OF SOCIAL CLEANSING

In September 1986, in the village of Liborina, in the Antioquia Department, two police officers killed Javier de Jesus Londoño Arango, an ex-offender. In June 1992, Colombia's highest judicial administrative body, the Council of State, ruled that the police officers were guilty of summary execution in targeting the victim solely "for being a well-known 'undesirable' and anti-social person with a criminal record."[90] The Council of State ordered the Ministry of Defense, whose remit covered the two perpetrators, to pay each of the victim's parents the equivalent of 500 grams of gold. This ruling was based on the following argument:

> No one in Colombia can assume the authority to define . . . just who is useful, good and deserves to live and who is bad, useless, "disposable" and must die. No one, and especially not those in authority. When the authorities take on this role, they . . . become the monstrous proprietor of these people's lives, integrity and property.[91]

However, the Ministry of Defense rejected the request for compensation and in doing so expressed a perception of social cleansing widespread in law enforcement:

> At no time was evidence presented that the police force or the public administration were at fault, hence there is no case for the payment of

122   CHAPTER 5

any compensation by the nation, particularly for an individual who was neither useful nor productive, either to society or to his family, but who was a vagrant whose presence nobody in the town of Liborina wanted.[92]

The killers enjoyed an impunity primarily explained by the police not recognizing social cleansing as a public problem and supporting the violent productivism that was its ideological underpinning. Although investigations were opened in the early 1980s—notably in Medellín, where judges and lawyers confirmed the existence of groups determined to exterminate criminals—the authorities constantly denied the evidence. The involvement of police and the military in cleansing operations was an even more taboo subject and, in the few cases of officers who were sanctioned down the years, they were usually merely disciplined, not tried by the legal system—a tendency by no means specific to Colombia, as reflected in the complacency shown by countries in South Asia toward "fake encounters" in the same period (see Chapter 6). However, the reticence of the security services to admit the existence of *limpiezas*, let alone their own responsibility in the killings, was not enough to stifle debate. The controversy was as old as the phenomenon itself, which had been denounced since it first appeared, notably by the Catholic clergy. In the city of Pereira, regarded as the birthplace of these punitive practices, the local bishop had opposed the plan to dye robbers' hands red and invited the congregation to ask themselves whether the criminals' families had received the support necessary to raise their children as "decent, honorable people."[93]

The public was never unanimously in favor of rough justice, and public support fluctuated with events and arguments. After the Santa Viviana massacre, local residents appeared deeply divided over social cleansing. Far from bringing people together or stifling local disagreement through terror, *limpiezas* reanimated dissent in the media, and then in the courts, as the vigilantes' practices came to light.[94] As often in cases of police violence, that the victims had no criminal record was key to the way the scandal played out. Adonai Vargas, for example, had left the army four months earlier at the request of his parents, who were concerned about his safety—in the preceding years Vargas had been tasked with protecting an oil pipeline against guerrilla attack in the Arauca region. Since leaving the army he had worked as a building manager in the Ciudad Salitre neighborhood. He owed money to the discotheque owner and was there on the night of February 17 to pay her back.[95]

Less than two weeks after the events, six people were arrested by the Bogotá *fiscalia* (prosecutor's office). They included González Martínez, La Gran Esquina's owner de los Angeles Iquira, Henao Orrego, and the *sicarios*

Edgar Guerrero and Alvaro Cárdenas. This was the start of a new controversy within the justice system, initially focusing on what happened. At first the six defendants were charged with carrying illegal weapons, criminal association, and aggravated homicide during a social cleansing. After the preliminary investigation, the case was transferred to a court in Cundinamarca, where the judge challenged this interpretation, preferring to see the event as a settling of scores between rival gangs: "We are dealing here with a territorial conflict between common criminals and, although the hypothesis of what is ill-named social cleansing [la mal llamada limpieza social] cannot be entirely ruled out, it is probable that the accused had promised remuneration for more banal, futile, and pointless motives than funding a [paramilitary or criminal] organization."[96] As always in such cases, the controversy extended to the victims, whose innocence was contested by several of those involved. The police and some media hinted that they might have been linked to the Aguapanelos or the Balcanes, two local street gangs. This interpretation completely ignored the witness statements of residents, who complained to the media and to investigators about the overwhelming presence of vigilantes and other cleansers in their neighborhood. Accumulated resentment against these violent entrepreneurs, often financed by local shopkeepers, probably played a major role in the denunciation of the massacre's sponsors to the police.

People's militias proliferated in the barrios of Ciudad Bolívar in the early 1990s. As reported in the press at the time, these militias asserted their roots in the community by claiming to consist of "housewives, street hawkers, and ordinary neighbors tired of seeing family members dying."[97] Initially charged with combating burglaries, the vigilantes sometimes dispensed heavy-handed justice. Summary executions quickly became such everyday occurrences that children played at "going to see the dead."[98] And although initial actions targeting well-known criminals mostly met with public approval, the violence of the militia groups escalated and became more arbitrary. They were accused of accidentally targeting "healthy" people (sanos) who stayed well away from the world of crime.[99] As the years went by, community self-defense diversified and accrued more actors. Alongside the self-defense groups of local residents, paramilitaries and gangsters were brought in by shopkeepers and small business owners. These clients had the necessary funds to recruit violent entrepreneurs, and their commercial activities also enabled them to identify troublemakers—an ability used by many vigilante clients far beyond Latin America.[100] The predominance of commercial actors in the Juntas de Acción Communal, which mediated between local populations and the state, also helped legitimate cleansing operations, which were often sponsored by the leaders of these bodies.[101] However, as in the

124 CHAPTER 5

disagreements around the January 2001 massacre, consensus around these practices was somewhat fragile.

The disputes concerning the events in the Santa Viviana neighborhood were once again extended and developed into judicial controversy when the case was transferred to another court in Soacha. The new judge determined it had been a cleansing operation targeting young people accused of disturbing the social order. In his view, the owner of La Gran Esquina had planned the operation and had raised the money to recruit hired killers. As the Soacha judge put it, "[These traders] agreed to perpetrate a "social cleansing" intended to eliminate some delinquents . . . by recruiting to that end a group with the necessary resources at their disposal." Although concurring with his colleague in Cundinamarca that the available evidence was too weak to establish that the offenders had acted in association, the judge noted the existence of a stable form of organization behind the homicides.[102] The conflicting judgments meant the case went to the supreme court, which concurred with the Soacha judge: the accused traders had "got together to pay a group that committed these homicides as indicated by the contracting party, with the aim of perpetrating 'social cleansing.'" Regarding the description of the group, the supreme court agreed with the hypothesis of a "criminal organization" performing a task "of an indeterminate, sustained nature," as reflected in the use of firearms, the number (7–9 people) charged with the murders, how the victims were identified, and the modus operandi—some attackers entered the discotheque while others kept watch at the entrance.[103] In the end, three of the accused were found guilty of multiple homicides, association with offenders, and illegally carrying weapons. La Gran Esquina's owner spent four years behind bars before having her conviction reversed on benefit of doubt.[104]

This case displays the impunity that the *limpieza* groups could claim and furthermore reveals the tensions in the Colombian judiciary about this violence. The unwillingness of judges to recognize some homicides as social cleansing and to try them as such (by describing them as a massacre or an aggravated homicide, perpetrated by a criminal association) was not solely the result of pressure from the killers and their protectors in the government.[105] Alongside the lack of legal clarity around the *limpiezas*, the hesitation of judges is explained by their acceptance of a criminology imbued with social hygiene and by the suspicion surrounding these acts of violence and their perpetrators. In this troubled context, the law was never more than a very partial help to magistrates looking for certainty. As admitted by the supreme court judge who ruled on the disagreement between the two judges in the case of the Santa Viviana massacre, it was an "inexact science,"[106] with limited power to determine the truth when dealing with one of those "crises of evidence"[107]—those disturbing moments when the members of a collectivity can no longer reach agreement on how to interpret the world or trust their own ability to understand it.

———

The controversies around the Santa Viviana massacre and the evolution of social cleansing in Colombia reflect the volatility of the relations between self-styled avengers and law enforcement agencies. This fluidity requires us to conceive policing practices as processes that are always being reorganized, exposed to criticism, and subject to negotiations between public actors who do not always agree and private interests. The existence of these "circumstantial coalitions"[108] among state authorities, vigilantes, and populations invites us to transcend the rather hackneyed dichotomy between so-called strong and weak states. *Limpiezas* confirm the heuristic value of Christian Lund's "twilight" approach, which looks at the mutual mimicry that blurs the dividing lines between the state and its monstrous doubles.[109]

The contingent effects to which these configurations are exposed relativize the impunity inherent in vigilante practices.[110] Permissive spaces negotiated with the police—and also with local residents—are always unstable and subject to changing attitudes on either side. This is reflected in the fluctuations in the relationship between the Colombian state and paramilitary groups, under pressure from the United States. But we also need to break down each of these larger categories of actors to identify the tensions internal to each. Colombian magistrates clearly did not adopt a shared position regarding paramilitarism and social cleansing, and their interventions were never perfectly synchronized with that of the governing political class.[111] Meanwhile, the position of US authorities, in particular the agencies working to suppress drug trafficking, was out of tune with the interests of multinational companies that, without formal arrangements, relied on the paramilitaries to dismantle labor unions.

The involvement of the Colombian paramilitaries in maintaining the industrial and mercantile order as part of their combat for social peace offers food for thought concerning both the economic repercussions of rough justice and the dark side of neoliberalism. The diffusion of the power to punish is sustained by the pauperization of the working classes, the destruction of public services, the promotion of self-help, and the outsourcing of law enforcement and justice itself to community institutions and private groups. Conversely, some rough justice enthusiasts directly involve themselves in the implementation of neoliberal reforms. Reinventing the historical figure of the goon and its local variants—the *pájaro* in Colombia, the *preman*

126 **CHAPTER 5**

in Indonesia,[112] the *dada* in India and Pakistan[113]—private enforcers then become auxiliaries to an enterprise of wealth accumulation based on the material dispossession of the laboring classes (for example, through the appropriation of land, natural resources, and indigenous knowledge) and the deprivation of their rights (labor rights, social security, and so on).

Merging different levels of law enforcement, from counterinsurrection to the moralization of society and the protection of economic arrangements, social cleansing openly undertakes the dirty work inherent in the exertion of domination. By implementing and claiming punishments, it reveals the violence underpinning the social order and turns the spotlight on the irregularities and excesses inherent in state formation. However, when it comes to the job of social control, such excesses are not the sole preserve of auxiliaries and amateurs. As we see in Chapter 6, law enforcers are also prone to unbound themselves from the legal straightjacket. These liberties with the law, which underpin the police power to punish, carry the seeds of a different form of summary justice, in which unofficial punishments are dispensed under cover of the law. And when a consensus emerges within the political and judicial authorities to back, encourage, and even reward such transgressive practices, the foundations of the vigilante state are laid.

6 PUNISHERS IN UNIFORM

Who's the boss? The cop or the law?

MIGUEL VARGAS (CHARLTON HESTON), in
Touch of Evil, Orson Welles, 1958

THERE'S NOTHING LIKE A WHATSAPP GROUP for trading rants and tips among pals. The promise of confidentiality that has been a major selling point of the instant messaging service reinforces the comfortable feeling of privacy and invites users to open up. Some fifty Salvadoran police officers and public servants in one group were all keen to see the eradication of the armed gangs (*maras* and *pandillas*), which had been officially identified as public enemies early in the first years of the 2000s under a hardline *mano dura* (iron hand) policy.[1] This group of law enforcers could have taken the famous Brazilian adage "A good bandit is a dead bandit" (*bandido bom é bandido morto*) as their motto. The most active among them used WhatsApp to share their knowledge and skills in faking evidence, getting hold of weapons, and planning "rat extermination" operations.[2] Some *pandilleros*, or members of the *pandillas*, who had served jail terms and been released were identified and killed after prison authorities sent snapshots of their tattoos to the police, with the instruction to "give them gas" (*dar gas*; execute them).[3] Every criminal liquidated was an occasion for mutual congratulations and an explosion of jubilant emojis.

Yet some delinquents managed to slip through the net, which inevitably exasperated the group's members and whipped up their anger against institutions that they regarded as complicit with the gangs, starting with the justice system. On June 2, 2017, a police officer shared the location of an injured *pandillero*, who had sought refuge in a church in the municipality of Sonsonate. The priest refused to hand over the suspect to the police, although he was said to be a notorious criminal, recently released from prison. His photograph was circulated. Tempers quickly flared. "The laws are worth shit (*valen verga las leyes*)," said one member, and others went further: "This is what happens when you release scum," "I hope the son of a bitch will finally croak." These vituperations against human laws led to appeals to higher authorities, portrayed as endorsing the right to eliminate the unproductive. "What is God's is God's, because frankly, what good can come from that kind of scum [*una rata de estas*]? Don't the Scriptures say 'Every tree that does not bear good fruit is cut down and thrown into the fire?'[4] And what kind of fruit can that scum bear?"[5]

Although this *pandillero* escaped death, one of his companions was not so lucky. He was killed on a motorcycle a few hours later by the Fuerzas Especializadas de Reacción El Salvador, an elite unit funded by the United States and responsible for most of the country's extrajudicial killings. Snapshots of the body, which a police officer present at the scene was quick to share on social media, show him lying in a pool of blood, a pistol an inch or so from his right hand. According to the police, he had just accelerated and opened fire on them. Using the same hand.[6]

———

Every cabal has a weak link. A civilian member of the group—a former door-to-door salesman of domestic appliances who had offered his services to the police after his motorcycle was stolen—gave journalists of the Salvadoran webzine *Factum* access to its discussions. The publication of the messages caused a scandal, and the police officers in the group were arrested. However, like most of the six hundred law enforcement professionals arrested in El Salvador in 2017 for participation in a death squad, complicity in extrajudicial violence, or criminal activities, they were released a few days later.[7] Indulgence from the authorities was taken as a given by these police officers, and their sense of impunity was reflected in the way that they displayed their hunting trophies on social media, even on publicly accessible Facebook pages.

Turning police killings into public spectacle is not specific to El Salvador. Until his disgrace in 2018, one of the police officers with the greatest media presence in Pakistan, Rao Anwar, liked to enhance his Facebook page with photos of his victims—young Pashtun workers portrayed as terrorists, lying in blood-spattered *shalwar kameez*[8] with a firearm always within reach. The formal similarity of these murders, evident in their macabre staging, extends to the field of discourse. From El Salvador to the Philippines via the Indian subcontinent, the language used to justify summary executions combines the register of legitimate self-defense with that of rough justice. Although claiming to be within the legal framework of self-defense, police officers are not afraid to simultaneously portray these homicides as punishments. Their words express a fierce critique of the justice system and address diverse audiences, ranging from criminals to the police hierarchy, magistrates, politicians, the media, and the public. Beyond this critique, the private conversations of the Salvadoran police officers on a WhatsApp group reflect an alternative idea of justice. Uncomfortable though it may be, these police officers, who claim they are getting their hands dirty in everyone's interests, must be taken seriously. To understand what is at stake here, it is important to listen to the political discourse they express when calling for circumvention of the law in order to protect society more effectively. Upholding the law is not the same as maintaining order; in reality they are two poles of a force field that characterizes modern policing.[9] And yet, even if some professional law enforcers can be tempted or requested to deliver order extralegally, these uniformed avengers have little in common with their civilian counterparts. The claim of a right to punish by the police tends to find legal and bureaucratic justifications, which make this form of rough justice less prone to sanctions than violent outbursts by concerned citizens.

This is not to say that punishers in uniform are immune to scrutiny. Whatever the degree of legitimacy that they claim and however skilled they may be in covering their tracks, justice done by the police is inevitably going to be controversial. Repeated scandals raise doubts concerning the forces that drive extrajudicial violence. In India and Pakistan, *fake encounter* refers to a summary execution dressed up as a shootout with the police. Media constructions and the treatment of fake encounters by the justice system reveal tacit assent combined with suspicion. And although this extrajudicial violence has acquired undeniable legitimacy in recent decades, a chronic uncertainty feeds suspicions that the "killing state" is leading a "double life."[10] By claiming to sacrifice the letter of the law in order to restore its majesty, aren't punishers in uniform impostors fomenting disorder?

THE SHADOW OF *DIRTY HARRY*

Because law enforcers contravene the norms regulating the use of force in the rest of society and tend to prioritize operational demands over adherence to formal rules, police work amounts to "legal lawlessness."[11] As an institution, the police service thus develops an ambivalent relationship to the law and, more specifically, to procedural rules that officers perceive as hindering their routine activities. The law and its professionals heighten this ambivalence. The law's vagueness "provides the police with the conditions of its subversion,"[12] and magistrates who rely on police work for their cases lack the material means to challenge the retrospective definition of events by law enforcers.[13] The equivocal relationship of the police to legal norms

130   CHAPTER 6

can be seen in police discretion, which is used by officers in every situation. As shown by Carl Klockars in a celebrated article inspired by the first film in the *Dirty Harry* series, police discretion constantly comes up against a moral dilemma: Is it justifiable to adopt "dirty means" to reach "good" ends?[14] Although he has lost patience with the rules governing the use of force, Inspector Harry Callahan faces this same dilemma in the second film in the series, *Magnum Force*, where he has to deal with a group of young police officers who use their prerogatives to execute criminals in cold blood. Dirty Harry himself stands on the fringes of an institution that he regards as too hampered by procedure—a position that earns him the sympathy of the new recruits, who try to enroll him—yet he is scandalized by colleagues who share his aim of cleaning up San Francisco but resort to methods that are even more dubious than his own. In the film these deviant vigilantes, inspired by the death squads of the Brazilian dictatorship and stripped of all individuality,[15] are supposed to contrast with the character of Harry and his libertarian ethos.[16] The contrast serves above all to exonerate Clint Eastwood, who plays Inspector Callahan and cowrote the script for *Magnum Force* after he was accused of fascism following the release of the first film. However, the clash between these two ways of maintaining order by breaking the law reveals a more widespread contradiction: although Hollywood cinema sets up the police officer who breaks with his tribe as the archetype of the punisher in uniform, in reality police rough justice tends to be a group phenomenon, organized and integrated into the state apparatus.

In every police force in the world, criticisms of the procedural aspects of official justice provide the most common justification for punitive practices. These focus on the leniency of the judicial system, its technicalities, its lack of appreciation for investigative police work, and its propensity to overemphasize the rights of the accused to the detriment of the victim. In the eyes of the police officers who use such tactics, verbal and physical humiliation, torture, and corporal punishment are all "unofficial retribution" in anticipation of the supposed indulgence and apathy of the judicial apparatus.[17] These punitive practices culminate in summary executions, asserting the right of the police to kill without hindrance.

In its unabashed violations of the law, police rough justice resembles its civilian counterparts. This has led some jurists and sociologists of the police to speak of *police vigilantism*, a term already used in the 1931 report of the Wickersham Commission, which launched the first systematic investigation of extralegal violence committed by US police forces. Updated by sociologists denouncing street justice[18] and the resurgence of brutality among the US and British police in the 1960s,[19] *police vigilantism* took on the more sociological meaning of "acts or threats of coercion in violation of the formal boundaries of an established sociopolitical order but intended to protect that order from some form of subversion."[20] Police vigilantism has reasserted itself in the sociology and anthropology of policing, where in the 2020s it refers to a range of disparate practices. Some authors interpret it as a response to a social demand for greater severity or, where the police have close relationships with the population, as correcting the behavior of wayward young people. In South Africa and Nigeria, working-class families sometimes haul their unruly children off to the police station, where both police officers and arrested criminals punish them to set them back on the right path.[21] Other authors are more critical, seeing police punishments as government sponsored. As Tom Bowden suggests in a book published in the late 1970s, "What might appear on the surface to be *spontaneous* acts of police vigilantism are often in effect managed, supervised or condoned by governments for ulterior political motives."[22] The sudden surge in murders by police officers in some countries of the Global South, starting with the Philippines under President Rodrigo Duterte (2016–2022), has thus been interpreted as an aggravated form of penal populism, in the sense of a hyper-repressive policy justified by rampant insecurity and grounded in electoral calculations.[23]

However, there are major differences between police rough justice and the other varieties we discuss in this book. The coercive resources of the police are underpinned by legal prerogatives that, combined with their bureaucratic skills, enable them to cover their tracks through administrative sleight of hand in writing reports. And when officers are required to account for themselves, it is to disciplinary bodies that are inclined to indulge their extralegal use of force. So rather than *police vigilantism*, we prefer *punitive police work*, a term borrowed from one of the Wickersham Commission's chief investigators, the American journalist Ernest J. Hopkins. In his book *Our Lawless Police*, published in 1931, he rails that "the [American] policeman has usurped, in amazing degree, the power to punish; and that without the formality of trial and conviction, often without the formality even of arrest."[24] The qualification of punitive practices as police work makes them part of the everyday activities of an institution that is tightly managed yet still gives considerable freedom to its agents on the ground.[25] It also rules out the bad apple hypothesis of individuals who go off the rails. Although the excesses of some punishers in uniform may prove controversial, their use of extrajudicial violence can only become established in the long term if it is seen as a service in the general interest, distinct from any personal score settling.

In the United States, reforms to penal procedure in the decades following the publication of Hopkins's book introduced the supervision of raids, arrests, and interrogations, noticeably limiting the capacity of the police to dispense their own justice. For the progressive judges behind this jurisprudence,

132   CHAPTER 6

starting with Supreme Court Chief Justice Earl Warren, "the police must obey the law while enforcing the law."[26] However, the lethal practices of the Special Investigation Section of the Los Angeles Police Department, known and tolerated by the Los Angeles police hierarchy over more than two decades, show the limitations of these safeguards, even in a country like the United States, which takes a highly procedural approach to policing. This elite squad, tasked with the surveillance and apprehension of the city's most hardened criminals, between 1965 and 1992 opened fire on fifty-five individuals, killing twenty-eight. Police officers adopted the cover of self-defense, claiming that the victims were all armed and dangerous. But across the entire period, only one member of the unit received a bullet wound, and that was due to an accidental shot fired by one of his colleagues. Scandal erupted in 1990, after a group of armed robbers targeting McDonald's restaurants were shot in dubious conditions by Special Investigation Section men. Far from being intimidated by the subsequent judicial procedure, which led to the police department being found guilty and fined $44,000, the department's very martial chief Daryl Gates stuck to his guns: "If we had taken them outside [the restaurant before they entered it], they would have been out on bail today, and probably robbing someone else. Now there won't be any more of these robberies at McDonald's. Perhaps we have accomplished something."[27]

In the United States and elsewhere, the use of potentially lethal force is the most regulated of police prerogatives. So the routinization of homicides by the police is a truth test for the police's claim to exert legitimate violence, all the more so when a consensus emerges in the media, the political class, and public opinion around the extrajudicial nature of recourse to lethal force. In democratic contexts, a police officer is authorized to use lethal force "with the mere proviso that force will be used in amounts measured not to exceed the necessary minimum, as determined by an intuitive grasp of the situation."[28] This authorization and the exercise of police discretion reach their limits in homicides committed by the police. The presumption that force has been used for legitimate and honest reasons, which judicial and political authorities generally grant to the police, is undermined in such cases, particularly when they cease to be exceptional.[29] The resulting controversies reveal the conditions that produce and legitimate police rough justice, a reordering project that relies on the law even as it transcends it.

FROM SELF-DEFENSE TO POLICE ROUGH JUSTICE

Around 1 p.m. on November 16, 1991, the head of Bombay's Anti-Terrorism Squad, Aftab Ahmed Khan, received a phone call from one of his informants. "I have spotted at least seven of the rats you're looking for," said the petty criminal, who had for a while been employed by one of the city's dons—gang leaders originally dealing in contraband and alcohol but who had moved into real estate, extortion, and money-laundering when the economy was liberalized. The suspects included Maya Dolas, a notorious contract killer, racketeer, and member of the gang headed by Bombay's most famous mafia boss, Dawood Ibrahim. Khan seized the opportunity and sent his men to Lokhandwala, a densely populated residential complex in the Andheri neighborhood. For four hours, officers of the Anti-Terrorism Squad, backed up by their colleagues from the Bombay police, fought a gun battle with the seven gangsters as cameras rolled. This was not only the first major police "encounter" in broad daylight but also the first event of its kind to be broadcast live on television. The publicity did not stop the seven gangsters from meeting the usual fate of Indian criminals in such circumstances. Their lives ended, in Khan's words, "totally submerged under an avalanche of bullets."[30] This fatal conclusion did not displease advocates of strong-arm tactics, of whom there were plenty among politicians and the urban middle classes, who feared that the "license raj" (state interventionism of the Jawaharlal Nehru period) would give way to the "mafia raj" (the reign of organized crime). Sudhakarro Naik, chief minister of Maharashtra at the time, and several prominent personalities congratulated Khan and his men. The Lion's Club, the Rotary Club, and other organizations also congratulated the police officers, and the head of a women's rights nongovernmental organization sent a message wishing long life to these men who, she said, "like Superman, reach everywhere at the right time and carry out operations successfully." Bolstered by this concert of praise, Khan used the interactions with his audience to recruit more informers: "Whenever, wherever we were honoured, I told the people repeatedly, that this kind of flushing out of the undesirable elements in society could be possible on a larger scale only if the common man co-operated fully with the men in uniform."[31] Note the use of "flushing out," with its hunting, military, and hygienist connotations (finding a prey, forcing a target to come out in the open, and washing away a foreign body). In addition to his fervent support for the paramilitarization of policing, Khan was an open advocate of social cleansing. In his memoirs, he highlights his determination to "de-weed," and it was no coincidence that the code name for the Lokhandwala operation was Operation Clean-Up.

This prophylactic conception of police work was not specific to Khan and his unit. Pradeep Sharma, who was recruited into the Bombay police as a subinspector in 1983, introduced the term *encounter specialist* into everyday language in India and Pakistan in the late 1990s. He headed an anti-gang unit nicknamed the Encounter Squad and was involved in the killing of around 112 supposed criminals, an exterminating role he was happy to claim, telling

134   CHAPTER 6

Time magazine in 2003, "Criminals are filth . . . and I am the cleaner."[32] This hygienist vocabulary offers an initial clue to what happened in the encounters between the Bombay (now Mumbai) police and the gangsters who had been causing trouble for law enforcement since the 1980s. In India and South Asia more widely (Pakistan, Bangladesh, Sri Lanka), *encounter* is a euphemism for a supposedly fortuitous shootout between police officers and criminals or supposed terrorists, in which the criminals are usually killed and the police suffer minor injuries at worst.[33] The term spread from police jargon to all the region and even gave rise to a specific verb in Hindi and Urdu: *encounter karna* (to do an encounter). The intentionality expressed by the verb reflects the suspicion that these shootouts are staged. Doubts are fostered by official first-information reports that contain a stereotypical police cover story[34] and that often are unquestioningly repeated in the media. In the eyes of the public, most of these confrontations are likely fake encounters, staged shootouts to conceal summary executions. Such suspicions are not enough to discredit the practice, as indicated by the following article published in 2001 in one of the most prestigious Indian daily papers:

> The Mumbai police call it "proactive policing." In everyday parlance, it is referred to as an "encounter" between policemen and gangsters that always results in the death of these gangsters. That these encounters do not have a surprise element, instead are planned, to a large extent, by the police, no longer raises eyebrows. But even by their own standards, Mumbai police have been far too "proactive" in 2001 compared to the past few years. . . . In 2000, the total number of alleged gangsters killed in encounters was 49. . . . The quantum leap to 94 has certainly sent shockwaves through the underworld. Extremely pleased at this leap, Police Commissioner M.N. Singh said: "Organised crime is well under check. This is the final blow."[35]

Police homicides of doubtful status have a long history in India. Midway between law enforcement and combat operations, they were originally a counterinsurgency method to deal with peasant uprisings: the Telangana rebellion of 1946–1951, Naga rebellion of 1958, Maoist uprising in the 1960s, and separatist movements of the 1980s in Punjab and Kashmir.[36] In the early 1980s, the practice was extended to the fight against urban organized crime, especially in Bombay, where the policy of neutralizing criminals reached its peak in 1994–2004 and resulted, according to official sources, in over five hundred deaths.[37]

Like their counterparts the world over, the Indian police claimed self-defense, guaranteed by sections 97, 100, and 103 of the country's penal code, to justify their homicides in the eyes of the law. They sometimes also invoked clause 46.3 of the Code of Criminal Procedure, which states that police officers have no right to cause the death of an individual who is "not accused of an offence punishable with death or with imprisonment for life." This clause is interpreted by Indian police officers as a right to use lethal force against any dangerous criminal evading arrest.[38] In accordance with the fleeing felon rule,[39] this interpretation, inherited from common law, is generally validated by the Indian courts. Until the scandals that raised questions about police actions in Mumbai and Gujarat late in the first decade of the 2000s, to which we return later, judges rarely contested the word of officers involved in encounters. In India and elsewhere, approval for extrajudicial violence proceeds through the silences and the ambiguities of the law, which favor discretionary interpretations by judges and police officers. The malleability of the law, then, legitimates what all parties recognize—covertly, as a public secret—as summary executions.

In Bombay, lethal violence by the police was also fostered by the requirement for results in what was seen as a context of ever more rampant criminality.[40] The anthropologist Julia Eckert, one of the first to research this issue, finds that this professional motive was supplemented by an impulse for justice: the guilty had to be punished and, because the courts were not up to the job, punishment became the task of the police. The principle of self-defense then had to be understood in a broader sense. It was no longer a matter of protecting police officers alone but extended to the "self-defence of society as a whole for which they take responsibility."[41] Aftab Ahmed Khan implicitly endorsed this approach to law enforcement by transcending the legal framework when he mentioned the possibility—indeed the necessity—of purging society through violence. This stance, based on a radical critique of the judicial system and the liberal regime of rights, was intended to counter the supposed failure of the correctional ideal. It is certainly the case that on the Indian subcontinent disciplinary institutions historically placed little emphasis on the "positive practices of rectification" that Michel Foucault sees as central to the treatment of "abnormal" individuals in eighteenth- and nineteenth-century Europe.[42] But Indian police officers, who remain convinced of the virtues of torture in extracting information and disciplining suspects,[43] also differentiate between reformable delinquents and irredeemable criminals. As explained by a police officer in Uttar Pradesh in an interview with the anthropologist Beatrice Jauregui,

> I do not bother with the petty criminals. They must be dealt with, so I will have them brought in, slap them around a bit, then let them go. I treat them like my children. They must be disciplined, but not really

136   CHAPTER 6

hurt, because our ultimate objective as police should be to bring the bad characters back into the mainstream of the society. . . . But the really bad criminals, they cannot be disciplined. And the legal system has completely degenerated, so it cannot stop them. But they must be stopped.[44]

Outlined here is a flexible approach to punishment, in which petty criminals who might mend their ways can receive corrective treatment. By contrast, the rehabilitation of hardened criminals is seen as a dangerous illusion, which society must guard against by emphasizing its absolute right of self-preservation. In most penal codes, the rationale of the "self-preservation instinct" that underpins the right of self-defense for civilians and the police is valid only if the violent response is immediate and hence distinct from punishment and vengeance, meaning it can be "excused."[45] The Indian police officers involved in summary executions are careful not to explicitly claim a right to kill, for fear of violating the public secret on which this unofficial punishment relies and thus exposing themselves to prosecution. However, this is the claim that emerges when we connect the dots in their memoirs, interviews, and works of fiction,[46] in which they are at pains to justify their actions by means of a necessarily incomplete theory of police rough justice.

The controversies over the genuineness of encounters show that these unofficial means of punishment owe much to a moral conception of police punitive work. As reflected in the messages of praise addressed to Aftab Ahmed Khan immediately after the encounter in Lokhandwala, police officers responsible for the deaths of notorious criminals were sometimes lauded to the skies by politicians and certain sections of the population. Such expressions of support can still be seen in the 2020s.[47] Although, in Khan's case, this support came primarily from fearful members of the urban middle class, some accounts note support from the rural poor for the elimination of dacoits and gangster politicians who exploit them and harass women.[48] So the lethal use of force in encounters is not always in itself seen as a deviant form of policing, even though the consensus prevailing in Indian society is that most of these incidents are illegal. Within the police, the legitimacy of an encounter is not a matter of strict respect for the legal framework but is based on the identity of the victims, the conformity of the reports written by the officers involved to the procedural norms, and crucially, the motives for the summary executions. As long as the victims are hardened criminals and the actions are within the legal framework and have been conducted in good faith, even a "staged encounter" can appear as a "genuine encounter," to use the categories employed by the Indian police themselves. Conversely, the murder of individuals without a criminal record, cases of mistaken identity, executions of suspects in custody, and murders carried out for personal enrichment or on behalf of gangs are regarded as unjustified and categorized as "fake encounters."[49]

In India as elsewhere, police reports receive various technical and legal authentications,[50] involving the input of experts from outside the police—starting with the medical examiners conducting autopsies on the victims. Occasional instances of insubordination by medical and legal experts resisting attempts at corruption and intimidation fuel suspicions of manipulation. However, dissonant voices largely go unheard because, with very rare exceptions, they are not picked up by the media.[51] Public support for murders committed by the police is also far from unequivocal, and many Indians perceive them as "a service at once necessary and abominable."[52] As discussed later, most encounter specialists have been prosecuted at some point in their careers, sometimes after complaints from ordinary citizens who doubted the veracity of their accounts and their supposed disinterest. However, the absence of public reaction to most encounters—especially when the targets are notorious criminals—remains striking. The few protests identified this century have related to victims with no criminal record who were killed in error or bad faith by police officers. Furthermore, local media, particularly cable television channels, have helped maintain an extreme form of "police fetishism,"[53] holding up the police as a bastion of social order against the forces of chaos.

In Mumbai and across all of South Asia, Bollywood cinema has done the most to shape the image of punishers in uniform in the minds of the public. Moreover, encounter specialists have very close links with the film industry; they advise screenwriters and adopt the stereotypes in myriad films showing punishments meted out by law enforcement. By promoting the entanglement of police rough justice and popular religion, Hindi cinema has also fostered a "metaphysical" dimension to the police critique of the justice system, depicting the "war" against crime or terrorism as a moral and spiritual fight.[54] One example of this is the film *Gangaajal: The Holy Weapon* (2003). The film is based on real events that took place in Bhagalpur (Bihar) in 1979–1980. It tells the story of the particularly brutal and highly symbolic punishment inflicted by police officers on a group of criminals who defy their authority. After putting out their victims' eyes, the officers pour into the sockets sulfuric acid, comparing it to the waters of the Ganges, the sacred river associated with the god Shiva, who is the simultaneously destructive and regenerative figure of the Hindu pantheon. This carnage is accompanied by puns on blind justice, and the joyful populace congratulates the police for having at last done their duty. The film ends with another act of violence with ritual echoes. Standing in the waters of the Ganges, the local police chief delivers a beating to the corrupt politician who dominates the city and his son, and by this action "uses the space of the holy river to destroy the demons and

138 CHAPTER 6

cleanse society at large,"[55] thereby combining ritual purification with collective self-preservation.

Far from being an isolated case, this film is one of a long list of Bollywood productions in which police officers act as avengers in defense of society and also restore dharma (the proper behavior expected of every social group as a guarantee of universal harmony). *Kurukshetra* (2000) has a title charged with symbolism because it refers to the most famous battle of the Mahabharata, in which the god Krishna persuades the archer Arjuna to exterminate his cousins in the name of dharma. The film once again portrays the punitive exploits of a police officer, driven by a highly personal sense of justice, who murders the head of the provincial government of Maharashtra, his son, and another politician to avenge the rape and murder of a girl. This triple homicide takes place during the festival of Dussehra, which celebrates the victory of good over evil and, more specifically, the defeat of the demon Ravana in the other great Indian epic, the Ramayana. The police officer appears before a popular court and is found guilty of murder, but the crowd applauds him and declares him innocent. As he is leaving the court to begin his sentence, verses in Sanskrit are heard, taken from the Bhagavad Gita:[56]

> O scion of the Bharata dynasty, whenever righteousness is on the decline, unrighteousness is in the ascendant, then I body Myself forth.
> For the protection of the pious, the destruction of the evil-doers, and establishing virtue, I manifest Myself in every age.[57]

These lines from the Bhagavad Gita are interpreted as advocating a just war against crime and often referred to by police officers closely or more distantly involved in encounters. In 1990, transcending religious divisions, they appeared in the writing of Aftab Ahmed Khan, one of the few Muslims to occupy a post of responsibility within security services described as "sensitive and strategic."[58] In the chapter of his memoirs on the Lokhandwala encounter, Khan writes,

> As long as one carries one's loads with élan, applies oneself earnestly to the present action rather than its future reward, the obstacles in the long race of life will never be insurmountable (isn't that the essence of the *nishkama karma* that Krishna prescribes for Arjuna on the battlefield in the *Gita*?).[59]

The notion of *nishkama karma*, disinterested action, is central to the teaching of the *Gita* and contrasts with *sakam karma*, selfish action driven by the search for personal gain. Here it is used to show the pure intentions of punishers in uniform, in accordance with an ethic of extrajudicial violence that sees the police right to punish as grounded as much in their selflessness, verging on self-sacrifice, as on the propensity of criminals to succumb to the temptations of the material world. However, this metaphysics of police rough justice cannot be reduced to the cultural codes in which it is expressed. We saw earlier how, in rebelling against the law, the Salvadoran police spoke of "rendering unto God that which is God's" and calling on the Gospels to justify the extermination of irredeemable individuals. Similarly in the Philippines, some foot soldiers of President Duterte's war on drugs present themselves as exterminating angels: "We are not that bad policemen or bad individuals. We are just a tool, we are just angels that God gave talent to, you know, to get these bad souls back to heaven and cleanse them,"[60] as one of them told a journalist from the *Guardian* in 2016. Although we cannot rule out the possibility that these police officers believe their own myths, the power of their words seems to lie beyond their subjective significance. Like all partisans of rough justice, these police officers evoke an ideal law to transcend the legal law. But whereas vigilantes and lynch mobs usually appropriate the power to punish in the name of a community in danger, or of the sovereign people, punishers in uniform are more inclined to invoke suprahuman norms, the highest of which is divine justice. For them the issue is not to replicate or appropriate sovereign power but to overstep it in order to assert their own right to kill, with no other form of trial.

This claim to overstep the norms of the state reflects the paradoxical position of these virtuosi of violence: however carried away by hubris, they still know that they are vulnerable to the ups and downs of political and judicial power. Their tendency toward hyperbole is a response to the contingent fragility of their protections, through an attempt to rise above the fray.

TOWARD A VIGILANTE STATE

The routinization of encounters within the Indian police is a major social fact in a society claiming the title of the world's largest democracy. It has redefined the power to punish while assigning dominated populations seeking emancipation (primarily Dalits and Muslims) to a subordinate position. The contribution of police murders to the reproduction of social inequalities is particularly evident in rural areas. In Bhagalpur, for example, where the police pierced and burned the eyes of around thirty supposed criminals in 1979–1980, most of the victims belonged to the caste of the Gangotras, a nomadic community at the very bottom of the social scale, who had been burdened by a reputation of incorrigibility since the colonial period, due to their supposed expertise in the art of thuggee.[61] The situation was more

140   CHAPTER 6

nuanced in urban India. In Mumbai, police indulgence with regard to dominant groups was more apparent in their handling of law enforcement during the riots between Hindus and Muslims in the early 1990s than in their policy of encounters.

Conversely, since the first years of the 2000s, the rise to power of Hindu nationalists in some provinces has given a strong anti-Muslim and anti-Dalit tone to the fight against crime. In Gujarat, ruled with an iron hand from 2001 to 2014 by current prime minister Narendra Modi and his right-hand man Amit Shah, the police murdered a great many supposed Muslim terrorists, and the most zealous officers were rewarded.[62] Another illustration of the systemic nature of police violence in states governed by the BJP (Indian People's Party) can be seen in Uttar Pradesh under the Hindu nationalist monk Yogi Adityanath, known for his extremist positions and past involvement in violence against the Muslim minority. Since Adityanath took power in 2017, the number of encounters acknowledged by the police has skyrocketed, a phenomenon he encourages by asserting his determination to eradicate crime from the province. This project is summed up in the phrase *thok diye jayenge*, which he used for the first time three months after becoming chief minister of Uttar Pradesh and suggests excesses of all kinds. Literally promising to "whack" criminals (in the sense of a hammer), it also indicates that they could be purely and simply "liquidated" in the most idiomatic sense of the word. Between mid-March 2017, when Adityanath came to power, and mid-July 2020, encounters across Uttar Pradesh killed 119 people. And although the head of the provincial government and his entourage constantly refer to this record in boasting of their success in the fight against crime, everything suggests that the victims of these shootouts were in fact minor players and sometimes even ordinary citizens with no criminal record who may have been mistaken for someone else with the same name. The overwhelming majority were members of structurally oppressed groups, around half being Muslims and the rest predominantly members of the lowest castes (Dalits and Other Backward Classes).[63]

The involvement of the police in the "saffronization"[64] of Indian political life is one aspect of a vast punitive configuration on a national scale, which also thrives on the networks connecting regional authorities and Hindu nationalist vigilante groups harassing Muslims and Dalits.[65] The police assist in the imposition of a moral order and a xenophobic ideology alongside self-proclaimed defenders of the sacred cow (*gau rakshak*) and rioting crowds determined to lynch eaters of beef, reducing Muslims to the rank of second-class citizens. The gap between law enforcement and Hindu nationalist vigilantes grows ever narrower. During the anti-Muslim pogrom of February 2020 in Delhi, the police did not simply close their eyes to the violence meted out by young Hindu nationalists; they overtly encouraged the crowd to be more aggressive. Sometimes they even joined in with the looting and destruction of madrasas and mosques, having first taken the precaution of sabotaging any CCTV cameras in the area.[66] Above and beyond its emphatically Islamophobic nature, this violence was intended to punish Muslims for their opposition to a law passed in December 2019 that enshrines religion as a criterion for access to citizenship, a landmark measure of Narendra Modi's second term in government. During the past few years, the routinizing of extrajudicial violence by the police—as a policy orientation rather than personal inclination—was confirmed by the repression of progressive intellectuals described as "urban Naxals."[67] In harassing supposed supporters of the Maoist movement and their families, the police have been acting on behalf of an ever more authoritarian government and also as the promoters of an increasingly intrusive moral order. During raids on the homes of activists arrested for supposed complicity with the insurgents, the police complain to their families about the kinds of books they read (on Mao and Marx) and accuse the women present of not conforming to the behavioral standards expected of high-caste Hindu wives.[68]

The situation in India is far from unique and shows similarities to the punitive configurations observed since the mid-2010s in Brazil, the Philippines, and to a lesser degree, in Turkey. In these societies that celebrate the return of strong men to power, we can see the emergence of a vigilante state, where a hypertrophied punitive apparatus is underpinned by the entanglement of public and private enforcers. A vigilante state takes the cleansing of the society as its mission and in governing its citizens gives a central role to terror, excess, and uncertainty. In franchising the sovereign sword of justice while maintaining rights for law-abiding citizens, this punitive pluralism relies on a rebellion by political elites against due process, a supposed social demand for severity, and an ever more diversified offer of coercion.

Narendra Modi, Jair Bolsonaro, Rodrigo Duterte, and Recep Tayyip Erdoğan have all been supporters of authoritarian liberalism, sharing a disdain for the rule of law and reservations with regard to due process. They gave free rein to the police, seeking to mutualize the war against crime, subversion, and antinationals[69] by bringing their populations into these missions. As Erdoğan said to an assembly of Turkish shopkeepers and artisans on November 26, 2014, "In our civilization, in our national and civilizational spirit, tradesmen and artisans are soldiers when needed. . . . They are the policemen who build order when needed; they are the judge and the referees who deliver justice when needed."[70] His Filipino counterpart Rodrigo Duterte (in power between 2016 and 2022) could speak harshly enough of the liberal regime of rights and the unwarranted concessions it would give criminals—especially

142   CHAPTER 6

the consumers and traffickers of *shabu* (methamphetamines), whom he had vowed to eradicate. "I don't care about human rights, believe me. There's no 'due process' in my mouth" said this ex-lawyer, who was quick to turn on any of his former colleagues who might have been tempted to defend the traffickers with the threat that they would end up on the famous blacklist of suspects to be punished by the police and death squads. Nothing could get in the way of his war on drugs, in which he sought to enlist not just the police but the entire society, called on to take the law in its own hands. In late June 2016 he said, "Don't hesitate to call us, the police, or do it yourself if you have a gun—you have my support. Shoot [the dealers] and I'll give you a medal."[71] The Brazilian president Jair Bolsonaro, on his part, undertook to save *pessoas de bem* (good people) by giving free rein to the police. On January 1, 2019, the evening of his investiture, he declared, "We need to urgently get rid of that ideology that defends criminals and criminalizes the police."[72] And as his minister of justice presented a series of draft laws weakening controls on the use of lethal force by the police, Bolsonaro gave ordinary citizens greater access to guns.

Sometimes governments encourage ordinary civilians to take responsibility and invest in their own security in areas beyond the fight against drugs and organized crime. Because neighborhoods are places where people know each other, they are a favored terrain for programs to promote community involvement in maintaining social and moral order. In 2015, Ismet Uçma, an Istanbul politician from the Adalet ve Kalkınma Partisi (AKP; Justice and Development Party) invoked "neighborhood honor" to encourage all men and women to "take ownership" of security and "neutralize" local trouble-makers.[73] But in practice, citizen involvement in law enforcement often leads to a proliferation of force-wielding agencies, blurring the line between public and private. The militias that became established in some working-class neighborhoods of Rio de Janeiro in the beginning of the twenty-first century, having ousted the drug traffickers, are mainly composed of former police officers. According to the Brazilian sociologist José Cláudio Souza Alves, close relations among groups such as the Escritório do Crime (Crime Bureau), the security services, and some political figures (Flávio Bolsonaro, one of the president's sons, among them) show that "these militias are not a parallel power. They are the state."[74]

The most elaborate and violent manifestation of this punitive configuration can be seen in the Philippines. In this domain the election of President Duterte in 2016 marked a change of scale—though not of direction—and a further step toward bureaucratization. Like Narendra Modi and his henchman Amit Shah in Gujarat in the first years of the 2000s, Duterte began by experimenting at the local level with punitive methods that he would later implement on a national scale. Like Modi's Gujarat, the city of Davao was a laboratory for new forms of collaboration between regular and unofficial law enforcers. Duterte was Davao's mayor for over twenty years, learning his craft by running—on his own admission—a death squad responsible for executing 1,400 people from 1998 to 2015. In the first decade of the 2000s, a division of labor for killing was gradually established. The mayor's office instructed the barangay captains (district leaders) to draw up lists of drug consumers and traffickers, which they passed to the *amo* (leader) of the local death squad—usually a police officer, heading a group of killers recruited among former communist guerrillas and reformed petty criminals. Before each operation the district police force would receive instructions telling them to keep their distance from the execution site.[75]

With the election of Duterte as president, these practices were extended nationwide and police forces were enlisted in social cleansing operations. As in India, the legal appearances of these operations were preserved, to the extent that the consumers and dealers killed were supposed to have resisted the police in encounters ("spontaneous" shootouts) or buy-bust operations (infiltration operations). The police were given bonuses indexed to the value of their target, fostering the proliferation of murders. Duterte also guaranteed impunity to the police and encouraged the few officers prosecuted for excessive use of force to plead guilty so that they could benefit from a presidential amnesty. As if that was not enough, he also invoked his own past as a killer as an example to emulate—for example, when speaking to a business audience in December 2016:

> In Davao I used to do it personally. Just to show to the [cops] that if I can do it why can't you? . . . I'd go around in Davao . . . [on] a big bike . . . and I would just patrol the streets, looking for trouble. I was really looking for a confrontation so I could kill.[76]

Overall, the police engaged enthusiastically with this project. At last they felt recognized in their work and received many material rewards, both licit and illicit. The political class was more divided. Some mayors had not waited for Duterte's election to carry out their own social cleansing operations. Rey Uy, mayor of Tagum City for twelve years, set up a death squad comprising police officers, former prisoners, gangsters, and ex-guerrillas who, as members of the local civil security unit, were an official organization armed and paid by the local authority. As in Davao, the group's main targets were small drug dealers and street children, whom the city mayor described as "weeds." Meanwhile, Sergio Tomas Osmeña, mayor and congressman of Cebu City, flattered himself that he was one of the first elected politicians to

144 CHAPTER 6

join President Duterte's war on drugs. After setting up a system of bonuses, which the president later implemented at the national level, he told police officers that "if you kill a criminal in the line of duty, no questions asked. I'm there to assist the police, not to prosecute."[77] However, some local representatives refused to enlist in this fight. The more vulnerable among them were forced to comply, on pain of being prosecuted for complicity with the drug traffickers. Others, who had the support of powerful dynastic families, stuck to their guns and asserted their differences. The propensity of regional elites to use violent entrepreneurs to consolidate their dominance, the solidity of their electoral base, and their vulnerability to pressure from central government were all factors in these variations.[78] The ratio of police victims to those killed by vigilantes also varied considerably from one province to the next. According to official sources, 7,884 people linked to drug trafficking were killed in shootouts with the police between July 2016 and July 2020, but human rights organizations put the number at 30,000 or more.[79] However, some of the regions most affected by this violence recorded an extremely low number of vigilante murders, reflecting the ability of local police forces to successfully monopolize extrajudicial violence in some localities.[80]

Despite these regional variations, the bureaucratic production of rough justice was undoubtedly a national phenomenon. The central government drew up blacklists and required civilian and police leaders to produce tangible and measurable results. Back in 2015, a circular from the Department of the Interior and Local Government called on barangay captains to compile lists of all users, sellers, funders, and protectors of the drug trade to give to the police. Under Duterte's presidency, barangay captains, representatives of civil society, and religious organizations were encouraged to "heighten community involvement" in the Masa Masid ("Masses Observe") program because their input provided knowledge that helped manage, dissuade, and ultimately, neutralize undesirables. This apparatus of control involved the society on a massive scale by mutualizing surveillance at a neighborhood level. It also encouraged self-discipline in families through "drug-free households" stickers that simultaneously made other households vulnerable to punishment by executioners of all kinds.[81]

Although this policy was based on past experiences—notably programs to mobilize the population in the struggle against communism during the 1990s[82]—it has been implemented on an unprecedented scale under Duterte. It fostered both conformity and competition by establishing an arena in which myriad specialists in extrajudicial violence fiercely competed for government recognition and subsidies and also for more hidden income generated by the punishment economy. The war on drugs enabled the Filipino police to turn murder into a proper business by extorting drug traffickers, abducting so-called suspects to obtain ransoms from their families, and even more literally, receiving a commission for every corpse they took to the morgue.[83]

Although manifested in its most extreme form in Duterte's Philippines, this approach to violence as a business exists elsewhere. In Rio de Janeiro, militias prosper through extortion, installing parallel connections to the gas supply, stealing gasoline, and illegally building luxury apartments.[84] In Karachi, the city's most scandalous "encounter specialist," Rao Anwar, whom we discuss in the last section of this chapter, capitalized on his reputation and coercive resources to extract ransoms from his victims' families, evict undesirable residents, appropriate their land on behalf of real estate barons, oversee oil smuggling with Iran, and control the industry of illegal sand and gravel quarrying that supplies the construction sector.[85]

Journalists and human rights advocates who run considerable risks to document this highly lucrative slaughter are wondering more and more openly whether there is any point to their work.[86] Not only do the terrifying records they compile arouse almost no protest but populations seem to be resigned to the punitive spectacle offered every day by the vigilante state. In the Philippines the theatricality of the carnage recalled the spectacular violence of the Latin American death squads. The corpses left in the streets bore signs saying "I am a dealer" or "I am a junkie, don't be like me." This ritual degradation of the victims also involved disfigurement. The corpses had their heads wrapped in packaging tape, with grotesque expressions drawn where their faces should be. The bodies were placed in poses and places chosen for maximum visibility, and every new macabre discovery attracted onlookers.

As in India, social representations of these violent performances were tinged with ambivalence. During the second half of the 2010s, Filipino and Brazilian voters have elected candidates who promised to restore order at any cost. In both countries the mandate, mostly from the middle and upper classes, favored the escalation of police and militia violence in poorer neighborhoods. The spectacular rise in violence in the months following the election of Duterte in the Philippines does not seem to have damaged his popularity.[87] However, more detailed studies show that this support was far from unconditional. Although his hyper-repressive policies seem to have found broad favor, the use of extrajudicial violence was still seen by the overwhelming majority of the Filipino population as an odious practice. This mismatch is explainable not by some abstract attachment to the rule of law—the structural failures of which fostered the emergence of the vigilante state in the first place—but rather by the fears for personal and family safety inspired by an unbridled, opaque apparatus of repression.[88] The vigilante state that claims to enforce the law and manifest truth is haunted by the specter of fakeness.

146   CHAPTER 6

It is racked by blunders and scandals that reveal the terrible ambiguity of its exterminating angels and their law enforcement project. Fraud and subterfuge undermine certainties and cloud the image of the forces engaged in this project. But the unpredictability of the punishments and the opacity of their underlying motives also serve to consolidate the authority of these regimes that thrive on disorder. In these configurations, the excesses of avengers of all kinds are consubstantial with political domination. In constraining rulers and law enforcement to account for themselves, public controversies act as truth tests while, in destabilizing the vigilante state, providing it with an opportunity to redeem itself—until the next scandal.

TOTAL IMPUNITY?

Like millions of Pashtun migrant workers before him, Naqeebullah Mehsud set off in 2017 from the highlands of his native Waziristan, leaving behind his young wife and their three children, to try his luck in Karachi, the great metropolis in south Pakistan which, despite decades of armed conflict, has retained the title of *gharib nawaz shehr* (the city hospitable to strangers). He took low-paid jobs in factories and on construction sites and, as an amateur model, took his mind off his dull routine by playing "hero" (*veer*, his pseudonym) on social media, in staged images where he showcased the joys of fatherhood and his penchant for big-engine motorcycles. He loved fashion and dreamed of opening a clothing store. With his family's help he had amassed a little savings, which he planned to invest in the store. But he had not reckoned with the vigilance of the police. Since 2007, upper ranks and militants of the Pakistani Taliban have been largely recruited among the Mehsuds,[89] who are therefore suspected of colluding with the insurgents and subject to particular surveillance in Karachi. They are also exposed to extortion by the police who, under cover of anti-terrorist operations, regularly abduct young people, releasing them on receipt of a ransom. The sum demanded is indexed to the number of encounters claimed by the officer overseeing the operation, and nonpayers risk seeing their children disappear in a fake encounter.[90]

The Pakistani police inherited the same legal framework as their Indian counterparts and began using encounters on a grand scale in the 1960s, at the instigation of the country's first military government.[91] Initially confined to the province of Punjab, the practice later developed in Karachi, the country's principal city and economic powerhouse, where in the 1980s a particularly complex and deadly entanglement of political, sectarian, and criminal violence became a major headache for law enforcement.[92] The local police, known for their brutality, developed a scale of punishments based on a distinction between "half-fry" and "full-fry."[93] "Half-fry" meant a bullet wound, usually in the leg, to mark the supposed guilty person for life. This would be administered to petty criminals and followed the same correctional logic as the aforementioned Uttar Pradesh police officer's tendency to "slap . . . around a bit" the hoodlums in his jurisdiction. "Full-fry" meant elimination of individual in a fake encounter. This unofficial capital punishment was reserved for irredeemable criminals, whose emblematic variants included dacoits, gang leaders, Islamist terrorists, and contract killers working for political parties.

Since the murder in 2014 of Chaudhry Aslam Khan, nicknamed the Dirty Harry of Karachi,[94] the most highly rated of these encounter specialists has been Rao Anwar, senior superintendent of police in charge of the Malir district. According to official sources, 444 suspects were killed in the course of operations carried out on his authority from 2011 to 2018.[95] The very low numbers of police injured or killed in these supposed shootouts cast doubt on the official versions, and this policeman's name in itself inspired such fear in the vulnerable Mehsud population that imposters began to use it to hold them to ransom on their own account. Despite his scandalous reputation, Anwar cultivated the image of a righteous avenger. His most famous gun battles date back to the mid-1990s, and he makes no secret of the "immense joy" he found in his early encounters, during which he killed some of the city's most famous contract killers. Emphasizing his inflexibility and disinterest, he also projects an image of incorruptible rigor. "You know it's very easy to strike a deal with a criminal and let him off the hook,"[96] he told a local journalist in 2016, implying that he preferred the virtues of summary justice to such petty and corrupting accommodations. This claim would, however, be sorely tested by the disappearance of Naqeebullah and its judicial consequences.

On January 4, 2018, the young Mehsud and two of his friends, Hazrat Ali and Muhammad Qasim, were arrested by plainclothes police officers as they enjoyed a cup of tea in a popular restaurant in north Karachi. The young men were questioned, handcuffed, blindfolded, and taken to an unknown destination. When they asked why, they were told they were being taken to Rao Anwar, who would make it his job to send them "to Paradise." The terrified Naqeebullah realized the police officers knew of his savings. They demanded that he pay a million rupees (11,000 USD) in exchange for his release. He claimed to have less than half that sum, but it made no difference. That evening Naqeebullah was taken to a nearby room, and Hazrat Ali and Muhammad Qasim had to endure their friend's screams as he was tortured by his jailers. An hour later it was their turn. The following day Naqeebullah was further tortured, after which his friends did not see him again. On January 6, Hazrat Ali and Muhammad Qasim were freed, but they were threatened with death if they said anything about Naqeebullah's disappearance.

148   CHAPTER 6

The following week they read of their friend's death in the press, alongside three other dangerous terrorists in an encounter overseen by Rao Anwar.[97]

As suggested by an investigation published in the national daily *Dawn* a few months later, Naqeebullah was probably executed on Anwar's orders; after days of torture, he could not be returned to his family because his physical condition would reveal he was tortured.[98] Although they were well practiced, the police officers' attempt to dress up this murder as an act of legitimate violence ended in blatant failure. Thousands of people recognized Naqeebullah from Facebook and Instagram and not as a Taliban commander. They tore the police story to shreds. Describing the young man's interest in fashion, they observed that the Taliban are not known for their interest in modeling, as the jihadists themselves confirmed through their spokesman in South Waziristan.

When it comes to state violence, "indignation is often proportionate to the visibility of the evidence"[99] and Naqeebullah's electronic traces fueled the outrage by contradicting the police version. Using these clues, the investigators sent in by the Sindh police ruled out "any extremist tendencies" on the part of a young man, whose activities on social media presented him as a "liberal citizen [who appeared] to lead a happy family life."[100] The mood of the times is as crucial as the victim's profile to an understanding of the mechanism of the scandal. Initially confined to social media, protests soon spilled over into Karachi's streets. Thousands of Pashtuns blocked the city's main arterial roads, denouncing police violence and the harassment of their communities in the name of the fight against terrorism. Although the movement was started by Naqeebullah's fan club, it became organized around the Mehsud Tahafuz Movement (Movement for the Protection of Mehsuds), founded a few years before by young Mehsuds. Renamed the Pashtun Tahafuz Movement (Movement for the Protection of Pashtuns), this organization spearheaded the protests, with demands that became increasingly broad as the weeks went by. While continuing to call for Rao Anwar to be charged with murder, the young Pashtuns developed a systematic critique of the anti-terrorist regime that had become established in Pakistan in the fight against jihadi groups. Protests spread throughout the country—not so much a Pashtun Spring as a Pashtun Lives Matter movement of combative citizenship, defending the principle of equal rights against a vigilante state.

This scandal also had other "instituting" effects.[101] The police investigation into the incident soon concluded that it was a fake encounter, which meant Rao Anwar and his subordinates could be charged with murder. Although Anwar himself spent only a few weeks behind bars and was acquitted in February 2023, the scandal seems to have tempered the ardor of the Karachi police for fake encounters. Some limits to the use of force and the accumulation of wealth were placed on the Pakistani security forces, and homicide victims killed by the Karachi police declined to a quarter of the number killed from 2017 to 2018, from 257 to 61. However, it would be a mistake to see this as an unequivocal success for supporters of the rule of law in Pakistan. The leaders of the Pashtun Tahafuz Movement did try to extend the debate to the structural problem of extrajudicial violence, which they denounced as a state policy used to control and punish the Pashtun minority. But they were blocked by a recurrent obstacle to juridical protest, which is the tendency of the law to individualize cases, to the detriment of collective causes. The lawyers acting for Naqeebullah's family paid less attention to the abuses of the police as an institution, instead lambasting one particular deviant police officer. For Faisal Siddiqui, the lawyer acting for Naqeebullah Mehsud's father and one of Pakistan's most celebrated "cause lawyers,"[102]

> even in a context as fucked up as Karachi, Rao Anwar was an aberration, in the sense that no police officer ever behaves this way. He really stood out from the rest. Even in this kind of society, however, there are some limits to the kind of aberration you can become. . . . You cannot get away with this when you behave like this under the nose of everyone. Everyone in the establishment, the police, the judiciary, considered him to be an aberration. Besides, he constantly flouted his hierarchy. It was only a matter of time [before he fell from grace].[103]

The victim's spotless record further helped mobilize the public and convince judges, at the price—once again—of narrowing the focus. Concentrating the attention of the judges and public on an innocent victim and on a police officer made atypical by his excesses of all kinds also served the interests of the police authorities, who, in the face of accusations of brutality and corruption, always prefer to sacrifice bad apples rather than take a critical look at the institution.[104] Although it can prove fruitful for civilian parties and human rights advocates keen to stand up to vigilante states and their legitimation of murders committed by the police, this individualization of both murderer and victim ultimately works to preserve the consensus around the need to kill hardened criminals without due process.

Like the Black Lives Matter movement in the United States and the debates raging around police violence in France since the mid-2010s, the Pashtun Tahafuz Movement mobilization shows that the social demand for protection *by* the state did not eclipse demands for protection *against* the state.[105] The vigilante state, that enfant terrible of penal populism, remains controversial. The debates are primarily concerned with the validity of police accounts (what happened? who were the victims?). They then interrogate the legality of the use of lethal force (was it justified and proportionate?) and, last, focus on responsibilities (was this an individual crime, a strategy of the police as an institution, or a state crime?). These debates take place within the police and, less frequently, in the judicial domain, when a scandal leads to some cases ending up in the courts.

In all these controversies it is the legitimacy of extrajudicial violence by the police that is being debated. The metamorphosis of repressive regimes into vigilante states stems precisely from the legitimation of police illegalities by political and judicial authorities. For the police hierarchy, magistrates, political elites, and a section of the public, the assessment of police killings tends to bypass legal rules. These assessments focus on the presumed intentions of the police officers, making them a moral rather than legal judgment. In this type of punitive configuration, police officers who claim to break the law for the sake of public order must be above reproach. However discretionary it may be, their power to punish cannot be exerted in an entirely arbitrary manner. It must be informed, proportionate, and—crucially—disinterested. The legitimate targets of punitive police work are thus theoretically confined to the categories of hardened criminals, who can be struck down in cold blood by the vigilante state's sword of justice.

That being said, citizens are not fooled. Indeed, did they ever believe in the capacity of punishers in uniform and the authorities that support them to fulfill their commitments? In casting off legal constraints, the police's mission to enforce the law is always open to suspicion, starting with the sense that it is being made to serve hidden political and economic agendas. In the 1990s, Mumbai's encounter specialists were thus accused of underhand action on behalf of gang bosses. Immediately after the Lokhandwala encounter, Aftab Ahmed Khan and his men were accused of killing Maya Dolas at the instigation of the don Dawood Ibrahim and of appropriating 7 million rupees found at the scene. Although hailed as a hero by some, Khan still had to account for his actions in court, after skeptics cast doubt on his probity.[106] Most of Mumbai's encounter specialists (Pradeep Sharma, Daya Nayak, Praful Bhosale, and Ravindra Angre, among others) suffered similar repercussions. In 2007, some thirty police officers from Gujarat who had been involved in fake encounters were arrested and jailed, including Dahyaji Gobari Vanzara, a former head of the Ahmedabad Anti-Terrorism Squad. In his letter of resignation, written six years later when he was still behind bars, this avowed Hindu nationalist claimed he had been betrayed by Narendra Modi and his right-hand man Amit Shah. Implicitly acknowledging his involvement in the dirty work of a government dealing with the "existential crisis" of Islamist terrorism, he presented himself and his men as dutiful soldiers and said he had served the government "with complete honesty, integrity and sincerity

PUNISHERS IN UNIFORM   151

without falling prey to any of the mundane temptations."[107] Far from reward-
ing him for his services, he said Modi and Shah had abandoned him to his
fate after the Central Bureau of Investigation and supreme court had become
troubled by the extralegal transgressions of regional police. This searing
charge did not prevent Modi and Shah from becoming prime minister and
interior minister, respectively, the following year. To make things right with
their enforcers, and above all to ensure their silence, Modi and his controversial lieutenant[108] soon set about ensuring their rehabilitation. In 2015,
Vanzara and his colleagues were released on bail, and some were promoted
for their good and loyal services.[109]

In the vicissitudes of these police officers' careers, we can clearly see
that the acceptability of punishers in uniform and the excesses arising from
their sense of omnipotence depends on the twists and turns of political for-
tunes and politico-judicial (re)configurations. After spending years boasting
of their exploits, encounter specialists sometimes find themselves behind
bars, although it is rare for them to receive sentences as long as those of the
Gujarat police officers previously mentioned. Similarly, whatever the gravity
of the accusations against them, they may be rehabilitated and even restored
to their functions following a change in the political majority.

Vigilante states themselves are not immune from the mechanics of scandal. In the Philippines, the first national debate to sully the image of the war
on drugs concerned a Korean businessman, Jee Ick-Joo, who was abducted
by police officers from the elite Anti-Illegal Drugs Group (AIDG), no doubt for
having refused to comply with their attempts at extortion. In October 2016,
he was garroted in the parking lot of the Philippine National Police headquarters. The police officers demanded a ransom from the victim's family when
he was already dead, and they had had the body cremated in collusion with a
funeral parlor business whose employees eventually panicked and scattered
Jee's ashes in the toilets when the national press began printing the revelations. This scandal infuriated President Duterte, who called in the heads of
all the security services to announce that the war on drugs was over and the
AIDG was being dissolved. This resolution did not last long. A month later,
the AIDG was reorganized and operations resumed. In March 2017, police
officers and their masked assistants once more began liquidating criminals
suspected of links with drug trafficking, although the pace of the killings
temporarily slowed.[110]

In subsidizing extrajudicial violence, the vigilante state fuels suspicions
of imposture. The bonuses handed out by the Indian, Pakistani, and Filipino authorities after each encounter, and the guarantee of accelerated promotion for police officers involved in these operations, foster doubts about
their motivations and heighten rivalries within the police. Although conflicts

between officers are key to the dynamics of police scandals, they cannot be reduced to personal differences and often reflect more structural divides between senior officers from the national police cadre and lower-ranking local officers whose careers are more dependent on the political authorities. In both Karachi and Mumbai, most encounter specialists are "rankers"—junior officers who have speedily risen up the police hierarchy owing to services rendered to politicians or high-ranking members of the military.[111] Beyond the capacity of police rough justice to hide behind bureaucratic procedures and legal prerogatives, it differs from vigilantism as generally understood in this book in its organic relationship to political authorities. This connivance is extended when uniformed avengers try to go into politics. In India, encounter specialists have sought to make their reputational capital pay electoral dividends; a prime example is Pradeep Sharma in Mumbai, who in 2019 stood in the regional elections under the banner of the Hindu nationalist party Shiv Sena. So far these attempts have generally ended in crushing defeats, demonstrating—at least in these cases—the limits to converting kill counts into a political resource.

———

The constraints imposed on the police by the legal framework for the use of force have led them to develop their own critiques of judicial institutions and indeed to replace those institutions by carrying out their own sentences. Routine punitive police work involves inflicting extralegal punishments (such as insults, bullying, and beatings) on their habitual prey. It may be seen as a legitimate way to deliver justice if it is publicly stated to be done for the benefit of society. Although police rough justice challenges the juridical framework by transcending legal law in the name of higher principles (such as public order, national security, or divine law), its existence is conditional on the good will of the authorities. This is only an apparent paradox. Police rough justice is not an expression of mutiny against state institutions but of a government-impelled rebellion against the liberal rule of law. The end point of this process is the emergence of the vigilante state, which guarantees impunity for the police and decent people who choose to dispense justice themselves and may even reward their transgressions. However, this good will has its limits. For excesses by all sides to be acceptable, they must also be conducive to the political and moral order promoted by the likes of Modi, Duterte, and Bolsonaro.

Aspirations of the police and their political protectors to cast off legal frameworks in order to promote their own notions of order always encounter some form of resistance. In Brazil, India, and the Philippines, the numbers of homicides committed by the police in recent decades have fluctuated quite considerably. This lack of consistency largely relates to the recurrent scandals that have tarnished the image of local police forces and their use of lethal force. Rare though such cases may be, when police officers are charged with and—crucially—found guilty of summary executions, there is a very clear reduction in lethal police violence over subsequent months and sometimes years. This was apparent after the massacre at the Carandiru prison in São Paulo in 1992, immediately after the execution of Javed Fawda in Mumbai in 1998, and in the months following the murder of Naqeebullah Mehsud in Karachi in 2018. These sharp rises and falls show that there is nothing inevitable about everyday police brutality. Even in societies branded by decades of military rule, such as Brazil, Argentina, Pakistan, and to a lesser extent, the Philippines, the routinization of extralegal violence by the police is not a matter of historical determinism so much as conjunctural political orientations.[112]

As the main body with the power of (dis)approving this violence, the justice system indisputably acts as a safeguard. However, we should be careful not to overvalue the impact of its decisions in pacifying police behavior and deradicalizing vigilante states. In matching their judgments to recommendations for police behavior in confrontations with armed criminals, judges provide officers with a checklist that they can use to ensure they are legally covered.[113] Each apparent victory for individual rights often conceals an increase in the invisibility of the police's power to punish. At the same time, these truth tests renew vigilante states by giving them an opportunity to reassert the legitimate conditions in which the right to punish can be exercised, both within and outside the framework of the law.

CONCLUSION
THE ROUGH JUSTICE CONTINUUM

ALTHOUGH DISTINCT ACADEMIC SUBFIELDS have studied separately Wild West vigilantes, twentieth-century Latin American death squads, cop killers, killer cops, lynch mobs, and people's courts, we argue that they are all of the same species. All these self-styled avengers diagnose failure of due process, which they aim to cure by administering a treatment of their own. In each of its avatars, rough justice involves both a radical critique of the rule of law and a set of practices aiming to repair the judicial system through extralegal means. In its ideological discourse, rough justice accuses the legal apparatus of leniency, delay, technicality, cost, and showing more concern for the rights of criminals than for the defense of their victims. Differing from the formal justice system, proponents of rough justice advocate a cheap, uncompromising form of law enforcement, which they regard as the embodiment of popular sovereignty. The persisting appeal of this spectacular, allegedly popular form of justice runs contrary to the general trend toward the rationalization of judicial proceedings in the course of the civilization process.[1]

This critique is not the sole preserve of reactionary tendencies on the extreme right of the political spectrum. Revolutionary movements share many of its premises in their attacks on bourgeois justice, which they seek to replace with popular justice. As a toolkit of simple, inexpensive methods for righting wrongs, rough justice is accessible to all. It appeals at once to the powerful and the oppressed, to conservative forces and progressive movements. What distinguishes these extralegal forms of law enforcement from each other is their positioning in relation to the state. Whereas most adepts of rough justice justify their actions by state failures, some seek the protection of law enforcers and others strive to preserve their autonomy. Far from being immunized against extralegal enforcement, the professionals of violence (the police, the military, and other state security forces) may also take the law into their own hands. The demand of order and the critique of state performance by vigilantes can thus converge with state use of extrajudicial violence. In both cases, the recourse to rough justice finds justification in a virulent critique of due process, in the primacy of order over legality and in a representation of the state as uncompromising.

Official police forces may tolerate or even support some of these groups, as long as their enemies are the same as their political patrons' enemies, and they are prepared to do their patrons' work. Not content with simply separating the wheat from the chaff, government forces may also authorize police officers to ignore legal constraints in order to eradicate the dregs of society. So the continuum of rough justice practitioners extends from self-appointed vigilantes to their counterparts in uniform. In our view, the variable distinguishing different "crime-fighting formations"[2] is their relationship with state institutions, because this influences their longevity, the degree of impunity they enjoy, the extent to which they are militarized, and the range of punishments they deliver. The greater the legitimacy granted to extrajudicial violence, the more professionalized it becomes, transitioning from an amateur affair to an integral part of penal policy. However, because it takes place beyond the constraints of the law, it retains the fundamental instability of rough justice and its propensity for excess and scandal.

Rough justice is intrinsically controversial. Scandals occur when vigilantes arouse the ire of those they claim to serve, be they neighborhood residents, fellow villagers, coethnics, or political patrons. Such scandals constitute a crisis of legitimacy in the relational sense adopted by Charles Tilly,[3] and they are a reminder of the contingent nature of the vigilantes' standing with the public. Although political patrons may temporarily empower their protégés, their approval remains volatile, and even the most established enforcers can swiftly be downgraded to self-appointed vigilantes. Controversy may ensue when hidden motives for target selection emerge or, more frequently, after miscarriages of justice. Should it transpire that enforcers are using extralegal means for personal enrichment or concealing personal vendettas behind righteous causes, their moral contract with their constituents is breached. Scandals also occur when rough justice goes obviously wrong, especially if the victim was clearly innocent or is actively defended by sections of the public. In such cases, the potential for public mobilization is limited by the defining characteristics of victims, who tend

156 CONCLUSION

to be foreigners, outcasts, or indefensibly evil figures such as witches, child abductors, or pedophiles.

THE TIME OF VIGILANTES?

Has the time of vigilantes now come? Throughout the world, avengers in their myriads perform for various audiences, attesting to a global craze for summary justice. From the desert expanses of the US-Mexican border to the crowded roads of North India, the neglected barrios of Latin American metropolises, and the bustling markets of West Africa, rough justice has gained visibility. This global craze is due, first and foremost, to a questioning of modern justice's focus on rehabilitating criminals. Even in so-called liberal democracies, this approach has faltered in the last few decades under public pressure for harsher sentences, and ostentatious punishment[4] has returned in response to a supposed social demand for severity. Espousing this punitive turn,[5] vigilantes oppose all attempts at rehabilitation, which they regard as both counterproductive and too expensive. The economic argument—sparing law-abiding taxpayers the financial burden of incarcerating irredeemable criminals—is certainly not new. It was made by the vigilantes of the American Wild West, whose inclination for rough justice was partly justified by budgetary concerns.[6] The demand for rough justice has found new impetus in the neoliberal era, because it resonates with efforts to reduce public spending and simultaneous calls for greater personal responsibility. In Russia, India, and Nigeria, vigilantes are increasingly involved in policing road traffic and in the fight against crime more broadly. Partnerships of this kind culminate in vigilante states, where the promotion of lateral surveillance may go as far as delegating police powers and administering punishment.

The rise of social media has also contributed to the standardization and global circulation of rough justice. There is nothing new about rumors or the enthusiasm for investigation and punitive spectacle, but digital technology has made it easier to collect and pass on information and to broadcast vigilante shows to ever-larger audiences. Whether in France, India, or Mexico, twenty-first-century lynchings are usually triggered by a rumor on social media concerning alleged incidents of child abduction involving a suspicious van lurking in the area. The alert inevitably appeals to wannabe detectives, keen to assist the investigation by tracking and tailing suspicious vehicles and their drivers. The manhunt culminates with the beating or killing of the alleged culprits, which is captured on video and widely shared and commented on. Digital vigilantism, in contrast, uses naming and shaming rather than actual physical violence, exposing alleged offenders to unsolicited visibility. This self-help justice in which social media networks are used to trap and publicly shame alleged offenders is exemplified by pedophile hunting, in which camera-toting hunters confront their prey and expose them to public disgrace.

VIGILANTE STATES AND THEIR PUNITIVE CONFIGURATIONS

At this time of growing visibility and legitimacy for punishers of all hues, the use of extrajudicial violence culminates in what we refer to as the vigilante state—a form of government that emerges at the meeting point of three interdependent trends: the reformulation of social tensions in the language of security in response to an alleged social demand for greater severity; a revolt against the rule of law promoted by segments of the ruling elite and advocates of a no-holds-barred response to crime; and a plethora of enforcement offers from "specialists in coercion,"[7] blurring the boundaries between the public and the private.[8] In their quintessential form, as observed in Narendra Modi's India, Rodrigo Duterte's Philippines, and Jair Bolsonaro's Brazil since the mid-2010s, these punitive configurations have been legitimated by governments inclined to share the sovereign power of the sword. By catalyzing forces and adjudicating the excesses inherent in such an exercise of domination, these vigilante states have removed constraints on extrajudicial violence while controlling it.

In India under the BJP (Indian People's Party), Hindutva (the politico-religious agenda of Hindu nationalists) is enforced by a coalition of murderous policemen and self-righteous citizens. In the face of a perceived threat from a many-headed hydra composed of jihadis, illegal aliens, cow smugglers, and Modi's so-called antinationals, the boundaries between state repression and vigilante justice tend to blur. Past incidents of communal violence always involved a degree of state complicity, even under the rule of the (allegedly secular) Congress Party, before 2014.[9] However, collaboration between law enforcement personnel and violent citizens has become routine and now plays a prominent role in the enforcement of the Hindu nationalist project and in the reassertion of social hierarchies in everyday life. Under the guise of a crackdown on crime and terrorism, extrajudicial violence primarily targets Muslims, Dalits, and members of Other Backward Classes, who are thus returned to their subjugated status.[10] This project, which strongly echoes the intensification of racial violence in the United States at the beginning of the twentieth century, manifests itself in the performance of extrajudicial violence. Since 2014, the lynching of Dalit and Muslim men by vigilantes and their extrajudicial killing or maiming[11] by police forces have become common forms of communal violence in the states under BJP rule.

In the Philippines of Rodrigo Duterte, the war on drugs has unleashed unprecedented numbers of police killings, involving both the state police and mysterious executioners reminiscent of the Latin American death squads of preceding decades. Doubts about the identity of these often-masked vigilantes, along with rumors of kill lists fueled by local community leaders and politicians, maintained a climate of fear and uncertainty that was key to this peculiar form of "ordered disorder."[12] This politics of fear, which taps into preexisting public anxieties and is reinforced by the shadowy nature of the vigilante state, however, is only one element in the mixed feelings of local populations toward iron-fisted leaders. Electoral support for uncompromising penal policies is also driven by a more aspirational "politics of hope" that "broadens citizens' time horizons, viewing the future as something within the realm of their control."[13]

In contrast to the Indian context, what seems to have characterized the Philippines under Duterte was the greater bureaucratization of the vigilante state and its embedding in the local administrative machinery, with the active involvement of barangay captains (the lowest tier of government), *puroks* (local representatives who maintain order in their area), and *tanods* (guards recruited by the barangay captains).[14] Possibly as an outcome of this bureaucratization, rough justice here essentially was extrajudicial killings (rather than lynchings) perpetrated by police personnel and vigilantes suspected to be working under their authority—and killings by vigilantes increased when police came under scrutiny.[15] Despite these attempts at rationalization and state monopolization, the orderliness of such a punitive configuration should not be overestimated. Its political impact was also premised on its unpredictability, and the informalization of criminal justice facilitated score settling between criminal groups and provided opportunities for illicit ventures within a notoriously extortive police force.[16]

Although these punitive configurations are most fully developed in illiberal democracies, it would be a grave mistake to regard other regimes as immune from this revolt against the rule of law. In the United States, the war on crime fueled a "prosecutorial shift" by the executive branch, which encouraged political elites to outbid each other with their ever more uncompromising and vengeful proposals for solving insecurity.[17]

In France, the terrorist attacks since 2015 have invigorated advocates of punitive measures and Talion Law among politicians, public intellectuals, and law enforcement agencies. Known for his repeated rants against due process, the far right polemicist and unsuccessful presidential candidate Eric Zemmour encourages the police to "use live bullets to shoot the thugs and gangbangers" who, in his view, have taken control of rundown suburbs seen as "foreign enclaves."[18] Meanwhile, some sections of the French police openly promote vigilantism. Following an arson attack on a bus in Lyon on Halloween in 2021, the Syndicat des commissaires de la police nationale (the main union of police commissioners in France) posted a tweet celebrating a retaliatory attack on the arsonist: "The thrashing of a scumbag who threatened others and damaged a bus. An understandable reaction in self-defense against the spread of violence."[19]

The Donald Trump presidency went a step further, demonstrating the potential for state-vigilante partnerships in enforcing a reactionary political and moral order in the United States. Those four years were characterized by recurring episodes of violence by White supremacists, which intensified in response to the Black Lives Matter movement. The "mutually supportive relationships"[20] between right-wing militias, sections of law enforcement, and the president's office were on display throughout the summer of 2020. These collusions came to a head during the assault on the US Capitol in January 2021, following various incitements to violence by President Trump, including his infamous call to the Proud Boys militia to "stand back and stand by."[21]

Although the most vocal advocates of rough justice seem to have been contained for now, from the United States to the Philippines,[22] this global punitive approach will continue to shape official penal policies and encourage self-proclaimed honest citizens to participate in the administration of punishment. These aspirations to fix the judicial system and restore order through low-cost, participative solutions to crime and deviance are accompanied by new punitive configurations that normalize, mutualize, and commercialize the spectacle of summary justice. The global revolt against due process is here to stay.

NOTES

Introduction

1. Cited by George O'Toole, *The Private Sector: Rent-a-cops, Private Spies and the Police-Industrial Complex*, New York, W. W. Norton, 1978, p. 150. Posse Comitatus (Force of the County) was formed in Portland, Oregon, in the late 1960s by antigovernment White supremacists.

2. The group's Facebook page has been deleted, but a screenshot of the page is in Steven Trask, "His New Home Is in the Boot of Our Car," *Daily Mail* (Australia), June 12, 2016.

3. Steven Schubert, "Vigilante Warning as NT Police Investigate Facebook Post of Hogtied 'Would-Be-Thief,'" *ABC News* (Australian Broadcasting Company), June 13, 2016.

4. Kieran Banks, "Former Organiser of Darwin Crime Rally Protest Group Stands by Hogtie Picture," *NT News* (Northern Territory, Australia), June 15, 2016.

5. Gilles Favarel-Garrigues and Laurent Gayer (eds.), "Justiciers hors-la-loi," *Politix*, no. 115, 2016, pp. 9–156.

6. We have in mind here the overwhelming presence of civilian and police vigilantes in Indian and Nigerian cinema. See Beatrice Jauregui, "Just War: The Metaphysics of Police Vigilantism in India," *Conflict and Society*, vol. 1, no. 1, 2015, pp. 41–59, https://doi.org/10.3167/arcs.2015.010105; John C. McCall, "Juju and Justice at the Movies: Nigerian Popular Videos," *African Studies Review*, vol. 47, no. 3, 2004, pp. 51–67, https://doi.org/10.1017/S0002020600030444.

7. Michel Foucault, *"Society Must Be Defended:" Lectures at the Collège de France 1975–76*, trans. David Macey, New York, Picador, 2006, p. 240.

8. This definition of legitimacy draws on Charles Tilly, "War Making and State Making as Organized Crime," in Peter B. Evans, Dietrich Rueschemeyer, and Theda Skocpol (eds.), *Bringing the State Back In*, Cambridge, Cambridge University Press, 1985, p. 171.

162 NOTES TO INTRODUCTION

9. H. Jon Rosenbaum and Peter C. Sederberg, "Vigilantism: An Analysis of Establishment Violence," *Comparative Politics*, vol. 6, no. 4, 1974, pp. 541–570, https://doi.org/10.9783/9781512806335-002.

10. Richard Maxwell Brown, *Strain of Violence: Historical Studies of American Violence and Vigilantism*, New York, Oxford University Press, 1975.

11. Regarding this change in the United States and in the United Kingdom, see David Garland, *The Culture of Control: Crime and Social Order in Contemporary Society*, Chicago, University of Chicago Press, 2001, pp. 8–9.

12. Grégoire Chamayou, *Manhunts: A Philosophical History*, trans. Steven Rendall, Princeton, NJ, Princeton University Press, 2012, chap. 9.

13. David Pratten and Atreyee Sen, "Global Vigilantes: Perspectives on Justice and Violence," in David Pratten and Atreyee Sen (eds.), *Global Vigilantes*, London, Hurst, 2007, p. 3.

14. Charles Tilly, *Coercion, Capital, and European States, AD 990–1990*, Cambridge, UK, Basil Blackwell, 1990, p. 19.

15. Michael Taussig, *Law in a Lawless Land: Diary of a Limpieza in Colombia*, Chicago, University of Chicago Press, 2003, p. 92.

16. Pierre Bourdieu, *On the State: Lectures at the Collège de France, 1989–1992*, trans. David Fernbach, London, Polity Press, 2014, pp. 57, 47.

17. Bourdieu, p. 57.

18. David Pratten, "'The Thief Eats His Shame': Practice and Power in Nigerian Vigilantism," *Africa*, vol. 78, no. 1, 2008, pp. 64–83, https://doi.org/10.3366/E0001972008000053; McCall, "Juju and Justice at the Movies."

19. Michel Foucault, *Discipline and Punish: Birth of the Prison*, trans. Alan Sheridan, New York, Vintage, 1995, p. 14.

20. Foucault, pp. 16–17.

21. Foucault, p. 8.

22. The term *vigilante*, from the Spanish, appeared in the United States after the Civil War to refer to members of vigilance committees. William Safire, "On Language: Vigilante," *New York Times*, February 10, 1985.

23. Jacques Le Goff and Jean-Claude Schmitt (eds.), *Le Charivari*, Paris, EHESS-Mouton, 1982.

24. Edward Palmer Thompson, "'Rough Music': Le charivari anglais," *Annales*, vol. 27, no. 2, 1972, pp. 285–312.

25. Stephen Frank, "Popular Justice, Community and Culture among the Russian Peasantry, 1870–1990," *Russian Review*, vol. 46, no. 3, 1987, pp. 239–265, https://doi.org/10.2307/130562.

26. Howard Becker, *Outsiders: Studies in the Sociology of Deviance*, New York, Free Press of Glencoe, 1963, chap. 8.

27. Michael Taussig, *Defacement: Public Secrecy and the Labor of the Negative*, Stanford, CA, Stanford University Press, 1999, p. 50.

28. Michel Foucault, *Abnormal: Lectures at the Collège de France 1974–1975*, trans. Graham Burchell, London, Verso, 2003, p. 83.

29. David Garland, "Penal Excess and Surplus Meaning: Public Torture Lynchings in Twentieth Century America," *Law and Society Review*, vol. 39, no. 4, 2005, pp. 819–826, https://doi.org/10.1111/j.1540-5893.2005.00245.x.

NOTES TO INTRODUCTION AND CHAPTER 1   163

30. See the account of one of these mercenaries in Claude Angeli and Nicolas Brimo, *Une milice patronale: Peugeot*, Paris, Maspero, 1975, p. 85.

Chapter 1

1. CaucasianNews, "Russian Skinheads Killing Non-Russian Tourists and Immigrants," September 9, 2010, https://www.youtube.com/watch?v=rs1tn-v6mko.

2. For the Purpose of Protecting Children from Information Advocating a Denial of Traditional Family Values, federal law no. 135, June 29, 2013.

3. Gilles Favarel-Garrigues, "Digital Vigilantism and Anti-paedophile Activism in Russia: Between Civic Involvement in Law Enforcement, Moral Policing and Business Venture," *Global Crime*, vol. 21, no. 3, 2020, pp. 306–326.

4. "Eks-zamglavy UFSSP Andrey Kaminov osuzhden za pedofiliyu" [Former deputy head of Moscow Regional Court Bailiffs convicted of pedophilia], *Life*, August 24, 2014, https://yandex.ru/turbo/life.ru/s/p/138895. Gilles Favarel-Garrigues made all Russian translations.

5. Grigory Levchenko, "Natsionalist Tesak naiden mertvym v kamere SIZO" [Nationalist Tesak found dead in a cell], *Meduza*, September 16, 2020, https://meduza .io/feature/2020/09/16/natsionalist-tesak-nayden-mertvym-v-kamere-sizo-on-ostavil -predsmertnuyu-zapisku-no-advokaty-i-rodnye-ne-veryat-v-versiyu-samoubiystva.

6. *Raid* is the term used by young, self-appointed law enforcers in Russia to refer to their policing operations, such as when they patrol a park to chastise people drinking alcohol.

7. Gilles Favarel-Garrigues, "Justiciers amateurs et croisades morales en Russie contemporaine," *Revue française de science politique*, vol. 68, no. 4, 2018, pp. 651–667.

8. Gilles Favarel-Garrigues and Laurent Gayer, "Violer la loi pour maintenir l'ordre: Le vigilantisme en débat," *Politix*, no. 115, 2016, pp. 9–34.

9. Michel Foucault, *Power/Knowledge: Selected Interviews and Other Writings, 1972– 1977*, New York, Pantheon, 1980, p. 39.

10. In a book published in 1938 and reissued in 1969, Frank Shay wrote that lynching was "as American as apple pie." Frank Shay, *Judge Lynch: His First Hundred Years*, New York, Biblo & Tannen, 1969, pp. 86–90.

11. Blaxploitation is a subgenre of the exploitation film that emerged in the United States in the 1970s, produced, performed, and particularly appreciated by African Americans. The question of vigilantism runs through a number of these productions. In *Coffy*, for instance (directed by Jack Hill one year before *Foxy Brown*), Pam Grier plays a nurse determined to eliminate dealers and pimps. The theme is also found in *Gordon's War* (1973), *Slaughter's Big Rip-Off* (1973), *Black Belt Jones* (1974), and *Disco Godfather* (1979).

12. Richard Maxwell Brown, *Strain of Violence: Historical Studies of American Violence and Vigilantism*, New York, Oxford University Press, 1975.

13. On this criterion distinguishing lynching from vigilantism, see Manfred Berg and Simon Wendt (eds.), *Globalizing Lynching History: Vigilantism and Extralegal Punishment from an International Perspective*, New York, Palgrave Macmillan, 2011.

14. See Michael J. Pfeifer, *The Roots of Rough Justice: Origins of American Lynching*, Urbana, University of Illinois Press, 2001; and Michael J. Pfeifer, *Rough Justice: Lynching and American Society, 1874–1947*, Urbana, University of Illinois Press, 2004.

164   NOTES TO CHAPTER 1

15. Brown, *Strain of Violence*, pp. 67–89.

16. Brown, p. 116; italics in the original.

17. Thomas J. Dimsdale, *The Vigilantes of Montana: Or Popular Justice in the Rocky Mountains*, Butte, McGee Printing, 1950 (1st ed. 1866), p. 102.

18. Brown, *Strain of Violence*, p. 117.

19. Philip J. Ethington, *The Public City: The Political Construction of Urban Life in San Francisco, 1850–1900*, Berkeley, University of California Press, 2001, pp. 88–89.

20. A photo of this pair of shoes was circulating on social media in early 2019 with the caption "Negro skin shoes. . . . Never forget," prompting fact-checkers to determine whether Parrott was Black. Dan Evon, "Does This Image Show 'Negro Skin Shoes'?," March 7, 2019, https://www.snopes.com/fact-check/big-nose-george-skin-shoes/.

21. Cited in William Safire, "On Language: Vigilante," *New York Times*, February 10, 1985.

22. Harel Shapira, *Waiting for José: The Minutemen's Pursuit of America*, Princeton, NJ, Princeton University Press, 2013; Damien Simonneau, "Entre suprématie blanche et cybersécurité: Mutations contemporaines des pratiques de vigilantisme en Arizona," *Politix*, no. 115, 2016, pp. 79–102.

23. The Southern Poverty Law Center tracks US hate groups; see http://www.splcenter.org/issues/hate-and-extremism.

24. Justin Akers Chacón and Mike Davis, *No One Is Illegal: Fighting Violence and State Repression on the U.S.-Mexico Border*, Chicago, Haymarket Books, 2006, pp. 11–87.

25. Wobblies is the nickname given to members of the Industrial Workers of the World, a group that promoted revolutionary trade unionism among workers and farm laborers in 1910–1920.

26. Michael Cohen, "'The Ku Klux Government': Vigilantism, Lynching, and the Repression of the IWW," *Journal for the Study of Radicalism*, vol. 1, no. 1, Spring 2007, pp. 31–56, https://doi.org/10.1080/00020184.2018.1519332.

27. Brown, *Strain of Violence*.

28. Regarding the actions carried out by the Jewish Defense League, see "Jewish Defense League," Southern Poverty Law Center, accessed June 4, 2023, https://www.splcenter.org/fighting-hate/extremist-files/group/jewish-defense-league.

29. Joshua Bloom and Waldo E. Martin Jr., *Black against Empire: The History and Politics of the Black Panther*, Berkeley, University of California Press, 2013.

30. Brit McCandless, "The Vigilantes of Chicago in '71," *60 Minutes*, CBS News, January 4, 2017.

31. In the weeks immediately following the death of George Floyd, nearly two hundred appearances by White supremacists, often with police blessing, were recorded. See Mara Hvistendahl and Alleen Brown, "Armed Vigilantes Antagonizing Protesters Have Received a Warm Reception from Police," *The Intercept*, June 19, 2020, https://theintercept.com/2020/06/19/militia-vigilantes-police-brutality-protests/.

32. Kurtis Lee, "Armed and Black: How a Group of Men Licensed to Carry Guns Say They Are Seeking Racial Justice," *Los Angeles Times*, September 21, 2020.

33. "After Nights of Violence in Minneapolis, Locals Take Up Arms to Defend Their Community," *Washington Post*, June 7, 2020, https://www.youtube.com/watch?v=ovtLTPrB2MA.

NOTES TO CHAPTER 1   165

34. Alex Acquisto, Silas Walker, and Brian Simms, "What Is the Gun Carrying NFAC That Was in Louisville for Derby, Breonna Taylor Protest?," *Lexington Herald Leader*, September 5, 2020.

35. "The American Vigilante Tradition," in Brown, *Strain of Violence*, chap. 4.

36. Laurent Fourchard, *Classify, Exclude, Police: Urban Lives in South Africa and Nigeria*, Hoboken, NJ, Wiley, 2021.

37. Fourchard, *Classify, Exclude, Police*, p. 187.

38. Nicholas Rush Smith, *Contradictions of Democracy: Vigilantism and Rights in Post-Apartheid South Africa*, New York, Oxford University Press, 2019.

39. Laurent Fourchard, "Le vigilantisme contemporain: Violence et légitimité d'une activité policière bon marché," *Critique internationale*, vol. 78, no. 1, 2018, p. 173, https://doi.org/10.3917/crii.078.0169.

40. Fourchard, pp. 173–174.

41. Kate Meagher, "Hijacking Civil Society: The Inside Story of the Bakassi Boys Vigilante Group of South-Eastern Nigeria," *Journal of Modern African Studies*, vol. 45, no. 1, 2007, p. 98. https://doi.org/10.1017/S0022278X06002291.

42. Daniel Jordan Smith, "The Bakassi Boys: Vigilantism, Violence and Political Imagination in Nigeria," *Cultural Anthropology*, vol. 19, no. 3, 2004, p. 443.

43. Benjamin Loveluck, "Le vigilantisme numérique, entre dénonciation et sanction: Auto-justice en ligne et agencements de la visibilité," *Politix*, no. 115, 2016, pp. 127–155, https://doi.org/10.3917/pox.115.0127; Daniel Trottier, "Digital Vigilantism as Weaponisation of Visibility," *Philosophy and Technology*, vol. 30, no. 1, 2017, pp. 55–72, https://doi.org/10.1007/s13347-016-0216-4; Gilles Favarel-Garrigues, Samuel Tanner, and Daniel Trottier (eds.), "Watchful Citizen: Policing from Below and Digital Vigilantism," special issue, *Global Crime*, vol. 21, nos. 3–4, 2020.

44. On the use of Foucault's concept of governmentality in the framework of citizen participation in law enforcement in the United States, see Joshua Reeves, *Citizen Spies: The Long Rise of America's Surveillance Society*, New York, New York University Press, 2017.

45. Olivia Solon, "Crime-Reporting App Vigilante Kicked Off App Store over Apple's Content Concerns," *Guardian*, November 1, 2016.

46. See the application at https://citizen.com.

47. See the video presenting the product at https://www.youtube.com/watch?v=fB6Sqhvm8l8.

48. Jay Caspian Kang, "Should Reddit Be Blamed for the Spreading of a Smear?," *New York Times*, July 25, 2013. See also Loveluck, "Le vigilantisme numérique, entre dénonciation et sanction," p. 139.

49. Lennon Y. C. Chang and Andy K. H. Leung, "An Introduction to Cyber Crowdsourcing (Human Flesh Search) in the Greater China Region," in Russell G. Smith, Ray Cheung, and Laurie Lau (eds.), *Cybercrime Risks and Responses: Eastern and Western Perspectives*, New York, Palgrave Macmillan, 2015, pp. 240–252.

50. Trottier, "Digital Vigilantism as Weaponisation of Visibility," p. 55.

51. Regarding the history of Anonymous and early doxing campaigns, see Gabriella Coleman, *Hacker, Hoaxer, Whistleblower, Spy: The Many Faces of Anonymous*, London, Verso, 2014.

166   NOTES TO CHAPTER 1

52. Regarding this distinction, see Les Johnston, "What Is Vigilantism?," *British Journal of Criminology*, vol. 36, no. 2, Spring 1996, p. 226, https://doi.org/10.1093/oxford journals.bjc.a014083.

53. Daniel M. Goldstein, "Flexible Justice: Neoliberal Violence and "Self-Help" Security in Bolivia," *Critique of Anthropology*, vol. 25, no. 4, 2005, pp. 389–411, https://doi .org/10.1177/0308275X05058656; Justice Tankebe, "Self-Help, Policing, and Procedural Justice: Ghanaian Vigilantism and the Rule of Law," *Law and Society Review*, vol. 43, no. 2, 2009, pp. 245–270, https://doi.org/10.1111/j.1540-5893.2009.00372.x.

54. Howard Becker, *Outsiders: Studies in the Sociology of Deviance*, New York, Free Press of Glencoe, 1963, chap. 8.

55. Emmanuelle Piccoli, *Les Rondes paysannes: Vigilance, politique et justice dans les Andes péruviennes*, Louvain-la-Neuve, L'Harmattan Academia, 2011.

56. Ray Abrahams, *Vigilant Citizens: Vigilantism and the State*, Malden, Polity Press, 1998.

57. Smith, "The Bakassi Boys," p. 439.

58. Meagher, "Hijacking Civil Society," p. 100.

59. Romain Le Cour Grandmaison, "'Vigilar y Limpiar': Identification and Self-Help Justice-Making in Michoacán, Mexico," *Politix*, vol. 115, no. 3, 2016, pp. 103–125, https://doi.org/10.3917/pox.115.0103. See also Matthew Heineman's documentary, *Cartel Land* (2015), which compares a self-defense committee in Michoacán to Arizona's Minutemen.

60. Shapira, *Waiting for José*.

61. Tommi Kotonen, "The Soldiers of Odin in Finland," in Tore Bjørgo and Miroslav Mareš (eds.), *Vigilantism against Migrants and Minorities*, London, Routledge, 2019, pp. 241–256.

62. Regarding La Meute, see Samuel Tanner and Aurélie Campana, "'Watchful Citizens' and Digital Vigilantism: A Case Study of the Far Right in Quebec," *Global Crime*, vol. 21, nos. 3–4, 2020, pp. 262–282.

63. Sofia Vasilopoulou and Daphne Halikiopoulou, *The Golden Dawn's "Nationalist Solution": Explaining the Rise of the Far Right in Greece*, New York, Palgrave Macmillan, 2015.

64. For a comparison of the DPNI (Movement Against Illegal Immigration) and Golden Dawn, see Sofia Tipaldou and Katrin Uba, "Movement Adaptability in Dissimilar Settings: The Far Right in Greece and Russia," *European Societies*, vol. 21, no. 4, 2019, pp. 563–582, https://doi.org/10.1080/14616696.2018.1494294.

65. Christophe Jaffrelot, *Modi's India: Hindu Nationalism and the Rise of Ethnic Democracy*, trans. Cynthia Schoch, Princeton, NJ, Princeton University Press, 2021, pp. 217–222.

66. Matthijs Gardenier, *Towards a Vigilant Society: From Citizen Participation to Anti-migrant Vigilantism*, Oxford, Oxford University Press, 2023. On French anti-migrant initiatives, see Pietro Castelli Gattinara, "Beyond the Hand of the State: Vigilantism against Migrants and Refugees in France," in Bjørgo and Mareš, *Vigilantism against Migrants and Minorities*, pp. 213–227.

67. On the notion of "police property," which refers to low-status groups most exposed to police brutality, see J.A. Lee, "Some Structural Aspects of Police Deviance in Relations with Minority groups," in Clifford Shearing (ed.), *Organizational Police Deviance*, Toronto, Butterworth, 1981, pp. 49-82.

NOTES TO CHAPTER 1   167

68. Shapira, *Waiting for José*, p. 14.

69. Heather Hamill, *The Hoods: Crime and Punishment in Belfast*, Princeton, NJ, Princeton University Press, 2011.

70. Ioulia Shukan, "Defending Ukraine at the Rear of the Armed Conflict in Donbas: Wartime Vigilantism in Odesa (2014–2018)," *Laboratorium: Russian Review of Social Research*, vol. 11, no. 3, 2020, pp. 71–104.

71. Yevgeny Roizman, *Gorod bez narkotikov* [A city without drugs], Yekaterinburg, 2005.

72. Favarel-Garrigues, "Justiciers amateurs et croisades morales en Russie contemporaine."

73. United Nations Stabilization Mission in Haiti (MINUSTAH) and Office of the High Commissioner for Human Rights, *Bay tèt yo jistis: Taking Justice into One's Own Hands or the Reign of Impunity in Haiti*, Executive Summary, January 2017, https://www.ohchr.org/sites/default/files/Documents/Countries/HT/170117Rapport_Se _faire_justice_soimeme_EN.pdf.

74. Lucien Febvre, "Histoire des sentiments: La Terreur," *Annales*, vol. 6, no. 4, 1951, p. 521, https://doi.org/10.3406/ahess.1951.2008.

75. Pascal Charrier, "Coronavirus: 12% des infirmiers déclarent avoir subi des pressions ou des menaces," *La Croix*, April 9, 2020.

76. Kirk Semple, "'Afraid to Be a Nurse': Health Workers under Attack," *New York Times*, April 27, 2020.

77. "Covid-19: Mob in Chennai Attacks Doctors, Officials Trying to Bury Man Who Died of the Disease," *Scroll.in*, April 20, 2020, https://scroll.in/latest/959752/covid-19 -mob-in-chennai-attacks-doctors-officials-trying-to-bury-man-who-died-of-the-dis ease.

78. Jeffrey Gettleman, Kai Schultz, and Suhasini Raj, "In India, Coronavirus Fans Religious Hatred," *New York Times*, April 12, 2020.

79. Viv Groskop, "Gone Too Tsar: The Erotic Period Drama That Has Enraged Russia," *Guardian*, April 19, 2018.

80. In 1998, M. F. Husain's home in Bombay was attacked by Hindu nationalist activists and several of his paintings were mutilated. These attacks and the hundreds of complaints filed against the artist forced him into exile in 2006. In 2007, a retrospective of his work in Delhi was attacked by Shiv Sena militants and two canvases were defaced.

81. The release of Deepa Mehta's film in 1996 was marred by violence in several cities across the country (Bombay, Delhi, Pune, Surat, and more). Movie theaters were vandalized, sometimes even torched.

82. In May 2007, Niraj Jain burst onto the University of Baroda campus with a group of Hindu nationalist militants aided by the police. They molested teachers and students, demanding that three controversial paintings be removed. They were ultimately successful. Anupama Katakam, "Attack on Art," *Frontline*, June 1, 2007, https://frontline.thehindu.com/the-nation/article30191617.ece.

83. Malvika Maheshwari, "Heroes in the Bedroom: Iconoclash and the Search for Exemplarity in India," *South Asia Multidisciplinary Academic Journal*, no. 4, 2010, p. 6, https://doi.org/10.4000/samaj.3044. See also Malvika Maheshwari, *Art Attacks: Violence and Offence-Taking in India*, Oxford, Oxford University Press, 2019.

NOTES TO CHAPTER 1

84. Atreyee Sen, *Shiv Sena Women: Violence and Communalism in a Bombay Slum*, London, Hurst, 2007.

85. "Dalit," literally, "broken man," replaces "Untouchable," deemed derogatory, for the lowest caste and as an administrative category.

86. See the Gulabi Gang website, https://gulabigang.in, and Atreyee Sen, "Women's Vigilantism in India: A Case Study of the Pink Sari Gang," *Violence de masse et Résistance–Réseau de recherche*, December 20, 2012, https://www.sciencespo.fr/mass-violence-war-massacre-resistance/en/document/womens-vigilantism-india-case-study-pink-sari-gang.html.

87. See the This Is Lebanon website, https://thisislebanon.site/.

88. Nishita Jha, "Name and Shame List: Indian Women Students Explain Why They Don't Trust Official Sexual Abuse Panels," *Scroll.in*, October 26, 2017.

89. Emma A. Jane, "Online Misogyny and Feminist Digilantism," *Continuum*, vol. 30, no. 3, 2016, pp. 284–297, https://doi.org/10.1080/10304312.2016.1166560.

90. Drew Magary, "Climate Vigilantism Is Your Future, Whether You Like It or Not," *GQ*, June 4, 2019.

91. Michael Colborne, "Levijatan: Serbian Animal Rights Vigilantes Go to the Polls," *Bellingcat*, June 18, 2020, https://www.bellingcat.com/news/2020/06/18/levijatan-serbian-animal-rights-vigilantes-go-to-the-polls/.

92. Center for Consumer Freedom Team, "Beware the Vegan Vigilantes," January 7, 2019, https://www.consumerfreedom.com/2019/01/beware-the-vegan-vigilantes.

93. Fabien Carrié, "Antispécisme," *Encyclopædia Universalis*, Paris, Encyclopædia Universalis, 2015, pp. 179–181.

94. Rachel Monaghan, "Not Quite Terrorism: Animal Rights Extremism in the United Kingdom," *Studies in Conflict and Terrorism*, vol. 36, no. 11, 2013, pp. 933–951, https://doi.org/10.1080/1057610X.2013.832117.

95. Christophe Traïni, "Les formes plurielles d'engagement de la protection animale," in Fabien Carrié and Christophe Traïni (eds.), *S'engager pour les animaux*, Paris, La Vie des idées–PUF, 2019, p. 52; Steven Best and Anthony J. Nocella II, *Terrorists or Freedom Fighters? Reflections on the Liberation of Animals*, New York, Lantern Books, 2004.

96. Lisa Visentin, "'Vegan Vigilantes': Green Groups Attack Proposed Trespassing Laws," *Sydney Morning Herald*, September 24, 2019.

97. Shapira, *Waiting for José*.

98. Emmanuelle Piccoli shows that the *rondas campesinas* in Peru, during which men get together to chew coca and confront the nocturnal forces as a group, also provide the participants with moments of male sociability in which their virility is put to the test. Piccoli, *Les Rondes paysannes*, pp. 37–52.

99. Shapira, *Waiting for José*.

100. Shapira, p. 64.

101. Joseph Hellweg, *Hunting the Ethical State: The Benkadi Movement of Côte d'Ivoire*, Chicago, Chicago University Press, 2011; Issifou Abou Moumouni, "L'offre informelle de la sécurité publique au Bénin: L'instrumentalisation des groupes d'autodéfense par l'État," *Déviance et Société*, vol. 41, no. 1, 2017, pp. 91–119; Romane Da Cunha Dupuy and Tanguy Quidelleur, "Self-Defence Movements in Burkina Faso:

Diffusion and Structuration of Koglweogo Groups," *Noria*, November 2018, https://noria-research.com/self-defence-movements-in-burkina-faso-diffusion-and-structuration-of-koglweogo-groups/.

102. Tim Eaton, "Prosecutor Kills Himself in Texas Raid over Child Sex," *New York Times*, November 7, 2006, https://www.nytimes.com/2006/11/07/us/prosecutor-kills-himself-in-texas-raid-over-child-sex.html.

103. See their Facebook page at https://www.facebook.com/LetzgoHunting Official.

104. Vanessa Barford, "Who Are Vigilante Group Letzgo Hunting?," *BBC News Magazine*, September 19, 2013.

105. See the Facebook page https://www.facebook.com/StinsonHunter. The film *The Paedophile Hunter*, put online July 3, 2015, is available on YouTube, https://www.youtube.com/watch?v=DIp4E5MwWDQ. For a critique of this "dark and disturbing" documentary, see Tim Dowling, "The Paedophile Hunter Review—Dark and Disturbing," *Guardian*, October 2, 2014.

106. Manisha Krishnan, "The Rise of Creep Catchers, Canada's Vigilante Paedophile Hunters," *Vice*, January 5, 2017, https://www.vice.com/en/article/mgvywn/the-real-story-behind-the-rise-of-creep-catchers-canadas-vigilante-pedophile-hunters.

107. See his YouTube user page, https://www.youtube.com/user/canadaohyayaya/featured.

108. See the video "Piéger un pédophile," YouTube, August 25, 2018, https://www.youtube.com/watch?v=tXWLHFK6NKM.

109. Karen Bertail, "Landes: 'Je chasse les pédophiles sur internet,'" *Sud-Ouest*, February 13, 2020.

110. Faustine Léo and Julie Olagnol, "Île-de-France: Le détenteur d'images pédo-pornographiques tombe dans un guet-apens," *Le Parisien*, August 4, 2020.

111. See the "wall of shame" on the Jewish Community Watch website, https://www.jewishcommunitywatch.org/wall-of-shame-gallery.

112. See the shame board on the Hand Over a Pedophile website, http://pedofilov.net/photoblog/487.

113. Lauren Walker, "Computer-Generated 10-Year-Old Girl Leads to Conviction of Online Predators," *Newsweek*, October 21, 2014, https://www.newsweek.com/computer-generated-10-year-old-girl-leads-conviction-online-predator-278811.

114. Piccoli, *Les Rondes paysannes*, pp. 95–96.

115. Hamill, *The Hoods*, pp. 68–69.

116. The administration of corporal punishment is still in effect among the republicans as well as the loyalists. In 2017, Northern Ireland police recorded 101 punishment beatings and shootings. Henry McDonald, "Northern Ireland 'Punishment' Attacks Rise 60% in Four Years," *Guardian*, March 12, 2018.

117. Hamill, *The Hoods*, p. 75.

118. Ronald J. Baar and R. A. Mollan, "The Orthopaedic Consequences of Civil Disturbance in Northern Ireland," *Journal of Bone and Joint Surgery*, vol. 71, no. 5, November 1989, pp. 739–744. See also John Williams, "Casualties of Violence in Northern Ireland," *International Journal of Trauma Nursing*, vol. 3, no. 3, 1997, pp. 78–82.

170 NOTES TO CHAPTER 1

119. Sinéad O'Shea, "I Found Out What Happened When a Mother Took Her Son to Be Kneecapped in Northern Ireland," *Guardian*, March 15, 2018.

120. Hamill, *The Hoods*, pp. 68–69.

121. "Bordeaux: Qui sont les Soldiers of Odin qu'on voit en ville," *Sud-Ouest*, October 28, 2016.

122. Garland, "Penal Excess and Surplus Meaning," pp. 793–833.

123. In 1191, when his army was setting off for the Holy Land, Richard I ordered that the heads of thieves and traitors be shaved, daubed with resin, and covered in feathers. This seems to be the first example identified in western Europe. See "Laws of Richard I. (Cœur de Lion) Concerning Crusaders Who Were to Go by Sea, 1189 AD," in Ernest F. Henderson, *Select Historical Documents of the Middle Ages*, London, George Bell & Sons, 1896, p. 135.

124. Benjamin H. Irvin, "Tar, Feathers, and the Enemies of American Liberties, 1768–1776," *New England Quarterly*, 76, no. 2, 2003, pp. 199–200, https://doi.org/10.2307/1559903.

125. Stephen Frank, "Popular Justice, Community and Culture among the Russian Peasantry, 1870–1990," *Russian Review* 46, no. 3, 1987, p. 245.

126. Rachel Monaghan, "Not Quite Lynching: Informal Justice in Northern Ireland," in Berg and Wendt, *Globalizing Lynching History*, pp. 153–171.

127. Laurent Gayer, *Karachi: Ordered Disorder and the Struggle for the City*, London, Hurst, 2014, p. 253.

128. Author's observation of a Lev Protiv raid in Moscow, September 29, 2017.

129. Tesak interview on Den' TV, September 8, 2013. Accessed September 16, 2014. No longer available.

130. Associated Press, "Texas Prosecutor Kills Himself after Sex Sting," *NBC News*, Tom Knowles, 'Paedophile Hunters' Undeterred by Man's Suicide," *Times* (London), November 6, 2006, https://www.nbcnews.com/id/wbna15592444; September 17, 2013, https://www.thetimes.co.uk/article/paedophile-hunters-undeterred-by-mans-suicide-b7vwnxdwkl6.

131. This information appears on the Jewish Community Watch website, https://www.jewishcommunitywatch.org/about-us/faq.

132. Chad Pawson, "'RCMP Does Not Condone This Activity,' Say Police to Creep Catchers," *CBC News*, September 3, 2016, https://www.cbc.ca/news/canada/british-columbia/surrey-rcmp-reaction-to-surrey-creep-catcher-1.3747822.

133. Author's observation of a Lev Protiv raid in Moscow, June 29, 2018.

134. Ray Abrahams, "Some Thoughts on Vigilantism," in David Pratten and Atreyee Sen (eds.), *Global Vigilantes*, London, Hurst, 2007, p. 423.

135. Abrahams, *Vigilant Citizens*, pp. 26–44.

136. Michael L. Fleisher, "Sungusungu: State-Sponsored Village Vigilante Groups among the Kuria of Tanzania," *Africa: Journal of the International African Institute*, vol. 70, no. 2, 2000, pp. 209–228, https://doi.org/10.3366/afr.2000.70.2.209. See also Nir Gazit, "State-Sponsored Vigilantism: Jewish Settlers' Violence in the Occupied Palestinian Territories," *Sociology*, vol. 49, no. 3, 2015, pp. 438–454, https://doi.org/10.1177/0038038514526648.

137. See the Khryushi Protiv webpage, https://www.youtube.com/channel/UCSd zksftzE7Tu2KAAZ4OvXQ.

NOTES TO CHAPTERS 1 AND 2

138. Rashid Gabdulhakov, "Heroes or Hooligans? Media Portrayal of StopXam (Stop a Douchebag) Vigilantes in Russia," *Laboratorium: Russian Review of Social Research*, vol. 11, no. 3, 2020, pp. 16–45, https://doi.org/10.25285/2078-1938-2019-11-3-16-45.

139. Laurent Fourchard, "Engagements sécuritaires et féminisation du vigilantisme en Afrique du Sud," *Politix*, no. 115, 2016, p. 71, https://doi.org/10.3917/pox.115.0057.

140. The Civic Chamber is a consultative body that represents civil society.

141. See the VKontakte page of the Hand Over a Pedophile project, https://vk.com/sdai_pedofila.

142. Fleisher, "Sungusungu," pp. 223–224.

143. Fiona Hamilton, "Criminals 'Pose as Vigilante Groups to Blackmail and Rob Paedophiles,'" *Times* (UK), January 25, 2019.

144. Favarel-Garrigues, "Digital Vigilantism and Anti-paedophile Activism in Russia."

145. Jaffrelot, *Modi's India*, pp. 217–218. See also Human Rights Watch, *Violent Cow Protection in India: Vigilante Groups Attack Minorities*, New York, 2019, https://www.hrw.org/report/2019/02/19/violent-cow-protection-india/vigilante-groups-attack-minorities.

146. Jaffrelot, *Modi's India*, p. 221.

147. Jaffrelot, *Modi's India*.

148. Author's observation of a Lev Protiv raid in Moscow, June 29, 2018.

149. Mikhail Lazutin, "Otvety na voprosy" [Answers to questions], YouTube, April 17, 2019, https://www.youtube.com/watch?v=8hXTGfBVQXs.

150. Tesak, "Vecherinka Okkupai Pedofilyai" (The Occupy Pedophilia party), YouTube, December 16, 2012, https://www.youtube.com/watch?v=-i4lB4OzEco.

Chapter 2

1. Cited by Frédérique Lebelley, *Tête à tête*, Paris, Grasset, 1989, p. 29. We learned of this story from Nicolas Picard, "L'Application de la peine de mort en France (1906–1981)," PhD diss., Université Paris 1-Panthéon Sorbonne, 2016, p. 42.

2. The names have been changed.

3. One page is discontinued, but two of these pages were accessed June 22, 2023: "Parents soyez vigilants," https://www.facebook.com/soyezvigilant/; and "Parents vigilants. Vigilance parentale. Mes enfants sont les tiens!!!," https://www.facebook.com/groups/2195402800771680.

4. The quotations throughout this scene come from police reports, court files, and trials pertaining to punitive expeditions carried out against the Roma community in March 2019.

5. Communiqué de presse du parquet de Bobigny (Bobigny public prosecutor's office, Press Communiqué), March 26, 2019, https://aulnaycap.files.wordpress.com/2019/03/53403654_2423451084354108_218973014891429888_n.jpg.

6. "Rumeurs sur les Roms: Le Conseil de l'Europe appelle à la 'vigilance,'" *Le Figaro*, March 29, 2019.

7. The "clarifying statement" made on March 29, 2019, is at https://www.facebook.com/soyezvigilant.

172   NOTES TO CHAPTER 2

8. Christopher Waldrep, *The Many Faces of Judge Lynch*, New York, Palgrave Macmillan, 2002, pp. 15–19.

9. Waldrep, pp. 27–47.

10. Sarah Silkey, "British Public Debates and the 'Americanization' of Lynching," in William D. Carrigan and Christopher Waldrep (eds.), *Swift to Wrath: Lynching in Global Historical Perspective*, Charlottesville, University of Virginia Press, 2013, p. 161.

11. See, for example, the novel of the same name by Gustave Aimard (1859) or the reference to the "loi de Lynch" in Victor Hugo's *Les Misérables* (1890).

12. Arnaud-Dominique Houte, "Citoyens policiers? Pratiques et imaginaires civiques de la sécurité publique dans la France du second XIXe siècle," *Revue d'histoire du XIXe siècle*, no. 50, 2015, pp. 110–111, https://doi.org/10.4000/rh19.4825.

13. Regarding the international spread of the term, see Carrigan and Waldrep, *Swift to Wrath*.

14. Meredith L. Roman, "U.S. Lynch Law and the Fate of the Soviet Union," in Carrigan and Waldrep, *Swift to Wrath*, pp. 215–236.

15. Vladimir Mayakovsky, *My Discovery of America*, trans. Neil Cornwell, London, Hesperus Press, 2005 (1st ed. 1926), p. 83.

16. Fumiko Sakashita, "Lynching across the Pacific," in Carrigan and Waldrep, *Swift to Wrath*, pp. 181–213.

17. Regarding the globalization of lynching, see Michael J. Pfeifer (ed.), *Global Lynching and Collective Violence*, vol. 1, Chicago, University of Illinois Press, 2017; Manfred Berg and Simon Wendt, "Introduction: Lynching from an International Perspective," in Berg and Wendt, *Globalizing Lynching History*, pp. 1–18; and Robert W. Thurston, *Lynching: American Mob Murder in Global Perspective*, Farnham, UK, Ashgate, 2011.

18. The term *mobocracy* first appeared in 1754 in the *Douglas Harper Etymology Dictionary*, which defined it as "mob rule, government by the disorderly class."

19. Gustave Le Bon, *Psychologie des foules*, Paris, Flammarion, 2009 (1st ed. 1895), p. 24.

20. Philippe Aldrin, *Sociologie politique des rumeurs*, Paris, PUF, 2005, p. 65.

21. Alain Corbin, *Le Village des "cannibales,"* Paris, Flammarion, 2009 (1st ed. 1990).

22. Maxime François, "Seine-Saint-Denis: Les étudiants préparaient leur expédition punitive contre les Roms sur les réseaux sociaux," *Le Parisien*, October 23, 2019.

23. Aldrin, *Sociologie politique des rumeurs*, p. 65.

24. David Garland, "Penal Excess and Surplus Meaning: Public Torture Lynchings in Twentieth Century America." *Law and Society Review* 39, no. 4, 2005, pp. 808, https://doi.org/10.1111/j.1540-5893.2005.00245.x.

25. Magdalena Chułek, "Mob Justice and Everyday Life: The Case of Nairobi's Kibera and Korogocho Slums," *African Studies*, vol. 78, no. 3, 2019, pp. 385–402, https://doi.org/10.1080/00020184.2018.1519332.

26. Chułek, "Mob Justice and Everyday Life."

27. The quote is in the *Dothan Eagle*, October 26, 1934, cited in Garland, "Penal Excess and Surplus Meaning," p. 804. For more, see James R. McGovern, *Anatomy of a Lynching: The Killing of Claude Neal*, Baton Rouge, Louisiana State University Press, 1992.

28. "John Hartfield Will Be Lynched by Ellisville Mob at 5 O'Clock This Afternoon," *New Orleans States*, June 26, 1919.

NOTES TO CHAPTER 2   173

29. Charles Tilly, *The Politics of Collective Violence*, New York, Cambridge University Press, 2003.

30. Frank Shay, *Judge Lynch: His First Hundred Years*, New York, Biblo & Tannen, 1969, pp. 86–90.

31. Randall Collins, *Violence: A Micro-Sociological Theory*, Princeton, NJ, Princeton University Press, 2008, pp. 413–430.

32. A lawyer involved in the case gave us this judicial record, which is not publicly available, pertaining to the punitive expeditions conducted against the Roma community in March 2019.

33. Daniel Goldstein, "'In Our Own Hands': Lynching, Justice, and the Law in Bolivia," *American Ethnologist*, vol. 30, no. 1, 2003, p. 34, https://doi.org/10.1525/ae .2003.30.1.22.

34. Daniel Goldstein, *The Spectacular City: Violence and Performance in Urban Bolivia*, Durham, NC, Duke University Press, 2005, pp. 204–205.

35. Collins, *Violence*, pp. 370–412.

36. James Scott, *Domination and the Arts of Resistance: Hidden Transcripts*, New Haven, NJ, Yale University Press, 1990, p. 150.

37. See in this regard Goldstein, "In Our Own Hands,'" p. 32.

38. Goldstein, *The Spectacular City*, p. 2.

39. Scott, *Domination and the Arts of Resistance*, p. 151.

40. Sarah-Jane Cooper-Knock, "Policing in Intimate Crowds," *African Affairs*, vol. 113, no. 453, October 2014, pp. 563–582.

41. *Whoonga* is a type of heroin cut with chemicals.

42. Cooper-Knock, "Policing in Intimate Crowds," pp. 570–571.

43. Cooper-Knock, p. 572.

44. Cooper-Knock, p. 574.

45. William Fitzhugh Brundage, *Lynching in the New South: Georgia and Virginia, 1880–1930*, Urbana, University of Illinois Press, 1993.

46. Michel Foucault, *Discipline and Punish: Birth of the Prison*, trans. Alan Sheridan, New York, Vintage, 1995, pp. 43, 207.

47. Goldstein, "In Our Own Hands," p. 36.

48. Carolien Jacobs and Christy Schuetze, "'Justice with Our Own Hands': Lynching, Poverty, Witchcraft, and the State in Mozambique," in Berg and Wendt, *Globalizing Lynching History*, p. 226.

49. Angelina Snodgrass Godoy, "When 'Justice' Is Criminal: Lynchings in Contemporary Latin America," *Theory and Society*, vol. 33, no. 6, 2004, p. 640, https://doi .org/10.1023/B:RYSO.0000049192.62380.29.

50. Goldstein, "In Our Own Hands," p. 23.

51. Goldstein, p. 34.

52. Amy Louise Wood, *Lynching and Spectacle: Witnessing Racial Violence in America, 1890–1940*, Chapel Hill, University of North Carolina Press, 2011, p. 1.

53. The figures vary depending on the source: the number of Roma killed was either three or four, the number of houses burned either thirteen or fourteen, and other houses were ransacked, which might explain the count of seventeen or eighteen houses destroyed. István Haller, *Lynching Is Not a Crime: Mob Violence against Roma in*

174 NOTES TO CHAPTER 2

Post-Ceauşescu Romania, Budapest, ERRC, 1998, pp. 35–42. See also the more detailed Romanian version in István Haller, *Cazul Hădăreni*, Tîrgu-Mureş, Editura Pro Europa, 1998, pp. 106–123.

54. Joël Michel, *Le Lynchage aux États-Unis*, Paris, La Table ronde, 2008, p. 142.

55. Michel, p. 142.

56. Regarding the Tuskegee Institute conference in 1940, see Christopher Waldrep, "War of Words: The Controversy over the Definition of Lynching, 1899–1940," *Journal of Southern History*, vol. 66, no. 1, February 2000, pp. 98, https://doi.org/10.2307/2587438.

57. Michel, *Le Lynchage aux États-Unis*, p. 38.

58. John Caughey, "Their Majesties the Mob," *Pacific Historical Review*, vol. 26, no. 3, 1957, pp. 217–234, https://doi.org/10.2307/3636213.

59. Michel, *Le Lynchage aux États-Unis*, pp. 43, 63.

60. Michel, pp. 222–225.

61. Jacobs and Schuetze, "Justice with Our Own Hands," p. 225.

62. Bjørn Enge Bertelsen, "Multiple Sovereignties and Summary Justice in Mozambique: A Critique of Some Legal Anthropological Terms," *Social Analysis*, vol. 53, no. 3, Winter 2009, p. 127, https://doi.org/10.1177/000276426801200107.

63. Bridget Welsh, "Local and National: Keroyokan Mobbing in Indonesia," *Journal of East Asian Studies*, vol. 8, no. 3, 2008, pp. 473–504, https://doi.org/10.1017/S1598240800006512.

64. Welsh, pp. 489–490.

65. Wood, *Lynching and Spectacle*, pp. 50–51.

66. Gema Kloppe-Santamaría, *In the Vortex of Violence: Lynching, Extralegal Justice, and the State in Post-revolutionary Mexico*, Oakland, University of California Press, 2020, pp. 48–50.

67. Garland, "Penal Excess and Surplus Meaning," pp. 813–814.

68. Garland, p. 829.

69. Garland, p. 816.

70. Chułek, "Mob Justice and Everyday Life," p. 392.

71. Welsh, "Local and National," p. 490.

72. Donald D. Mathews, "The Southern Rite of Human Sacrifice: Lynching in the American South," *Mississippi Quarterly*, vol. 61, nos. 1–2, 2008, pp. 27–70, http://www.jstor.org/stable/26476642. See also Amy Louise Wood, "Critical Conversation on Donald Mathews's 'The Southern Rite of Human Sacrifice,'" *Journal of Southern Religion*, vol. 17, 2015, http://jsreligion.org/issues/vol17/Wood.html.

73. Wood, *Lynching and Spectacle*, p. 65.

74. Kloppe-Santamaría, *In the Vortex of Violence*, pp. 40–62.

75. Foucault, *Discipline and Punish*, p. 251.

76. Romain Bertrand, *Indonésie: La démocratie invisible. Violence, magie et politique à Java*, Paris, Karthala, 2002, p. 90.

77. Jean Comaroff and John L. Comaroff, *The Truth about Crime: Sovereignty, Knowledge, Social Order*, Chicago, University of Chicago Press, 2016, pp. 195–196.

78. Nancy Scheper-Hughes, "The Global Traffic in Human Organs," *Current Anthropology*, vol. 41, no. 2, 2000, p. 203, https://doi.org/10.1086/300123.

79. Leigh Binford and Nancy Churchill, "Lynching and States of Fear in Urban Mexico," *Anthropologica*, vol. 51, no. 2, 2009, p. 308, https://doi.org/10.2307/25605293.

NOTES TO CHAPTER 2   175

80. Nancy Scheper-Hughes, "Theft of Life: The Globalization of Organ Stealing Rumours," *Anthropology Today*, vol. 12, no. 3, 1996, p. 3, https://doi.org/10.2307/2783143.

81. John Comaroff and Jean Comaroff, "Policing Culture, Cultural Policing: Law and Social Order in Post-colonial Africa," *Law and Social Inquiry*, vol. 29, no. 3, 2004, pp. 513–545, https://doi.org/10.1111/j.1747-4469.2004.tb00999.x.

82. Jacobs and Schuetze, "Justice with Our Own Hands," p. 231.

83. See the description of what happened to Grushka, an indigent widow accused of witchcraft in her village, in Stephen Frank, "Popular Justice, Community and Culture among the Russian Peasantry, 1870–1990," *Russian Review*, vol. 46, no. 3, 1987, pp. 239–240, https://doi.org/10.2307/130562.

84. Welsh, "Local and National," pp. 487–488.

85. Julien Bonhomme, *The Sex Thieves: The Anthropology of a Rumor*, trans. Dominic Horsfall, Chicago, HAU Books, 2016, p. 113.

86. Bonhomme, p. 21.

87. Bonhomme, p. 21.

88. See, for example, the video "Lord Nazi Ruso es linchado en Cancún," *El País* (Madrid), May 20, 2017, https://www.youtube.com/watch?v=t2UsYc4zJVk.

89. Elena Reina, "En la cueva caribeña del nazi ruso," *El País* (Madrid), June 14, 2017.

90. See the project's website, https://withoutsanctuary.org.

91. Richard Lacayo, "Blood at the Root," *Time*, April 2, 2000.

92. Ray Stannard Baker, "What Is a Lynching?," *McClure's Magazine*, February 1905.

93. Baker, "What Is a Lynching?"

94. Lacayo, "Blood at the Root."

95. Shawn Michelle Smith, "The Evidence of Lynching Photographs," in Dora Apel and Shawn Michelle Smith, *Lynching Photographs*, Berkeley, University of California Press, 2007, p. 23–24.

96. Linda Kim, "A Law of Unintended Consequences: United States Postal Censorship of Lynching Photographs," *Visual Resources*, vol. 28, no. 2, 2012, pp. 171–193, https://doi.org/10.1080/01973762.2012.678812.

97. James Cameron, born in 1914, is the sole survivor of a lynching in Marion, Indiana, in 1930. Two of his friends were hanged, as a famous photograph shows, and he probably would have met with the same fate if a young woman hadn't proclaimed his innocence.

98. James Cameron, *A Time of Terror*, Baltimore, Black Classic Press, 1994, p. 74, cited in Smith, "The Evidence of Lynching Photographs," p. 14.

99. Kerry Segrave, *Lynchings of Women in the United States: The Recorded Cases, 1851–1946*, Jefferson, NC, McFarland, 2010, p. 15.

100. After the lynching of Luther Holbert and his wife, burned alive in Vicksburg, Mississippi, in 1904, their fingers became commodities.

101. Collins, *Violence*, p. 426.

102. On lynching trophies and souvenirs, see Elijah Gaddis, *Gruesome Looking Objects: A New History of Lynching and Everyday Things*, Cambridge, Cambridge University Press, 2022.

103. Wood, *Lynching and Spectacle*, pp. 29–31.

104. Garland, "Penal Excess and Surplus Meaning," p. 808.

NOTES TO CHAPTER 2

105. Wood, *Lynching and Spectacle*, p. 11.

106. Amy Louise Wood, "They Never Witnessed Such a Melodrama," *Southern Spaces*, April 27, 2009, https://doi.org/10.18737/M7Z31N.

107. Wood, *Lynching and Spectacle*, pp. 72–73.

108. Wood, pp. 134–143.

109. Smith, "The Evidence of Lynching Photographs," pp. 18–24.

110. Dora Apel, "Lynching Photographs and the Politics of Public Shaming," in Apel and Smith, *Lynching Photographs*, p. 61.

111. Goldstein, *The Spectacular City*, p. 214.

112. Goldstein, p. 213.

113. Arjun Sidharth, "Viral Message, Images That Led to Lynching in Southern States Now Target Bihar, Jharkhand and Odisha," *Alt News*, June 2, 2018.

114. According to the independent information website *IndiaSpend*, 86 percent of the twenty-eight Indians lynched between 2010 and 2017 by cow vigilantes belonged to the Muslim minority. Delna Abraham and Ojaswi Rao, "Cow-Related Violence: 86% Dead since 2010 Are Muslim; 97% Attacks Reported after 2014," *The Wire*, June 28, 2017, https://thewire.in/government/cow-related-violence.

115. See the investigation into twenty-seven murder cases in one year: "Murderous Mob—9 States, 27 Killings, One Year: And a Pattern to the Lynchings," *Indian Express*, July 15, 2018.

116. Alison Saldanha, Pranav Rajput, and Jay Hazare, "Child-Lifting Rumours: 33 Killed in 69 Mob Attacks since January 2017. Before That Only 1 Attack in 2012," *IndiaSpend*, July 9, 2018.

117. Saldanha, Rajput, and Hazare, "Child-Lifting Rumours."

118. Shakuntala Banaji and Ram Bhat, *WhatsApp Vigilantes: An Exploration of Citizen Reception and Circulation of WhatsApp Misinformation Linked to Mob Violence in India*, London, London School of Economics, 2019, pp. 41–44.

119. Jignesh Patel, "Images Shared to Claim Mob Justice Stopped Rape Incidents in Nagaland—Fact-Check," *Alt News*, December 5, 2019.

120. "As Lynchings Rise, Govt Tells WhatsApp to Curb Rumours," *Times of India*, July 4, 2018.

121. Banaji and Bhat, *WhatsApp Vigilantes*, p. 20.

122. See "Fact Check," https://www.indiatoday.in/fact-check.

123. Prabir Purkayastha, "Lynching as a Public Spectacle," *NewsClick*, January 4, 2019.

124. Dilip D'Souza, "When They Lynch, It's the 'Best Fun'—Whether in the US or India," *The Wire*, June 16, 2018.

125. "Dimapur Mob Lynching: Government Taking Necessary Steps, Says Rajnath," *India Today*, March 6, 2015.

126. "Mob Drags Alleged Rapist out of Jail in Nagaland, Thrashes Him to Death," *Times of India*, March 6, 2015.

127. Samudra Gupta Kashyap, "Dimapur: Lynched Nagaland Man Came from Family of Armymen, not Bangladesh," *Indian Express*, March 8, 2015.

128. Dolly Kikon, "The City of Sorrow: Revisiting the 2015 Dimapur Lynching," *Scroll.in*, June 24, 2015.

NOTES TO CHAPTERS 2 AND 3   177

129. Dola Mitra, "A Story from Outside," *Outlook*, March 30, 2015.

130. Nusrat Sabina Chowdhury, *Paradoxes of the Popular: Crowd Politics in Bangladesh*, Stanford, CA, Stanford University Press, 2019.

131. Marcos Martinez, "Burned to Death Because of a Rumour on WhatsApp," *BBC Monitoring*, November 12, 2018.

132. Scott, *Domination and the Arts of Resistance*, p. 151.

133. Grace Elizabeth Hale, "Without Sanctuary: Lynching Photography in America," *Journal of American History*, vol. 89, no. 3, December 2002, pp. 993–994, https://doi.org/10.2307/3092350. See also Wendy Wolters, "Without Sanctuary: Bearing Witness, Bearing Whiteness," *JAC*, vol. 24, no. 2, 2004, pp. 399–425.

Chapter 3

1. "Obraschenie primorskikh partizan k zhitelyam Rossii" [Allocution of Primorsky Partisans to Russians], https://www.ya.ru/video/preview/17782590363229654195.

2. Evgueni Moroz, "Le néo-paganisme, 'foi ethnique,' contre-culture ou entrisme politique?," in Marlène Laruelle (ed.), *Le Rouge et le Noir: Extrême droite et nationalisme en Russie*, Paris, CNRS Éditions, 2007, pp. 225–249.

3. It is generally acknowledged that the two rebels indeed committed suicide, but some are convinced they were killed by special forces during the raid.

4. We refer to the controversy in the United States around the song "Cop Killer" by Body Count (1992), which we analyze later in this chapter.

5. The attacks of the Pakistani Taliban against police forces across the country are a case in point. See Zia ur Rehman and Christina Goldbaum, "Militants Wage Deadly Battle in Karachi Police Headquarters," *New York Times*, February 17, 2023.

6. "Obraschenie primorskikh partizan k zhitelyam Rossii." This video, whose first title translated to "The last interview of the Primorsky Partisans," went online on October 9, 2010, and was placed on the Russian government's list of extremist documents in a court decision of March 2012, making it illegal to save or repost it. In July 2013 a resident of Tomsk was sentenced to six months' community service for reposting it. However, it was always easily accessible on the Internet and remains so in 2023. A written document titled "The Appeal of the Primorsky Partisans" was put online in June 2010, but its origins are disputed.

7. "Primorskie 'partizany': Kak bandity prevratilis' v geroev" [The Primorsky "partisans": How bandits became heroes], *Komsomolskaya Pravda* (Moscow), June 25, 2010.

8. The Omon is a special-purpose mobile unit that police use to maintain order in Russia.

9. "Obraschenie primorskikh partizan k zhitelyam Rossii."

10. Anne Le Huérou, "Police Brutality and Police Reform in Russia and the CIS: Introduction," *Journal of Power Institutions in Post-Soviet Societies*, no. 1, 2012, https://doi.org/10.4000/pipss.3813.

11. The phrase "bandits in law" (*bandity v zakone*) is a reference to "thieves in law" (*vory v zakone*), a phrase used by criminals to describe an elite who are thought to live in respect for the law of the underworld. Traditional thieves are contrasted with the bandits who emerged in the late 1980s and took over criminal markets without respect for this law. On the contrast between thieves and bandits, see Vadim Volkov, *Violent*

178 NOTES TO CHAPTER 3

Entrepreneurs: The Use of Force in the Making of Russian Capitalism, Ithaca, NY, Cornell University Press, 2002, pp. 54–63.

12. "Obraschenie primorskikh partizan k zhitelyam Rossii."

13. "Obraschenie primorskikh partizan k zhitelyam Rossii."

14. "Obraschenie primorskikh partizan k zhitelyam Rossii."

15. "Obraschenie primorskikh partizan k zhitelyam Rossii."

16. Today it is a sports school for children and young patriots. See its website, http://патриот.киробр.рф/. On military and patriotic clubs, see Marlene Laruelle, "Patriotic Youth Clubs in Russia: Professional Niches, Cultural Capital and Narratives of Social Engagement," *Europe-Asia Studies,* vol. 67, no. 1, 2015, pp. 8–27, https://doi .org/10.1080/09668136.2014.986965.

17. Rostislav Antonov, *Primorskie partizany* [The Primorsky Partisans], Moscow, Fond ROD, 2011, p. 11.

18. Smuggling involves not only illegally cut Russian timber but also rare imported wood, which is treated in Russia and exported back to China despite a ban. See, for example, "SK vozbudil ugolovnye dela o kontrabande lesa na 458 mln roublei v Primorie" [The investigative committee opens a criminal investigation into wood smuggling worth 458 million rubles in Primorsky Krai], *Izvestiya,* January 30, 2020.

19. Antonov, *Primorskie partizany,* p. 34.

20. Antonov, p. 40.

21. The GRU (Glavnoe razvedyvatel' noe upravlenie; Main Intelligence Directorate of the General Staff of the Armed Forces of the Russian Federation) is the main Russian military intelligence service.

22. Some sources suggest that his parents divorced and he was raised by his grandmother. His former teachers describe him as a "problem child." See Dina Karpitskaya, "Banda 'primorskikh partisan': Robin Gudy po lokot' v krovi" [The "Primorsky Partisans" gang: Robin Hoods up to their elbows in blood], *Komsomolskaya Pravda* (Moscow), September 19, 2019.

23. Véra Nikolski, *National-bolchévisme et néo-eurasisme dans la Russie post-soviétique,* Paris, Mare & Martin, 2013.

24. The National Bolshevik Party's Moscow base, known as the Bunker, was both a meeting place and a home to some activists. See Nikolski, *National-bolchévisme et néo-eurasisme dans la Russie post-soviétique.*

25. The photograph appears, for example, in "Mat' Andreya Sukhorada o smerti syna" [Andrey Sukhorada's mother on the death of her son], YouTube, June 11, 2011, https://www.youtube.com/watch?v=hbhFPLhgd5I.

26. See accounts in Anastasia Kirilenko and Aleksandr Kulygin, "'Partizan' Andrey Sukhorada v 16 let byl buntarem" [The "partizan" Andrey Sukhorada was a rebel at the age of 16], *Radio Svoboda,* June 13, 2010.

27. Iliya Falkovsky and Aleksandr Litoy, *Grazhdanskaya voina uzhe nachalas'* [Civil war has already started], Moscow, Algoritm, 2013, pp. 182–184.

28. "Delo 'primorskikh partizan' vo Vladivostoke: Storona obvineniya rasskazala o materialakh 'natsionalisticheskogo kharaktera'" [The trial of the "Primorsky Partisans" in Vladivostok: The prosecution mentions documents "of a nationalist nature"], *ussur.net,* February 21, 2013, https://ussur.net/news/27127/.

29. Karpitskaya, "Banda 'primorskikh partisan.'"

NOTES TO CHAPTER 3   179

30. Vladislav Maltsev, "Ariiskii djikhad: Zachem russkim ul'trapravym islam" [Aryan jihad: How does Islam relate to the far right?], *Lenta.ru*, February 22, 2016, https://lenta.ru/articles/2016/02/22/nazi_islam/.

31. Antonov, *Primorskie partizany*, p. 36.

32. On all these stories, see Karpitskaya, "Banda 'primorskikh partisan.'"

33. See, for example, Human Rights Watch, *Confessions at Any Cost: Police Torture in Russia*, New York, HRW, 1999.

34. On the historical figure of the "crooked cop" in France, see, for example, Jean-Marc Berlière, "Images de la police: Deux siècles de fantasme?," *Criminocorpus*, January 2009, https://doi.org/10.4000/criminocorpus.206; and Quentin Deluermoz, *Policiers dans la ville: La construction d'un ordre public à Paris (1854–1914)*, Paris, Publications de la Sorbonne, 2012, pp. 29–32.

35. Aleksandr Khinshtein, *Okhota na oborotnei: Samoe gromkoe zhurnalistskoe rassledovanie polednikh let* [The werewolf hunt: The biggest journalistic inquiry of recent years], Moscow, Detektiv-Press, 2005.

36. Gilles Favarel-Garrigues, "La police russe en procès," *Le Courrier des pays de l'Est*, no. 6, 2005, pp. 66–74; Brian Taylor, *State Building in Putin's Russia: Policing and Coercion after Communism*, New York, Cambridge University Press, 2011; Leonid Kosals and Anastasia Dubova, "Commercialization of Police and Shadow Economy: The Russian Case," *Economic Sociology*, vol. 13, no. 2, 2012, pp. 21–28, https://www.econstor.eu/handle/10419/155987.

37. "Obraschenie primorskikh partizan k zhitelyam Rossii."

38. Known as *slonik*—the diminutive of the word for "elephant"—this widespread method is described in, among others, "Byvshii uchastkovyi rasskazal o vidakh pytok v politsii" [A former local policeman described methods of torture current in the police], *NTV*, April 1, 2012.

39. Olga Semukhina and Michael Reynolds, *Understanding the Modern Russian Police*, Boca Raton, LA, CRC Press, 2013; Theodore Gerber and Sarah Mendelson, "Public Experiences of Police Violence and Corruption in Contemporary Russia: A Case of Predatory Policing?," *Law and Society Review*, vol. 42, no. 1, March 2008, pp. 1–44, https://doi.org/10.1111/j.1540-5893.2008.00333.x.

40. From 2008 to 2012, Dmitri Medvedev was president of the Russian Federation and Vladimir Putin was prime minister.

41. Speech to parliament by the president, April 25, 2005, http://www.kremlin.ru/acts/bank/36354.

42. Le Huérou, "Police Brutality and Police Reform in Russia and the CIS."

43. Aleksey Dymovsky was born in 1977 and joined the Ministry of the Interior in 2000. In 2009, he posted an address to the president on YouTube in which, wearing his police uniform, he openly denounced the corruption rife in the police department where he worked. The video was very widely viewed. See Yulia Chistyakova and Annette Robertson, "YouTube Cops and Power Without Limits: Understanding Police Violence in 21st Century Russia," *Journal of Power Institutions in Post-Soviet Societies*, no. 13, 2012, https://doi.org/10.4000/pipss.3949.

44. The police had been targets of *Russkii shanson*, a popular musical genre that portrays life in prison, glorifies the underworld, and vilifies the police, since the 1990s. Mikhail Krug and Lesopoval were leading exponents.

180   **NOTES TO CHAPTER 3**

45. See especially the performance by the group Voina, which had links to Pussy Riot, in January–February 2011, during which they hurl themselves at Moscow police-women to hug and kiss them. The policewomen react with shock and embarrassment. "Gruppa Voina zatselovyvaet mentov" [The Voina Group cover cops with kisses], You-Tube, February 28, 2011, https://www.youtube.com/watch?v=loA8Qf893cs.

46. "Stolychnym politseiskim prislali 100 g. trotila" [100 grams of TNT were sent to police officers in the capital], *Izvestiya*, August 29, 2011. Other attacks on police cars and buildings were later imputed to anarchist groups.

47. Rus' is the name of the principality that developed into Russia (ninth–thirteenth centuries).

48. These press releases are included in Falkovsky and Litoy, *Grazhdanskaya voina uzhe nachalas'*, pp. 165–177.

49. The Movement Against Illegal Immigration made its name with attacks on immigrants from about 2005 to the early 2010s. Martin Laryš and Miroslav Mareš, "Right-Wing Extremist Violence in the Russian Federation," *Europe-Asia Studies*, vol. 63, no. 1, 2011, pp. 129–154, https://doi.org/10.1080/09668136.2011.534308.

50. Launched on November 4, 2005, the Russian march is an annual gathering of nationalists in Moscow.

51. In late August 2006, in the city of Kondopoga in Karelia, a fight between young Russians and Chechens degenerated into fatal violence. This incident was widely dis-cussed by nationalists, who saw it as a symptom of the migrant peril facing Russia.

52. The group that has done the most work in this area is the SOVA Center for Information and Analysis.

53. Viktor Shnirel'man, *Porog tolerantnosti: Istoriya i praktika novogo rasizma* [The threshold of tolerance: History and practice of the new racism], vol. 2, Moscow, Novoe literaturnoe obozrenie, 2011, pp. 412–431.

54. Falkovsky and Litoy, *Grazhdanskaya voina uzhe natchalas'*. Their book was placed on the list of extremist documents in September 2015.

55. Kavkaz-Tsentr was founded in 1999 as a portal for information on the disputed territory of Chechnya, and it was accused of relaying communications from Islamist groups and justifying terrorist acts committed on Russian soil.

56. See the speech by the leader of the Russian branch of Blood and Honor on the fighting qualities of North Caucasians, in Falkovsky and Litoy, *Grazhdanskaya voina uzhe natchalas'*, p. 177.

57. Moroz, "Le néo-paganisme, 'foi ethnique', contre-culture ou entrisme poli-tique?," pp. 245–246.

58. The video was posted online on September 1, 2005. On this, see Falkovsky and Litoy, *Grazhdanskaya voina uzhe natchalas'*, pp. 91–92.

59. On the links between skinheads and soccer fans, see Shnirel'man, *Porog tol-erantnosti*, pp. 406–411.

60. "Zhirinovsky vyskazalsya v podderzhku 'primorskikh partizan'" [Zhirinovsky declares his support for the "Primorsky Partisans"], *RIA Novosti*, July 7, 2010.

61. Aleksandr Sladkikh was the second of the partisans to kill himself during the raid.

62. Cited in Marina Terpinkot, "Istoriya 'primorskogo partizana' Andreya Suk-horada" [The story of the "Primorsky partisan" Andrey Sukhorada], *Gorod 812*, June

NOTES TO CHAPTER 3   181

15, 2010, https://gorod-812.ru/istoriya-primorskogo-partizana-andreya-suhorada/. See also Vsevolod Emelin's poem, *Korotkaya pesnya* [Short song], June 16, 2010, https://emelind.livejournal.com/170486.html?style=mine; and the poem "Primorskie Partizany" [The Primorsky Partisans], December 22, 2010, https://www.neizvestniy-geniy.ru/cat/literature/stihi/268097.html.

63. Yuliya Tsarenko, "Primorskie 'partizany' ostavili posle sebya vserossiiskoe dvizhenie" [The Primorsky "partisans" have engendered a movement across all of Russia], *Gazeta*, June 12, 2010, https://baikal24.ru/text/14-06-2010/primorskie/.

64. See, for example, Aleksey Usov, "'Partizany' 'prosnoulis' v Astrakhani" [The "partisans" have "awakened" in Astrakhan], *Novyi den'*, July 28, 2010, https://newday news.ru/incidents/293944.html.

65. This is a reference to the English name of Hitler's party.

66. Falkovsky and Litoy, *Grazhdanskaya voina uzhe natchalas'*, p. 167–168.

67. Judicial action against the far right at the start of the twenty-first century generally ignored the racist dimension of the violent acts being prosecuted, describing them as "hooliganism." See Shnirel'man, *Porog tolerantnosti*, pp. 432–452.

68. Adopted by Soviet dissidents to challenge the crackdown on the Prague Spring in 1968, this last slogan is still used by the opposition to the current Russian regime.

69. Svetlana Simakova, "Prigovor orlovskim partizanam" [The verdict on the Orlov partisans], *Istoki*, June 29, 2012. See also Vera Chelishcheva, "Partizany iz FSO" [Partisans from (Federal Protective Service)], *Novaya Gazeta* (Moscow), July 2, 2012.

70. This trial, full of twists and turns, ended in 2018. The accused received prison sentences of more than twenty years for their involvement in the crimes of the partisans and also in the murder of four people in 2009, which was linked to drug trafficking.

71. In early June 2010, the idea that the Primorsky Partisans were led by a mysterious *spetsnaz* veteran, Roman Muromtsev, was frequently mentioned. See, for example, "Banda Muromtseva okhotitsya na militsionerov" [Muromtsev's gang hunt the police], *Gorod 812*, June 9, 2010, https://gorod-812.ru/banda-muromtseva-ohotitsya-za-militsionerami/.

72. Eric Hobsbawm, *Bandits*, London, Abacus, 2000. Social bandits are defined by relationships; the term reflects a particular perception of rebel activity by the peasant society of which they are a part, which contrasts with the categories used for them by the lord and the state.

73. Karpitskaya, "Banda 'primorskikh partisan."

74. In April 2011 in Irkutsk, two ultranationalist, neo-pagan brothers killed two Central Asians and laid a trap for police officers. They blatantly broke a traffic law in front of a police car, which followed them to an apartment block courtyard. There they opened fire, killing two officers and wounding a third, before going into hiding.

75. In 2020 a group of survivalist strikeball enthusiasts promoted their lifestyle online using the name Mean Partisans and were accused of inciting attacks on the local police. "Troikh zhitelei Sakhalina, igravshikh v straikbol, obvinili v sozdanii terroristicheskogo soobschestva" [Three Sakhalin residents and strikeball fans are accused of founding a terrorist organization], *Meduza*, April 6, 2020, https://meduza.io/feature/2020/04/06/troih-zhiteley-sahalina-igravshih-v-straykbol-obvinili-v-sozdanii-terroristicheskogo-soobschestva-eto-delo-sravnivayut-s-delom-seti.

182   NOTES TO CHAPTER 3

76. See Human Rights Foundation, "2016 Havel Prize Awarded to Atena Fargha-dani, Petr Pavlensky, and Umida Akhmedova," press release, May 5, 2016.

77. "Russian Artist Pavlensky Stripped of Award over Support for Police Killers," *Moscow Times*, July 8, 2016.

78. "V Primorskom krae nashli mogilu pogibshego v Ukraine 'partizana' Aleksan-dra Kovtuna" [In Primorye was found the tomb of ex-"partisan" Aleksandr Kovtun who died in Ukraine], *Meduza*, February 21, 2023.

79. Jo Tuckman, "Mob Kills Two Policemen Mistaken for Kidnappers," *Guardian*, November 25, 2004.

80. Zoha Waseem, *Insecure Guardians: Enforcement, Encounters and Everyday Polic-ing in Postcolonial Karachi*, London, Hurst, 2022, p. 225.

81. Gema Kloppe-Santamaría, *In the Vortex of Violence*: *Lynching, Extralegal Jus-tice, and the State in Post-revolutionary Mexico*, Oakland, University of California Press, 2020, p. 19.

82. Ice-T famously observed, "If you believe that I'm a cop killer, you believe David Bowie is an astronaut."

83. Mathieu Deflem, "Popular Culture and Social Control: The Moral Panic on Music Labeling," *American Journal of Criminal Justice*, vol. 45, no. 1, 2020, pp. 2–24, https://doi.org/10.1007/s12103-019-09495-3; Mark S. Hamm and Jeff Ferrell, "Rap, Cops, and Crime: Clarifying the 'Cop Killer' Controversy," in Richard C. Monk (ed.), *Taking Sides: Clashing Views on Controversial Issues in Crime and Criminology*, Guilford, UK, Dushkin-McGraw-Hill, 1998, pp. 23–28; Barry Shank, "Fears of the White Un-conscious: Music, Race, and Identification in the Censorship of 'Cop Killer,'" *Rad-ical History Review*, no. 66, 1996, pp. 124–145, https://doi.org/10.1215/01636545-1996 -66-124.

84. Mary Angela Bock, "Film the Police! Cop-Watching and Its Embodied Narra-tives," *Journal of Communication*, vol. 66, no. 1, 2016, pp. 13–34, https://doi.org/10.1111/ jcom.12204.

85. Rebecca Stein, *Screen Shots: State Violence on Camera in Israel and Palestine*, Stan-ford, CA, Stanford University Press, 2021.

86. ACAB stands for "all cops are bastards."

87. Ronan Maël, "Des milliers de policiers s'échangent des messages racistes sur un groupe Facebook," *Streetpress*, June 4, 2020.

88. Nicolas Giorgi, "Yvelines. Versailles: La 'chasseuse de flics' part directement en prison," *78actu*, December 4, 2019, https://actu.fr/ile-de-france/_78/yvelines-ver sailles-chasseuse-flics-part-directement-prison_29905875.html.

89. "Harcèlement et acharnement judiciaire contre Amélie 'Marie Acab-Land': Quand la police se fait justice," *Désarmons-les*! June 25, 2020, https://desarmons .net/2020/06/25/harcelement-etacharnement-judiciaire-contre-amelie-quand-la-po lice-se-fait-justice.

90. The author's observation of the demonstration of December 17, 2019.

91. See the debate in the French National Assembly, Assemblée Nationale, XVᵉ législature, *Session ordinaire de 2020–2021, Séance du vendredi 20 novembre 2020*, Novem-ber 20, 2020, https://www.assemblee-nationale.fr/dyn/15/comptes-rendus/seance/ session-ordinaire-de-2020-2021/deuxieme-seance-du-vendredi-20-novembre-2020.

92. The term *paco* refers to the Chilean "cops."

NOTES TO CHAPTERS 3 AND 4   183

93. The explanatory note is available online at https://web.archive.org/web/2019103000 2909/https://pacos.rebelside.pw/pacoleaks/informativo-2.html.

94. Brady Ng, "Hong Kong Protesters Are Naming and Shaming Police Officers," *Nikkei Asia*, December 18, 2019.

95. Benjamin Mueller and Al Baker, "2 N.Y.P.D. Officers Killed in Brooklyn Ambush; Suspect Commits Suicide," *New York Times*, December 20, 2014.

96. Jason Hanna, "Baton Rouge Cop Killer Left Note, Fired at Least 43 Rounds," *CNN*, July 9, 2017.

97. Talal Ansari, "Gavin Long's Alleged Manifesto Calls Baton Rouge Shootings a 'Necessary Evil,'" *BuzzFeed News*, July 20, 2016, https://www.buzzfeednews.com/article/talalansari/gavin-longs-alleged-manifesto.

98. Ansari, "Gavin Long's Alleged Manifesto."

Chapter 4

1. Cited by Mario Aguilera Peña, "Guerra, insurgencia y prácticas juciciales," in Eric Lair and Gonzalo Sanchez Comez (eds.), *Violencia y estrategias colectivas en la región andina*, Bogotá, Editorial Norma, 2004, p. 577.

2. Philip E. Jones, *The Pakistan People's Party: Rise to Power*, Karachi, Oxford University Press, 2003, p. 175.

3. Kamran Asdar Ali, "The Strength of the Street Meets the Strength of the State: The 1972 Labor Struggle in Karachi," *International Journal of Middle East Studies*, vol.37, no. 1, 2005, pp. 83–107, http://www.jstor.org/stable/3880083.

4. On the history of the paid anti-union gangs in India and Pakistan, see Rajnarayan Chandavarkar, *Imperial Power and Popular Politics: Class, Resistance and the State in India*, Cambridge, Cambridge University Press, 1998, chap. 4.

5. Anushay Malik, "Public Authority and Local Resistance: Abdur Rehman and the Industrial Workers of Lahore, 1969–1974," *Modern Asian Studies*, vol. 52, no. 3, 2018, p. 840, https://doi.org/10.1017/S0026749X16000469.

6. On corporate policing and "yellow unionism," see Matteo Millan and Alessandro Saluppo (eds.), *Corporate Yellow Unionism, and Strikebreaking 1890–1930: In Defence of Freedom*, London, Routledge, 2021.

7. Muhummad Idrees, "The Abdur Rehman Story (I) Dial 'M' for Murder," in *The Night Was Not Loveless*, Lahore, Rhotas Books, 1991, p. 188.

8. On the debates around feudalism in rural areas of the Punjab, see Nicolas Martin, *Politics, Landlords and Islam in Pakistan*, Abingdon, UK, Routledge, 2016.

9. Malik, "Public Authority and Local Resistance," p. 832.

10. Khalid Mahmud, *Pakistan mein Mazdur Tehrik* [The workers' movement in Pakistan], Lahore, Idarah Fikr-e-Mazdoor Kisan, 1983, p. 64. Laurent Gayer made all Urdu translations.

11. Tariq Hamid, interview by Anushay Malik, March 2014. We thank her for sharing this interview with us.

12. Idrees, "The Abdur Rehman Story (I)," p. 191.

13. This nickname characterizes Abdur Rehman as the providential figure who will bring about the ideal world that Bhutto promised. For some on the Left, Bhutto betrayed his commitments on becoming president in 1971.

14. Malik, "Public Authority and Local Resistance," p. 843.

184   NOTES TO CHAPTER 4

15. Abdur Rehman rose to prominence in union elections at Packages in defiance of the group led by Altaf Baloch, the left-wing activist who headed the company, or house, union. Their rivalry extended to the leadership of the wider union movement in Kot Lakhpat. At the time of his death, Rehman headed approximately a dozen other organizations in the area. In allying himself with a gangster like Dogar, Baloch may have sought to avenge the humiliation he had repeatedly suffered at the hands of the upstart Rehman.

16. "Khushi Muhammad Dogar and Another v. The State, 1984," *Monthly Law Digest* 1337, p. 1349.

17. Idrees, "The Abdur Rehman Story (I)," p. 197; Jones, *The Pakistan People's Party*, p. 252n93.

18. On revolution as a project meant to radically overhaul and totally transform the way people live, which cannot be reduced to the acts of violence that lead to the break with what went before, see Igor Cherstich, Martin Holbraad, and Nico Tassi, *Anthropologies of Revolution: Forging Time, People and Worlds*, Oakland, University of California Press, 2020.

19. Cited by Zhang Ning, "The Political Origins of Death Penalty Exceptionalism: Mao Zedong and the Practice of Capital Punishment in Contemporary China," *Punishment and Society*, vol. 10, no. 2, 2008, p. 119, https://doi.org/10.1177/1462474507087195.

20. Ning, "The Political Origins of Death Penalty Exceptionalism."

21. Mao Zedong, *Report on an Investigation of the Peasant Movement in Hunan*, March 1927, http://academics.wellesley.edu/Polisci/wj/China/Mao/hunan.html.

22. Mao Zedong, *Report on an Investigation of the Peasant Movement in Hunan.*

23. Ning, "The Political Origins of Death Penalty Exceptionalism," p. 180.

24. Yang Su, *Collective Killings in Rural China during the Cultural Revolution*, Cambridge, Cambridge University Press, 2012, chap. 6.

25. Mario Aguilera Peña, *Contrapoder y justicia guerrillera: Fragmentación política y orden insurgente en Colombia (1952–2003)*, Bogotá, IEPRI–Universidad Nacional de Colombia, 2014.

26. Aguilera Peña, *Contrapoder y justicia guerrillera*, p. 109.

27. Michel Foucault, "On Popular Justice: A Discussion with Maoists," in Michel Foucault, *Power/Knowledge: Selected Interviews and Other Writings*, 1972–1977, ed. Colin Gordon, New York, Pantheon Books, 1980, p. 29.

28. Thomas Blom Hansen, "Sovereigns beyond the State: On Legality and Authority in Urban India," in Thomas Blom Hansen and Finn Stepputat (eds.), *Sovereign Bodies: Citizens, Migrants and States in the Postcolonial World*, Princeton, NJ, Princeton University Press, 2005, pp. 169–191.

29. Hansen, "Sovereigns beyond the State," p. 170.

30. James Scott, "Revolution in the Revolution: Peasants and Commissars," *Theory and Society*, vol. 7, nos. 1/2, 1979, pp. 97–134, http://www.jstor.org/stable/657000.

31. Vanessa Codaccioni, "Justice populaire et mimétisme judiciaire: Les maoïstes dans et hors la Cour de sûreté de l'État," *Droit et société*, no. 89, 2015, p. 18, https://doi .org/10.3917/drs.089.0017. Codaccioni refers here to Timothy Tackett's classic work, *Par la volonté du peuple: Comment les députés de 1789 sont devenus révolutionnaires*, Paris, Albin Michel, 1997.

NOTES TO CHAPTER 4   185

32. Codaccioni, "Justice populaire et mimétisme judiciaire," p. 18.

33. Codaccioni, "Justice populaire et mimétisme judiciaire."

34. Cited by Gabriela Saidon, *La Montonera: Biografía de Norma Arrostito, la primera jefa de la guerrilla peronista*, Buenos Aires, Sudamericana, 2005, p. 17.

35. Beatriz Sarlo, *La pasión y la excepción*, Buenos Aires, Siglo XXI, 2003, p. 135.

36. "Mario Firmenich y Norma Arrostito cuentan como murió Aramburu," *La Causa Peronista*, vol. 1, no. 9, 1974, p. 9.

37. "Mario Firmenich y Norma Arrostito cuentan como murió Aramburu," p. 29.

38. The Montoneros had complicated origins. Several of their leaders, including one of the main protagonists from this time, Mario Firmenich, came from the Catholic Right, and the organization's fascination with death was interpreted by some of its critics as proof of its fascist tendencies. This did not prevent the Montos from becoming the main party of the Left in Argentina in the 1970s. See Guillaume de Gracia, *De sueur et de sang: Mouvements sociaux, résistances populaires et lutte armée dans l'Argentine de Perón*, Paris, Syllepse, 2016, pp. 193–198.

39. On June 9, 1956, Juan José Valle orchestrated an uprising against the military dictatorship of General Aramburu. Valle was executed at the same time as other civilian and military figures accused of taking part in the insurrection. These executions earned the regime the nickname La Fusiladodra, which was used by Aramburu's kidnappers.

40. On the turbulent story of this embalmed body, see the historical fiction by Tomás Eloy Martínez, *Santa Evita*, New York, Alfred A. Knopf, Inc., 1996.

41. "Mario Firmenich y Norma Arrostito cuentan como murió Aramburu," p. 29.

42. The "years of lead" refers first to a period in Italian history—mainly the second half of the 1970s—that was marked by terrorism. By extension, the phrase refers to a global historical conjuncture characterized by a resurgence of political violence in the wake of 1968, notably from the far left.

43. "In Spanish, [the suffix -*azo*] is added to a word to indicate a blow struck with an object or part of the body. The most classic example is *puñetazo*, punch, from the noun *puño*, meaning fist. Through semantic derivation, notably in Argentina (but also in Venezuela), -*azo* is often added to talk about an event with 'punch.'" De Gracia, *De sueur et de sang*, p. 155.

44. Sarlo, *La pasión y la excepción*, p. 145.

45. "Ante los crímenes del enemigo: El brazo justiciero del ERP," editorial, *Estrella Roja*, no. 41, October 7, 1974, p. 2.

46. Cited in Aguilera Peña, *Contrapoder y justicia guerrillera*, p. 302.

47. Vera Carnovale, "Las ejecuciones selectivas del Ejército Revolucionario del Pueblo: Nociones implicadas en el ejercicio de la justicia revolucionaria," *Caleidoscopio*, no. 21, 2007, p. 41, https://doi.org/10.33064/21crscsh363.

48. The social composition of these groups is doubtless not totally unconnected to their view of the people: these were all urban guerrilla groups recruiting primarily from the educated middle classes.

49. "Mario Firmenich y Norma Arrostito cuentan como murió Aramburu," p. 25.

50. John Caughey, "Their Majesties the Mob," *Pacific Historical Review*, vol. 26, no. 3, 1957, pp. 217–234, https://doi.org/10.2307/3636213.

186   NOTES TO CHAPTER 4

51. Reverbel was captured by the Movimiento de Liberación Nacional–Tupamaros, an urban guerrilla group in Uruguay, founded in 1966 and particularly active in the 1970s.

52. On the Monteneros' "aristolelico-Thomist" vision, which was influenced by the philosophical and theological doctrine developed by Saint Thomas Aquinas and involved testing their militants' revolutionary spirit through physical pain, see de Gracia, *De sueur et de sang*, p. 197.

53. Daniela Slipak, "La justice de la révolution: *Evita Montonera* dans l'Argentine des années 1970," *Problèmes d'Amérique latine*, no. 93, 2014, pp. 91–108, https://doi .org/10.3917/pal.093.0091.

54. Yoshikuni Igarashi, "Dead Bodies and Living Guns: The United Red Army and Its Deadly Pursuit of Revolution, 1971–1972," *Japanese Studies*, vol. 27, no. 2, 2007, p. 129, https://doi.org/10.1080/10371390701494135.

55. Christopher Perkins, *The United Red Army on Screen: Cinema, Aesthetics and the Politics of Memory*, Basingstoke, UK, Palgrave Macmillan, 2015. The most important film about the organization undoubtedly remains *United Red Army* (Koji Wakamatsu, 2007).

56. The term *rinchi* (lynching) notably appears in the account of Takaya Shiyomi, ex-head of the United Red Army, cited in Rengo Sekigun jiken no zentai zo o nokosu kai [Commemoration Committee of the Red Army Affair] (ed.), *Shogen: Rengo Sekigun* [Eye-witness accounts: The Red Army], Tokyo, Koseisha, 2013, p. 225. We thank Mayuka Ueno-Gayer for helping with the translation of this text.

57. Cited by Aguilera Peña, *Contrapoder y justicia guerrillera*, p. 151.

58. "Strengthen the People's Army and Intensify the People's War," special issue, *Ang Bayan*, March 29, 2012, p. 11.

59. Eric Hobsbawm, "Revolution Is Puritan," *New Society*, May 22, 1969.

60. Aguilera Peña, *Contrapoder y justicia guerrilla*, p. 238. On the affinities between revolution and puritanism, see also Srila Roy, *Remembering Revolution: Gender, Violence and Subjectivity in India's Naxalbari Movement*, Delhi, Oxford University Press, 2012.

61. Laurent Gayer, "Militariser les femmes: Doctrines, pratiques et critiques du féminisme martial en Asie du Sud," in Caroline Guibet Lafaye and Alexandra Frénod (eds.), *S'émanciper par les armes? Sur la violence politique des femmes*, Paris, Inalco Presses, 2019.

62. Jeff Goodwin, "The Libidinal Constitution of a High Risk Social Movement: Affectual Ties and Solidarity in the Huk Rebellion, 1946 to 1954," *American Sociological Review*, vol. 62, no. 1, 1997, pp. 53–69, https://doi.org/10.2307/2657452.

63. Max Weber, *Essays in Sociology*, London, Routledge, 1948, p. 258.

64. Marie Lecomte-Tilouine, "Ruling Social Groups—from Species to Nation: Reflections on Changing Conceptions of Caste and Ethnicity in Nepal," in David Gellner (ed.), *Ethnic Activism and Civil Society in South Asia*, New Delhi, Sage, 2009, pp. 291–336.

65. Aguilera Peña, *Contrapoder y justicia guerrilla*, p. 238.

66. Heather Hamill, *The Hoods: Crime and Punishment in Belfast*, Princeton, NJ, Princeton University Press, 2011, p. 26.

67. Rachel Monaghan, "'An Imperfect Peace': Paramilitary 'Punishments' in Northern Ireland," *Terrorism and Political Violence*, vol. 16, no. 3, 2004, p. 440, https:// doi.org/10.1080/09546550490509775; Hamill, *The Hoods*, p. 33.

NOTES TO CHAPTER 4   187

68. Monaghan, "An Imperfect Peace," p. 444; Hamill, *The Hoods*, p. 137.

69. Michael Taussig, *Law in a Lawless Land: Diary of a Limpieza in Colombia*, Chicago, University of Chicago Press, 2003, p. 92.

70. Aguilera Peña, *Contrapoder y justicia guerrilla*, p. 197.

71. Anne Simonin, "Les acquittés de la Grande Terreur: Réflexions sur l'amitié dans la République," in Serge Aberdam (ed.), *Les Politiques de la Terreur, 1793–1794*, Rennes, PUR, 2008, pp. 185–205.

72. Marie Lecomte-Tilouine, "Political Change and Cultural Revolution in a Maoist Model Village, Mid-Western Nepal," in Mahendra Lawoti and Anup K. Pahari (eds.), *The Maoist Insurgency in Nepal: Revolution in the Twenty-First Century*, Milton Park, UK, Routledge, 2010, p. 117.

73. In Nepalese, the Maoist insurgents are known as the *maobadi*.

74. We are grateful to Marie Lecomte-Tilouine for providing this information.

75. International Commission of Jurists, "Nepal: Justice in Transition," February 2008, Geneva, Switzerland, pp. 11–13, https://www.icj.org/wp-content/uploads/2012/04/Nepal-Justice-in-Transition-Thematic-reports-2008.pdf.

76. The foundations of the FARC's justice system were laid in the early 1980s, after the first ceasefire of 1984–1990.

77. The resistance of the local population to the FARC's hegemony was confirmed in the legislative elections of 2018, in which the party favored by the guerrillas won barely 0.34 percent of the vote.

78. Juanita León, *Country of Bullets: Chronicles of War*, Albuquerque, University of New Mexico Press, 2009, p. 83.

79. René Provost, *Rebel Courts: The Administration of Justice by Armed Insurgents*, New York, Oxford University Press, 2021, p. 55.

80. María Clemencia Ramírez, *Between the Guerrillas and the State: The Cocalero Movement, Citizenship and Identity in the Colombian Amazon*, Durham, NC, Duke University Press, 2011, p. 45.

81. Nicolás Espinosa Menéndez, "Del control (los castigos insurgentes) a la autonomía (las sanciones comunitarias): Elementos para la transición de la Justicia local en La Sierra de La Macarena," *Agora USB*, vol. 16, no. 2, 2016, pp. 416–417.

82. In the everyday language of the rural populations of La Macarena, *pelarlo* (skinning) refers to butchery of farm animals. It is also commonly used to refer to summary executions.

83. Garry Leech, *The FARC: The Longest Insurgency*, London, Zed Books, 2011, p. 44.

84. Cited by Aguilera Peña, *Contrapoder y justicia guerrilla*, p. 192.

85. Codaccioni, "Justice populaire et mimétisme judiciaire," pp. 18–19.

86. Taussig, *Law in a Lawless Land*, p. 92.

87. Andrés López Bermúdez, "Las Leyes del Llano, 1952–1953: Conceptos fundamentales," *Dialéctica Libertadora*, no. 8, 2015, p. 170, http://hdl.handle.net/10495/10023. On the work and contribution of this lawyer, see also Corporación Colectivo de Abogados, "José Alvear Restrepo," in *José Alvear Restrepo: Una gesta silenciada*, Bogotá, Rodríguez Quito Editores, 2000.

88. Boaventura de Sousa Santos, "Law: A Map of Misreading. Toward a Postmodern Conception of Law," *Journal of Law and Society*, vol. 14, no. 3, 1987, pp. 279–302, https://doi.org/10.2307/1410186.

188   NOTES TO CHAPTER 4

89. Idrees, "The Abdur Rehman Story (I)," p. 192.

90. Nicolás Espinosa Menéndez, "La justicia guerrillera en Colombia: Elementos de análisis para los retos de la transición política en una zona de control insurgente (el caso del piedemonte amazónico)," *Estudios Latinoamericanos*, no. 37, 2016, pp. 96–97, https://doi.org/10.22201/cela.24484946e.2016.37.54724.

91. León, *Country of Bullets*, p. 86.

92. Boris Mamlyuk, "The Cold War in Soviet International Legal Discourse," in Matthew Craven, Sundhya Pahuja, and Gerry Simpson (eds.), *International Law and the Cold War*, Cambridge: Cambridge University Press, 2020, p. 349.

93. In the mid-1950s, B. P. Koirala, a major figure of the Nepali congress (who would become the country's first elected prime minister in 1959), encouraged his party to adopt the notion of "revolutionary legality" to implement agrarian reform. John Whelpton, *A History of Nepal*, Cambridge, Cambridge University Press, 2005, p. 89.

94. Communist Party of Nepal (Maoist) Public Legal Code of 2060, chap. 2, general principles 5 and 7, cited by International Commission of Jurists, "Nepal," p. 9.

95. We are grateful to Marie Lecomte-Tilouine for this information.

96. Lecomte-Tilouine, "Political Change and Cultural Revolution in a Maoist Model Village, Mid-Western Nepal," p. 117.

97. Charles Haviland, "Parallel Justice, Maoist Style," *BBC News*, October 14, 2006.

98. International Commission of Jurists, "Nepal," p. 13.

99. Aguilera Peña, *Contrapoder y justicia guerrilla*, p. 130.

100. Provost, *Rebel Courts*, p. 53.

101. Espinosa Menéndez, "La justicia guerrillera en Colombia," p. 99.

102. Hamill, *The Hoods*, p. 35.

103. Pat Gambao, "Justice Is the Heart of the Revolution," *Liberation*, May 7, 2018,≈p. 5.

104. Teresa Lorena Jopson, "Revolutionary Justice in the Philippines," *Peace Review*, vol. 26, no. 2, 2014, pp. 245–246, https://doi.org/10.1080/10402659.2014.906992.

105. Espinosa Menéndez, "Del control (los castigos insurgentes) a la autonomía (las sanciones comunitarias)," p. 414.

106. Chris Kamalendran, "The Inside Story of 'Eelam Courts,'" *Sunday Times* (Sri Lanka), November 14, 2004. According the Liberation Tigers of Tamil Eelam, between 2002 and 2005, over 32,000 cases were tried by the district courts they had established in their stronghold and 1,500 by the Court of Appeals. These courts ceased to operate in May 2009, following the offensive of the Sri Lankan army. See Provost, *Rebel Courts*, p. 231.

107. Max Weber, "L'économie et les ordres," in *Concepts fondamentaux de sociologie*, Paris, Gallimard, 2016, pp. 225–264.

108. Espinosa Menéndez, "La justicia guerrillera en Colombia," p. 95.

109. Cited in Su, *Collective Killings in Rural China during the Cultural Revolution*, p. 183.

110. Su, *Collective Killings in Rural China during the Cultural Revolution*."

111. Hong Lu and Terance D. Miethe, *China's Death Penalty: History, Law and Contemporary Practices*, New York, Routledge, 2007, p. 45.

112. Eduardo Barriobero, cited by François Godicheau, *La Guerre d'Espagne: République et révolution en Catalogne (1936–1939)*, Paris, Odile Jacob, 2004, p. 251.

NOTES TO CHAPTER 4   189

113. Sergio Nieves Chaves, "La justicia republicana durante la Guerra Civil: Los tribunales especial popular y especial de guardia de Cuenca," in Eduardo Higueras Castañeda, Ángel Luis López Villaverde, and Sergio Nieves Chaves (eds.), *El pasado que no pasa: La Guerra Civil española a los ochenta años de su finalización*, Cuenca, Ediciones de la Universidad de Castilla–La Mancha, 2020.

114. "Et maintenant ils massacrent nos enfants!," *La Cause du peuple*, May 1, 1972, p. 15.

115. For a discussion on this, see François Athané and Michel Kail, "Sartre au péril du lynchage: L'engagement et le droit," *Lignes*, no. 48, 2015, https://doi.org/10.3917/lignes.048.0179.

116. Jean-Paul Sartre, "Lynchage ou justice populaire?," *La Cause du peuple*, May 17, 1972, p. 12.

117. Foucault, "On Popular Justice," p. 35.

118. Foucault, p. 32.

119. Foucault, p. 29. For a contextualization of this discussion, see Jean Bérard, "Tordre ou briser le bâton de la justice? Les mouvements de l'après-68 et les illégalismes des dominants, entre justice populaire et refus de la pénalité (1968–1972)," *Champ pénal*, vol. 10, 2013, https://doi.org/10.4000/champpenal.8418.

120. Mario Moretti, *Brigades rouges: Une histoire italienne. Entretien avec Carla Mosca et Rossana Rossanda*, Paris, Éditions Amsterdam, 2018, p. 38.

121. Aguilera Peña, *Contrapoder y justicia guerrilla*, p. 225.

122. This is the term used by the Nepalese *maobadi*. We are grateful to Marie Lecomte-Tilouine for this information.

123. Espinosa Menéndez, "La justicia guerrillera en Colombia," p. 99.

124. Aguilera Peña, *Contrapoder y justicia guerrilla*, p. 244n367.

125. Adam Baczko, "Juger en situation de guerre civile: Les cours de justice Taleban en Afghanistan," *Politix*, no. 104, 2013, p. 30, https://doi.org/10.3917/pox.104.0025.

126. Malik, "Public Authority and Local Resistance," p. 842; Mahmud, *Pakistan mein Mazdur Tehrik*, p. 64.

127. Paul Rollier, "Vies de caïds et justice informelle à Lahore (Pakistan)," *L'Homme*, nos. 219–220, 2016, p. 69, https://doi.org/10.4000/lhomme.29034.

128. Tathiana Flores Acuña, *The United Nations Mission in El Salvador: A Humanitarian Law Perspective*, The Hague, Kluwer Law International, 1995, pp. 59–60.

129. Philip Alston, "Promotion and Protection of All Human Rights, Civil, Political, Economic, Social and Cultural Rights, Including the Right to Development," addendum, April 16, 2008, United Nations General Assembly, p. 14.

130. Flores Acuña, *The United Nations Mission in El Salvador*.

131. Elaine Pearson, "Philippines: People's Courts or Cold-Blooded Murder?," *Philippine Star*, April 18, 2012.

132. Sandesh Sivakumaran, "Courts of Armed Opposition Groups: Fair Trials or Summary Justice?," *Journal of International Criminal Justice*, vol. 7, no. 3, 2009, p. 491, https://doi.org/10.1093/jicj/mqp039.

133. Yves Dezalay, "Les courtiers de l'international: Héritiers cosmopolites, mercenaires de l'impérialisme et missionnaires de l'universel," *Actes de la recherche en sciences sociales*, nos. 151–152, 2004, p. 30, https://doi.org/10.3917/arss.151.0004.

134. Aguilera Peña, *Contrapoder y justicia guerrilla*, p. 116.

190   NOTES TO CHAPTERS 4 AND 5

135. Tania Tapia Jáuregui, "Al menos 30 personas han sido asesinadas bajo el pretexto de 'violar la cuarentena,'" *070*, August 20, 2020.

136. Juanita Vélez, "Los armados ahora también juegan a autoridad sanitaria," *La Silla Vacia*, May 1, 2020.

137. International Commission of Jurists, "Nepal," p. 13.

138. Shanta Sinha, *Maoists in Andhra Pradesh*, Delhi, Gyan, 2013, p. 317.

139. In addition to the examples from Colombia and Pakistan described in this chapter, an example is a property dispute that was arbitrated by the Nepalese Maoists and presented in International Commission of Jurists, "Nepal," p. 13 (box).

Chapter 5

1. Reproduced in "Crecen amenazas de limpieza social en Kennedy," *El Espectador* (Bogotá), April 25, 2014.

2. Our main sources here are the accounts of this massacre and its judicial repercussions in the Colombian press—for example, "La mano negra que rondó a Soacha," *El Tiempo* (Colombia), March 24, 2001.

3. Corte Suprema de Justicia, Sala de Casación Penal, Proceso no. 20161, Resuelve la Sala el conflicto negativo de competencia suscitado entre los Juzgados 1° Penal del Circuito Especializado de Cundinamarca y 2° Penal del Cicuito de Soacha (Cundinamarca), January 21, 2003, p. 2.

4. Christian Lund, "Twilight Institutions: Public Authority and Local Politics in Africa," *Development and Change*, vol. 37, no. 4, 2006, pp. 685–705, https://doi.org/10.1111/j.1467-7660.2006.00497.x.

5. Lesley Gill, *A Century of Violence in a Red City: Popular Struggle, Counterinsurgency and Human Rights in Colombia*, Durham, NC, Duke University Press, 2016.

6. On the "art and culture of paramilitary terror," see Michael Taussig, *Law in a Lawless Land: Diary of a Limpieza in Colombia*, Chicago, University of Chicago Press, 2003, p. 12.

7. R. S. Rose, *The Unpast: Elite Violence and Social Control in Brazil, 1954–2000*, Athens, Ohio University Press, 2005, p. 234.

8. Diário Oficial do Estado do Rio de Janeiro, Poder Legislativo, November 23, 2016, p. 29, https://www.jusbrasil.com.br/diarios/131425294/doerj-poder-legislativo-23-11-2016-pg-29.

9. Etelvina Maria de Castro Trindade, "Modèles et emprunts: L'hygiénisme au Brésil (fin XIXe–début XXe siècle)," in Patrice Bourdelais (ed.), *Les Hygiénistes: Enjeux, modèles et pratiques*, Paris, Belin, 201, pp. 267–296.

10. Serge Paugam, Bruno Cousin, Camila Giorgetti, and Jules Naudet, *Ce que les riches pensent des pauvres*, Paris, Seuil, 2019, p. 34.

11. María-Teresa Gutiérrez, "Proceso de institucionalización de la higiene: Estado, salubridad e higienismo en Colombia en la primera mitad del siglo XX," *Estudios Socio-Juridicos*, vol. 12, no. 1, 2010, pp. 73–97, http://www.scielo.org.co/scielo.php?script=sci_arttext&pid=S0124-05792010000100005&lng=en&nrm=iso.

12. Gutiérrez, p. 78.

13. Sandra Caponi, "Hygiénisme et réorganisation urbaine au Brésil et en Argentine," *Cahiers du centre de recherches historiques*, no. 33, 2004, https://doi.org/10.4000/ccrh.259.

NOTES TO CHAPTER 5   191

14. Gutiérrez, "Proceso de institucionalización de la higiene," p. 76.

15. Paugam et al., *Ce que les riches pensent des pauvres*, p. 118.

16. Dominique Colas, *Le Léninisme*, Paris, PUF, 1998, pp. 201–206.

17. Rose, *The Unpast*, p. 235.

18. Officially, "E. M." referred to the Esquadrão Motorizado, a unit where Le Cocq had once served.

19. Charles Antoine, "Au Brésil, le procès de l''escadron de la mort' est celui du régime," *Le Monde*, April 27, 1971.

20. Cited in Bruno Paes Manso, *A República das Milícias: Dos Esquadrões da Morte à Era Bolsonaro* [The republic of militias: Death squads in Brazil], São Paulo, Todavia, 2020, p. 120.

21. Martha K. Huggins, "Modernity and Devolution: The Making of Police Death Squads in Modern Brazil," in Bruce B. Campbell and Arthur D. Brenner (eds.), *Death Squads in Global Perspective: Murder with Deniability*, New York, Palgrave Macmillan, 2000, p. 208.

22. Nancy Scheper-Hughes and Daniel Hoffman, "Brazilian Apartheid: Street Kids and the Struggle for Urban Space," in Nancy Scheper-Hughes and Caroline Fishel Sargent (eds.), *Small Wars: The Cultural Politics of Childhood*, Berkeley, University of California Press, 1998, p. 376.

23. Gilberto Dimenstein, *Brésil, la guerre des enfants*, Paris, Fayard, 1991, pp. 154–157.

24. Scheper-Hughes and Hoffman, "Brazilian Apartheid," p. 374.

25. Human Rights Watch, *"Social Cleansing" and Street Youths in Guatemala*, New York, HRW, 1998, p. 1.

26. "Paramilitares de Honduras asesinan a 200 delincuentes," *El País*, September 21, 1999.

27. Delphine Minotti–Vu Ngoc, "Marginalité et répression en Colombie: Le cas du nettoyage social," PhD diss., Université Stendhal-Grenoble III, 2002, p. 263.

28. Mario Fumerton, "Rondas Campesinas in the Peruvian Civil War: Peasant Self-Defence Organisations in Ayacucho," *Bulletin of Latin American Research*, vol. 20, no. 4, 2001, p. 475, http://www.jstor.org/stable/3339025.

29. Jaime Ulises Marinero, "La Sombra Negra: La historia detrás del mito," *La Pagina* (El Salvador), August 24, 2008.

30. Romain Le Cour Grandmaison, "'Vigilar y Limpiar': Identification and Self-Help Justice-Making in Michoacán, Mexico," *Politix*, vol. 115, no. 3, 2016, https://doi.org/10.3917/pox.115.0103.

31. Jacobo Grajales, *Gouverner dans la violence: Le paramilitarisme en Colombie*, Paris, Karthala, 2016, p. 88. See also Carlos Miguel Ortiz Sarmiento, *La violence en Colombie: Racines historiques et sociales*, Paris, L'Harmattan, 1990.

32. The *pájaros* (birds) took their name from their reputation for furtiveness, maintained by their surprise attacks. The word *aplanchadores* comes from a torture technique in which the victim is struck with the flat blade of a machete. The term *chulavitas* refers to the village of the same name in the Boyacá region, home to the group's earliest members. Ortiz Sarmiento, *La Violence en Colombie*, pp. 114, 128, 153.

33. Ortiz Sarmiento, p. 176. However, as Carlos Miguel Ortiz Sarmiento shows, the language of cleansing and its moral implications (eradicating evil) are shared by conservative and liberal armed gangs.

NOTES TO CHAPTER 5

34. Carlos Eduardo Rojas Jr., *La violencia llamada "limpieza social,"* Bogotá, Centro de Investigación y Educación Popular, 1994, pp. 15–16.

35. "Homicidios por exterminio social en Colombia," *El Espectador* (Bogotá), April 19, 2016.

36. Rojas, *La violencia llamada "limpieza social,"* p. 74.

37. In the Colombian press of the 1980s, the comparison to Argentina was most frequently made in relation to political assassinations. We thank Jacobo Grajales for this information.

38. Rojas, *La violencia llamada "limpieza social,"* p. 55.

39. Rojas, p. 57.

40. Rojas, p. 54.

41. Rojas, p. 54.

42. Martha K. Huggins and Myriam P. Mesquita, "Scapegoating Outsiders: The Murders of Street Youth in Modern Brazil," *Policing and Society,* vol. 5, no. 4, 1995, p. 265, https://doi.org/10.1080/10439463.1995.9964730.

43. Martha Nieves Ochoa was the daughter of a major landowner and sister of three members of the Medellín cartel. At age twenty-six she was abducted by the guerrilla group M-19, who demanded $12 million for her release. She was released without a ransom payment after the MAS abducted twenty-five people connected to the kidnappers.

44. Minotti–Vu Ngoc, "Marginalité et répression en Colombie," p. 56.

45. Gérard Marin, "Quand le trafic de cocaïne est arrivé à Medellín: Réseaux mafieux, violences et politiques de sécurité (1975–2014)," PhD diss., EHESS, 2014.

46. Lesley Gill, "Right There with You: Coca-Cola, Labor Restructuring and Political Violence in Colombia," *Critique of Anthropology,* vol. 27, no. 3, 2007, p. 241, https://doi.org/10.1177/0308275X07080354.

47. "La violencia contra los 'indeseables,'" *Verdadabierta.com,* March 15, 2016, https://verdadabierta.com/la-violencia-contra-los-indeseables/.

48. Cited by Aldo Civico, *The Para-State: An Ethnography of Colombia's Death Squads,* Berkeley, University of California Press, 2015, p. 109.

49. Cited in Centro Nacional de Memoria Histórica, *Limpieza social: Una violencia mal nombrada,* Bogotá, CNMH-EIPRI, 2015, p. 42.

50. Minotti–Vu Ngoc, "Marginalité et répression en Colombie," p. 356.

51. "Marquémoslos legalmente," *La Republica,* January 25, 1980, cited in Minotti–Vu Ngoc, p. 21.

52. "Healthier living," or *práticas humanas de aseo,* literally translates as "human hygiene practices." Rojas, *La violencia llamada "limpieza social,"* p. 46.

53. Alain Brossat, *Le Corps de l'ennemi: Hyperviolence et démocratie,* Paris, La Fabrique, 1998, chap. 4.

54. Rojas, *La violencia llamada "limpieza social,"* p. 46.

55. Ingrid Carolina Pabón Suárez, "'Limpieza social' en Bogotá: La construcción del indeseable," PhD diss., Universidad Nacional de Colombia, 2015, p. 167.

56. Minotti–Vu Ngoc, "Marginalité et répression en Colombie," p. 87.

57. Minotti–Vu Ngoc, p. 28.

58. Rojas, *La violencia llamada "limpieza social,"* pp. 17, 62; Minotti–Vu Ngoc, "Marginalité et répression en Colombie," pp. 364, 375.

NOTES TO CHAPTER 5   193

59. Cited by Rojas, *La violencia llamada "limpieza social,"* p. 62.

60. Grajales, *Gouverner dans la violence*, p. 88.

61. Civico, *The Para-State*, p. 110.

62. The former president of Sri Lanka, Gotabaya Rajapaksa, confirmed that the intelligence services had used these practices, including under his authority as defense minister (2005–2015). Journalists for Democracy in Sri Lanka, "Sri Lanka: Gotabaya Acknowledges Use of White Vans to 'Take In' Suspects," February 14, 2019.

63. Le Cour Grandmaison, *"Vigilar y Limpiar."*

64. Lesley Gill, "The Parastate in Colombia," *Anthropologica*, vol. 51, no. 2, 2009, pp. 313–325.

65. Taussig, *Law in a Lawless Land*, p. 67.

66. This practice was first identified in Medellín in 1981. Rojas, *La violencia llamada "limpieza social,"* p. 18.

67. Minotti–Vu Ngoc, "Marginalité et répression en Colombie," p. 370.

68. Rojas, *La violencia llamada "limpieza social,"* pp. 28–29.

69. Minotti–Vu Ngoc, "Marginalité et répression en Colombie," p. 68.

70. Minotti–Vu Ngoc, p. 65.

71. Minotti–Vu Ngoc.

72. Taussig, *Law in a Lawless Land*, p. 92.

73. Rojas, *La violencia llamada "limpieza social,"* p. 27.

74. Emmanuel-Pierre Guittet, *Antiterrorisme clandestin, antiterrorisme officiel: Chroniques espagnoles de la coopération en Europe*, Montreal, Athena Editions, 2010.

75. Begoña Aretxaga, "Playing Terrorist: Ghastly Plots and the Ghostly State," *Journal of Spanish Cultural Studies*, vol. 1, no. 1, 2000, pp. 49, 48, https://doi.org/10.1080/713683435.

76. Taussig, *Law in a Lawless Land*, p. 142.

77. Ortiz Sarmiento, *La Violence en Colombie*, p. 153.

78. Taussig, *Law in a Lawless Land*, p. 142.

79. Minotti–Vu Ngoc, "Marginalité et répression en Colombie," pp. 63–232.

80. *El Tiempo*, "La Mano Negra que rondó a Soacha."

81. Gill, *A Century of Violence in a Red City*, p. 19.

82. Gill, "Right There with You," pp. 238–239.

83. Grajales, *Gouverner dans la violence*, pp. 85–88.

84. Gill, "The Parastate in Colombia."

85. Stephen Dudley, *Walking Ghosts: Murder and Guerrilla Politics in Colombia*, New York, Routledge, 2005, p. 171; Gill, "Right There with You."

86. Gill, *A Century of Violence in a Red City*, p. 119.

87. Cited in Centro Nacional de Memoria Histórica, *Aniquilar la diferencia: Lesbianas, gays, bisexuales y transgeneristas en el marco del conflicto armado colombiano*, Bogotá, Centro Nacional de Memoria Histórica, 2015, p. 214.

88. Gill, *A Century of Violence in a Red City*, p. 28.

89. Gill, "The Parastate in Colombia," p. 214.

90. Amnesty International, "Political Violence in Colombia: Myth and Reality," Amnesty International Report 23/0001/1994, March 1, 1994, https://www.amnesty.org/en/documents/amr23/001/1994/en/.

91. Cited by Amnesty International, "Political Violence in Colombia."

92. Cited by Amnesty International, "Political Violence in Colombia."

NOTES TO CHAPTERS 5 AND 6

93. Cited by Minotti–Vu Ngoc, "Marginalité et répression en Colombie," p. 21.

94. "Detenidos presuntos asesinos de jovenes," *El Tiempo*, March 2, 2001.

95. "Comerciantes financiaron matanza en Soacha," *El Tiempo*, March 3, 2001.

96. Cited in Corte Suprema de Justicia, Sala de Casación Penal, p. 5.

97. "Ciudad Bolívar: Cara . . . ," *El Tiempo* (Colombia), September 20, 1992.

98. Centro Nacional de Memoria Histórica, *Limpieza social*, p. 163.

99. Centro Nacional de Memoria Histórica, p. 164.

100. Insa Nolte, "Without Women Nothing Can Succeed: Yoruba Women in the Oodua People's Congress (OPC), Nigeria," *Africa*, vol. 78, no. 1, 2008, pp. 84–106.

101. Centro Nacional de Memoria Histórica, *Limpieza social*, p. 163.

102. Cited in Corte Suprema de Justicia, Sala de Casación Penal, p. 7.

103. Corte Suprema de Justicia, p. 16.

104. Consejo de Estado, Radicación número 25000-23-26-000-2006-01696-01 (45217), Actor: María de los Angeles Iquira Collazos y Otros; Demandado: Nación—Fiscalía General de la Nación y Otro, Bogotá D.C., December 5, 2017.

105. On the Colombian magistrates' capacity to resist pressure from the paramilitaries, see Grajales, "Quand les juges s'en mêlent."

106. Corte Suprema de Justicia, Sala de Casación Penal, p. 10.

107. Michel de Certeau, *The Possession at Loudun*, trans. Michael B. Smith, Chicago, University of Chicago Press, 2000, p. 2.

108. Laurent Fourchard, "Le vigilantisme contemporain: Violence et légitimité d'une activité policière bon marché," *Critique internationale* vol. 78, no. 1, 2018, p. 185, https://doi.org/10.3917/crii.078.0169.

109. Lund, "Twilight Institutions."

110. For an illustration of this thesis taken from Colombia, see Human Rights Watch, *Colombia's Killer Networks: The Military-Paramilitary Partnership and the United States*, Washington, DC, HRW, 1996, p. 61.

111. Grajales, "Quand les juges s'en mêlent."

112. Nicolaas Warouw, "Community-Based Agencies as the Entrepreneur's Instruments of Control in Post Soeharto's Indonesia," *Asia Pacific Business Review*, vol. 12, no. 2, 2006, pp. 193–207, https://doi.org/10.1080/13602380500532313.

113. Rajnarayan Chandavarkar, *The Origins of Industrial Capitalism in India: Business Strategies and the Working Classes in Bombay, 1900–1940*, Cambridge, Cambridge University Press, 1994, pp. 200–211.

Chapter 6

1. Sonja Wolf, *Mano Dura: The Politics of Gang Control in El Salvador*, Austin, University of Texas Press, 2017.

2. The term most commonly used by the police to refer to gang members is *ratas* (literally, "rats").

3. Bryan Avelar and Juan Martínez d'Aubuisson, "En la intimidad del escuadrón de la muerte de la policía," *Factum*, August 22, 2017, https://www.revistafactum.com/en-la-intimidad-del-escuadron-de-la-muerte-de-la-policia/.

4. This is a quotation from the Book of Matthew (7:19), frequently mentioned by Latin American vigilantes to justify their purificatory practices (see also Chapter 4).

NOTES TO CHAPTER 6   195

5. Avelar and d'Aubuisson, "En la intimidad del escuadrón de la muerte de la policía."

6. Avelar and d'Aubuisson, "En la intimidad del escuadrón de la muerte de la policía."

7. "In Some Countries, Killer Cops Are Celebrated," *Economist*, March 8, 2018.

8. The *shalwar kameez* is a unisex garment traditionally worn in Afghanistan and Pakistan. It consists of loose trousers and a long tunic, often in a pale color.

9. Paul Chevigny, *Edge of the Knife: Police Violence in the Americas*, New York, New Press, 1995, p. 19.

10. Julia Eckert, "The *Trimurti* of the State: State Violence and the Promises of Order and Destruction," Working Paper no. 80, Max Planck Institute for Social Anthropology, Halle, Germany, 2005, p. 183.

11. Jean-Paul Brodeur, *The Policing Web*, Oxford, Oxford University Press, 2010, p. 6.

12. Fabien Jobard and Jacques de Maillard, *Sociologie de la police*, Paris, Armand Colin, 2015, pp. 142–143.

13. Fabien Jobard, "Comprendre l'habilitation à l'usage de la force policière," *Déviance et Société*, vol. 25, no. 3, 2001, p. 339, https://doi.org/10.3917/ds.253.0325.

14. Carl Klockars, "The Dirty Harry Problem," *Annals of the American Academy of Political and Social Science*, no. 452, 1980, pp. 33–47, https://doi.org/10.1177/000271628045200104.

15. For Clint Eastwood, the members of the death squad represent the transgressions of the Brazilian punishers in uniform, who he says lost their original "nobility" by claiming to replace the justice system to establish a "dictatorship." Kevin Avery (ed.), *Conversations with Clint: Paul Nelson's Lost Interviews with Clint Eastwood, 1979–1983*, London, Continuum, 2011, p. 91.

16. On the ideological effects of the series and the construction of its central character as an icon of the conservative revolution, see Joe Street, *Dirty Harry's America: Clint Eastwood, Harry Callahan and the Conservative Backlash*, Gainesville, University Press of Florida, 2016.

17. Didier Fassin, *Punir: Une passion contemporaine*, Paris, Seuil, 2017, p. 50.

18. Jerome Skolnick, *Justice Without Trial: Law Enforcement in Democratic Society*, New York, John Wiley & Sons, 1966.

19. Tom Bowden, *Beyond the Limits of the Law: A Comparative Study of the Police in Crisis Politics*, Harmondsworth, UK, Penguin Books, 1978; Kanti C. Kotecha and James L. Walker, "Police Vigilantes," *Society*, vol. 13, March–April 1976, pp. 48–52, https://doi.org/10.1007/BF02693881.

20. Kotecha and Walker, "Police Vigilantes," p. 48.

21. Sarah-Jane Cooper-Knock and Olly Owen, "Between Vigilantism and Bureaucracy: Improving Our Understanding of Police Work in Nigeria and South Africa," *Theoretical Criminology*, vol. 19, no. 3, 2014, pp. 355–375, https://doi.org/10.1177/1362480614557306.

22. Bowden, *Beyond the Limits of the Law*, p. 94.

23. Julian Roberts, Loretta J. Stalans, David Indermaur, and Mike Hough, *Penal Populism and Public Opinion: Lessons from Five Countries*, Oxford, Oxford University Press, 2003; John Pratt, *Penal Populism*, London, Routledge, 2007.

196 NOTES TO CHAPTER 6

24. Ernest J. Hopkins, *Our Lawless Police: A Study of the Unlawful Enforcement of the Law*, New York, Viking, 1931, p. 17.

25. Dominique Monjardet, "À la recherche du travail policier," *Sociologie du travail*, vol. 27, no. 4, 1985, pp. 391–407, https://doi.org/10.3406/sotra.1985.2015.

26. This quotation is taken from the Supreme Court judgment, delivered by Chief Justice Warren, in the case *Spano v. New York*, 360 U.S. 315 (1959), https://supreme.justia.com/cases/federal/us/360/315/. The case concerned the violation of a young man's rights while he was under arrest for homicide. And see G. Edward White, *Earl Warren: A Public Life*, New York, Oxford University Press, 1982, p. 267.

27. Chevigny, *Edge of the Knife*, p. 49.

28. Egon Bittner, "Florence Nightingale in Pursuit of Willie Sutton: A Theory of the Police," in *The Potential for Reform of Criminal Justice*, vol. 3, ed. Herbert Jacob, Sage Criminal Justice System Annuals, Beverly Hills, CA, Sage, 1974, p. 35.

29. Jobard, "Comprendre l'habilitation à l'usage de la force policière," p. 336.

30. A. A. Khan, *Surrender*, Mumbai, Yogi Impressions, 2004, p. 72.

31. Khan, p. 74.

32. Alex Perry, "Urban Cowboys," *Time*, January 6, 2003.

33. Jyoti Belur, *Permission to Shoot? Police Use of Deadly Force in Democracies*, London, Springer, 2010, p. v.

34. A first-information report is a statement based on a complaint that enables a preliminary investigation to be opened. This procedure applies only to criminal offenses (cognizable offenses) and allows the police to make arrests without authorization and to open an investigation without gaining approval from a judge. Cover stories are the lies told by the police to magistrates, their superiors, and their colleagues to protect themselves against criminal, administrative, or symbolic sanctions. Jennifer Hunt and Peter K. Manning, "The Social Context of Police Lying," *Symbolic Interaction*, vol. 14, no. 1, 1991, p. 53, https://doi.org/10.1525/si.1991.14.1.51.

35. "Mumbai Police Pats Itself as Encounter Deaths Double," *Indian Express*, December 29, 2001, cited in Belur, *Permission to Shoot?*, p. v.

36. Mohan Guruswamy, "Close Encounters," *Outlook*, June 8, 2007.

37. Sandeep Unnithan and Kiran Tare, "Mumbai's Encounter Specialists Fight a Losing Battle for Redemption," *India Today*, March 2, 2012.

38. Eckert, "The *Trimurti* of the State," p. 186.

39. This legal rule allows the police to use force, including lethal force, against a fleeing criminal.

40. The construction of uncontrollable criminality by the media and politicians relates to events in Mumbai affecting the middle class (shopkeepers) and the economic and cultural elites (including business people, real estate agents, and film stars).

41. Eckert, "The *Trimurti* of the State," p. 187.

42. Michel Foucault, *Abnormal: Lectures at the Collège de France 1974–1975*, trans. Graham Burchell, London, Verso, 2003, p. 325.

43. Rachel Wahl, *Just Violence: Torture and Human Rights in the Eyes of the Police*, Stanford, CA, Stanford University Press, 2017.

44. Beatrice Jauregui, "Law and Order: Police Encounter Killings and Routinized Political Violence," in Isabelle Clark-Decès (ed.), *A Companion to the Anthropology of India*, Oxford, Blackwell, 2011, p. 381.

NOTES TO CHAPTER 6   197

45. Vanessa Codaccioni, *La Légitime Défense: Homicides sécuritaires, crimes racistes et violences policières*, Paris, CNRS Éditions, 2018, pp. 20–21.

46. Omar Shahid Hamid, *The Prisoner*, New York, Arcade Publishing, 2015; Y. P. Singh, *Carnage by Angels*, Mumbai, Shree Book Centre, 2011.

47. In December 2019 the killing of four presumed rapists and murderers by the Telangana police, in the place where their crime was committed, gave rise to many demonstrations of support from politicians and the entertainment world. Taran Deol, "Politicians, Actors Celebrate 'Encounter' of 4 Accused in Hyderabad Vet Rape-Murder," *Print*, December 6, 2019.

48. Belur, *Permission to Shoot?*; Jauregui, "Just War."

49. Belur, *Permission to Shoot?*, pp. 80–83.

50. Dominique Linhard and Cédric Moreau de Bellaing, "Légitime violence? Enquêtes sur la réalité de l'État démocratique," *Revue française de science politique*, vol. 55, no. 2, 2005, p. 297, https://doi.org/10.3917/rfsp.552.0269.

51. For example, in 2015 a Karachi coroner raised an alarm concerning an explosion of extrajudicial violence by the local police. See Noman Ahmed, "Murder He Wrote: Medico-Legal Officer Blows the Whistle on Police Encounters," *Express Tribune*, February 22, 2015.

52. Beatrice Jauregui, *Provisional Authority: Police, Order and Security in India*, Chicago, Chicago University Press, 2016, p. 89.

53. Robert Reiner, "Media Made Criminality: The Representation of Crime in the Mass Media," in Mike Maguire, Rod Morgan, and Robert Reiner (eds.), *The Oxford Handbook of Criminology* (3rd ed.), Oxford, Oxford University Press, 2002, p. 323.

54. Jauregui, "Just War," pp. 48, 49. This epic aspect is, however, far from the only type of representation of the encounter specialist in Indian popular cinema. Some films use "disenchanted realism" to portray punishers in uniform as tragic figures embroiled in urban chaos. See Anustup Basu, "Encounters in the City: Cops, Criminals, and Human Rights in Hindi Films," *Journal of Human Rights*, vol. 9, no. 2, 2010, pp. 175–190, https://doi.org/10.1080/14754831003761688.

55. Jauregui, "Just War," p. 48.

56. The Bhagavad Gita is one section of the epic of the Mahabharata. It describes the dialogue between Arjuna the archer and the god Krishna, who persuades Arjuna to do battle with his cousins in the name of the dharma.

57. Bhagavad Gita, chap. 4, verses 7 and 8, https://bhagavadgita.io/chapter/4/verse/7/ and https://bhagavadgita.io/chapter/4/verse/8/.

58. Since independence, Muslims have been deliberately kept out of the intelligence services and elite police units. They are also underrepresented in the elite corps of the Indian Police Service. See Omar Khalidi, *Khaki and the Ethnic Violence in India*, Delhi, Three Essays Collective, 2003, chap. 2.

59. Khan, *Surrender*, p. 73.

60. Cited in Kate Lamb, "Philippines Secret Death Squads: Officer Claims Police Teams behind Wave of Killings," *Guardian*, October 4, 2016.

61. Farzand Ahmed and Dilip Bobb, "Bhagalpur Blindings Represents One of the Darkest Chapters in India's History," *India Today*, December 31, 1980. *Thuggee* historically refers to the Thugs, or groups of stranglers, who attacked travelers and were said to sacrifice their victims to the goddess Kali. On the moral panic engendered by

198 NOTES TO CHAPTER 6

this supposed brotherhood of murderers in the nineteenth century, see Martine van Woerkens, *Le Voyageur étranglé: L'Inde et les Thugs, le colonialisme et l'imaginaire*, Paris, Albin Michel, 1995.

62. Srinath Jagannathan, Rajnish Rai, and Christophe Jaffrelot, "Fear and Violence as Organizational Strategies: The Possibility of a Derridean Lens to Analyze Extra-Judicial Police Violence," *Journal of Business Ethics*, October 10, 2020, https://doi.org/10.1007/s10551-020-04655-6.

63. Subhashini Ali, "Yogi Adityanath's War on Crime Excluded Powerful, Connected Criminals like Vikas Dubey," *The Wire*, July 9, 2020, https://thewire.in/government/yogi-adityanath-vikas-dubey-war-on-crime.

64. "Saffronization" refers to the Hindu domination of the state apparatus and society, in reference to the color saffron, a symbol of purity in Hinduism.

65. Christophe Jaffrelot, *Modi's India*: Hindu Nationalism and the Rise of Ethnic Democracy, trans. Cynthia Schoch, Princeton, NJ, Princeton University Press, 2021, p. 229.

66. Jaffrelot, *Modi's India*, chap. 10.

67. In the language of the Hindu nationalists in power in 2023, *urban Naxals* refers to the (supposed) support for Maoist rebels in left-wing circles.

68. Jaffrelot, *Modi's India*, p. 403

69. *Antinational* is a pejorative used by the Narendra Modi government to discredit left-wing opponents by suggesting their involvement in seditious activities.

70. Cited by Élise Massicard, "Quand les civils maintiennent l'ordre: Configurations vigilantes à Istanbul," *Revue des mondes musulmans et de la Méditerranée*, no. 145, 2019, https://doi.org/10.4000/remmm.10212.

71. Cited in David T. Johnson and John Fernquest, "Governing through Killing: The War on Drugs in the Philippines," *Asian Journal of Law and Society*, vol. 5, no. 2, 2018, p. 359, https://doi.org/10.1017/als.2018.12.

72. Jonathan Wheatley, "Rio de Janeiro's Militias: A Parallel Power in Bolsonaro's Brazil," *Financial Times*, March 25, 2019.

73. Massicard, "Quand les civils maintiennent l'ordre."

74. Mariana Simões, "No Rio de Janeiro a milícia não é um poder paralelo: É o Estado," *Pública*, January 28, 2019, https://apublica.org/2019/01/no-rio-de-janeiro-a-milicia-nao-e-um-poder-paralelo-e-o-estado/.

75. Human Rights Watch, *"You Can Die Any Time": Death Squad Killings in Mindanao*, New York, HRW, 2009, p. 2.

76. Cited in Miriam Grace A. Go, "Duterte Says He 'Maybe' Killed a Man at 17," *Rappler*, December 18, 2016, https://www.rappler.com/newsbreak/inside-track/155843-duterte-maybe-killed-man-age-17/.

77. Cited in Danilo Andres Reyes, "The Spectacle of Violence in Duterte's 'War on Drugs,'" *Journal of Current Southeast Asian Affairs*, vol. 35, no. 3, 2016, p. 127, https://doi.org/10.1177/186810341603500306.

78. Peter Kreuzer, "'If They Resist, Kill Them All': Police Vigilantism in the Philippines," Peace Research Institute Frankfurt Report no. 142, 2016.

79. Rambo Talabong, "Unreal Numbers: Around 2,000 Drug War Deaths Missing in Duterte Gov't Tally," *Rappler*, September 11, 2020, https://www.rappler.com/nation/missing-drug-war-deaths-duterte-government-tally/.

NOTES TO CHAPTER 6 199

80. Kreuzer, "If They Resist, Kill Them All," p. 11.

81. Jayson S. Lamcheck, "A Mandate for Mass Killings? Public Support for Duterte's War on Drugs," in Nicole Curato (ed.), *A Duterte Reader: Critical Essays on Rodrigo Duterte's Early Presidency*, Manila, Bughaw, 2017, pp. 212–213.

82. Ronald J. May, *Vigilantes in the Philippines: From Fanatical Cults to Citizens' Organizations*, Manoa, University of Hawaii, 1992.

83. Sheila S. Coronel, "Murder as Enterprise: Police Profiteering in Duterte's War on Drugs," in Curato, *A Duterte Reader*, p. 178.

84. Chris Dalb and Ariane Francisco, "Militias Become Luxury Real Estate Barons in Rio de Janeiro," *Insight Crime*, April 23, 2019.

85. Fahim Zaman and Naziha Syed Ali, "Rao Anwar and the Killing Fields of Karachi," *Dawn*, February 16, 2018, https://www.dawn.com/news/1389761.

86. Lamcheck, "A Mandate for Mass Killings?"

87. Seven months after his election, in which time almost 7,000 people were killed in the war on drugs (including 2,500 killed by police officers on duty), Duterte had an approval rating of 83 percent. Lamcheck, "A Mandate for Mass Killings?," p. 199.

88. Lamcheck, p. 202.

89. The Mehsuds are a Pashtun tribe, concentrated in the Waziristan region (Khyber Pakhtunkhwa Province).

90. Zia ur Rehman, "Footprints: The Crime of Being Mehsud," *Dawn*, January 4, 2015; Mahim Maher, "Encounters Raise Your Rishwat Rate," *Friday Times*, January 22, 2018.

91. According to a former inspector general of police, in the Punjab in the late 1960s hundreds of supposed criminals were killed in fake encounters. According to this retired senior officer the wave of murders by the police was guided by General Muhammad Musa, at that time governor of West Pakistan, in response to rumors of a plot to kill the president, Field Marshal Ayub Khan. M. A. K. Chaudhry, *Of All Those Years*, Lahore, Classic, 2006, pp. 54–55.

92. Laurent Gayer, *Karachi: Ordered Disorder and the Struggle for the City*, London, Hurst, 2014.

93. Moosa Kaleem, "Police 'Fry' Suspects to Fight Crime," *Herald*, September 2016, https://herald.dawn.com/news/1153535.

94. On the controversial figure Chaudhry Aslam Khan, murdered by the Pakistani Taliban in 2014, see Declan Walsh, *The Nine Lives of Pakistan: Dispatches from a Divided Nation*, London, Bloomsbury, 2020, chap. 8.

95. A lawyer gave us these official police files, not publicly available, "Inquiry Report Regarding Alleged Encounter of Naseemullah alias Naqeebullah Mehsood," Sind Police, Karachi, 2018.

96. Rabia Ali, "'Smoking' Gun: After Target Killings, Encounters Come to Haunt Karachi," *Express Tribune*, January 16, 2016.

97. The account of the two young men is attached to the indictment of Rao Anwar (Charge Sheet 77/2018, 13.03.2018, Malir District, Karachi), which a lawyer provided to us.

98. Zaman and Ali, "Rao Anwar and the Killing Fields of Karachi."

99. Fabien Jobard, *Bavures policières? La force publique et ses usages*, Paris, La Découverte, 2002, p. 173.

200 NOTES TO CHAPTER 6 AND CONCLUSION

100. Sind Police, "Inquiry Report Regarding Alleged Encounter of Naseemullah alias Naqeebullah Mehsood," p. 3.

101. On the "instituting power" of scandals, see Damien de Blic and Cyril Lemieux, "The Scandal as Test: Elements of Pragmatic Sociology," *Politix*, no. 71, 2005, pp. 9–38, https://doi.org/10.3917/pox.071.0009.

102. "Cause lawyers" are activist lawyers who use the law as a weapon to achieve political ends. See Austin Sarat and Stuart Scheingold (eds.), *Cause Lawyering and the State in a Global Era*, New York, Oxford University Press, 2001.

103. Interview by Laurent Gayer with the lawyer Faisal Siddiqui, Karachi, July 2018.

104. Jobard and de Maillard, *Sociologie de la police*, p. 141.

105. David Garland, *The Culture of Control: Crime and Social Order in Contemporary Society*, Chicago, University of Chicago Press, 2001, p. 12.

106. S. Hussain Saidi, "'Mr. Controversy' Seeks a Clean Ticket," *Indian Express*, February 5, 1998.

107. "Read DG Vanzara's Letter," *Times of India*, September 3, 2013.

108. Amit Shah was arrested by the Central Bureau of Investigation in July 2010 on suspicion of complicity in the summary execution of a gangster and his wife. Three months later, following a decision by the High Court of Gujarat, he was released on bail. In 2019, Shah became India's minister of home affairs.

109. In 2020 (six years after his retirement), Vanzara was promoted to inspector general of police, with retrospective effect from 2007.

110. Coronel, "Murder as Enterprise," p. 179.

111. Zoha Waseem, *Insecure Guardians: Enforcement, Encounters and Everyday Policing in Postcolonial Karachi*, London, Hurst, 2022, p. 117.

112. Teresa P. R. Caldeira, *City of Walls: Crime, Segregation and Citizenship in São Paolo*, Berkeley, University of California Press, 2001, p. 158. See also Daniel M. Brinks, *The Judicial Response to Police Killings in Latin America: Inequality and the Rule of Law*, Cambridge, Cambridge University Press, 2007.

113. This is what happened in Mumbai after the judgment by the High Court of Maharashtra in the Javed Fawda case. See Belur, *Permission to Shoot?*, p. 42.

Conclusion

1. On rough justice as an enduring exception to the Eliasian thesis on the civilization process, see David Garland, "Penal Excess and Surplus Meaning: Public Torture Lynchings in Twentieth Century America," *Law and Society Review*, vol. 39, no. 4, 2005, pp. 819–826.

2. Lars Buur and Stephen Jensen, "Introduction: Vigilantism and the Policing of Everyday Life in South Africa," *African Studies*, vol. 63, no. 2, 2004, p. 139, https://doi .org/10.1080/00020180412331318724.

3. Charles Tilly, "War Making and State Making as Organized Crime," in Peter B. Evans, Dietrich Rueschemeyer, and Theda Skocpol (eds.), *Bringing the State Back In*, Cambridge, Cambridge University Press, 1985, p. 171.

4. John Pratt, "Emotive and Ostentatious Punishment: Its Decline and Resurgence in Modern Society," *Punishment and Society*, vol. 2, no. 4, 2000, pp. 417–439, https://doi .org/10.1177/14624740022228088.

NOTES TO CONCLUSION 201

5. David Garland, *The Culture of Control: Crime and Social Order in Contemporary Society*, Chicago, University of Chicago Press, 2001.

6. Thomas J. Dimsdale, *The Vigilantes of Montana: Or Popular Justice in the Rocky Mountains*, Butte, McGee Printing, 1950 (1st ed. 1866), p. 102.

7. Charles Tilly, *Coercion, Capital, and European States, AD 990–1992*, Cambridge, UK, Basil Blackwell, 1990, p. 19.

8. Tessa Diphoorn and Erella Grassiani (eds.), *Security Blurs: The Politics of Plural Security Provision*, New York, Routledge, 2019.

9. Veena Das (ed.), *Mirrors of Violence: Communities, Riots and Survivors in South Asia*, Delhi, Oxford University Press, 1990; Paul Brass (ed.), *Riots and Pogroms*, New York, NYU Press, 1996.

10. Subhashini Ali, "Yogi Adityanath's War on Crime Excluded Powerful, Connected Criminals like Vikas Dubey," *The Wire*, July 9, 2020, https://thewire.in/government/yogi-adityanath-vikas-dubey-war-on-crime.

11. Arunabh Saikia, "'Thok Do': Adityanath Government's 'Zero Tolerance' of Crime Leaves a Trail of Victims," *Scroll.in*, September 16, 2021, https://scroll.in/article/1005307/thok-do-adityanath-governments-zero-tolerance-of-crime-leaves-a-trail-of-victims.

12. Laurent Gayer, *Karachi: Ordered Disorder and the Struggle for the City*, London, Hurst, 2014.

13. Nicole Curato, "Politics of Anxiety, Politics of Hope: Penal Populism and Duterte's Rise to Power," *Journal of Current Southeast Asian Affairs*, vol. 35, no. 3, 2016, p. 102, https://doi.org/10.1177/186810341603500305.

14. Steffen Jensen and Anna Braemer Warburg, "Ambiguous Fear in the War on Drugs: A Reconfiguration of Social and Moral Orders in the Philippines," *Journal of Southeast Asian Studies*, vol. 5, nos. 1–2, 2020, p. 6, https://doi.org/10.1017/S0022463420000211.

15. Lian Buan and Jodesz Gavilan, "In Duterte's Drug War, Justice Is 'Nearly Impossible,'" *Rappler*, July 15, 2021, https://www.rappler.com/newsbreak/in-depth/duterte-drug-war-killings-justice-nearly-impossible-2021/.

16. Steffen Jensen and Karl Hapal, "Police Violence and Corruption in the Philippines: Violent Exchange and the War on Drugs," *Journal of Current Southeast Asian Affairs*, vol. 37, no. 2, 2018, pp. 39–62, https://doi.org/10.1177/186810341803700202.

17. Jonathan Simon, *Governing through Crime: How the War on Crime Transformed American Democracy and Created a Culture of Fear*, New York, Oxford University Press, 2007, p. 34.

18. Quoted in "'Tirer à balles réelles': Zemmour conseille à la police d'appliquer la loi du talion," *Valeurs actuelles*, January 9, 2020, p. 66.

19. @ScpnCommissaire, Twitter, November 1, 2021.

20. Dolores Janiewski and Chad Pearson, "The Right-Wing Violence Trump Has Encouraged Has Deep Roots in American History," *Jacobin*, November 3, 2020, https://jacobin.com/2020/11/violence-trump-blm-weatherford-kenosha.

21. Kathleen Ronayne and Michael Kunzelman, "Trump to Far-Right Extremists: 'Stand Back and Stand By,'" *AP News*, September 30, 2020, https://apnews.com/article/election-2020-joe-biden-race-and-ethnicity-donald-trump-chris-wallace-0b32339da25fbc9e8b7c7c7066a1dbof.

202 NOTES TO CONCLUSION

22. Rodrigo Duterte cannot run for office again, and all the candidates in the 2022 presidential election agreed to put an end to the almost-routine extrajudicial killings under the Duterte administration. Jodesz Gavilan, "Presidential Bets Call for Due Process, End to Killings in Drug War," *Rappler*, April 3, 2022, https://www.rappler .com/nation/elections/presidential-candidates-responses-war-on-drugs-comelec-pre sidential-debate-2022/.

SELECTED BIBLIOGRAPHY

We omit in this bibliography nonacademic sources, which can be found in the endnotes.

Abou Moumouni, Issifou. "L'offre informelle de la sécurité publique au Bénin: l'instrumentalisation des groupes d'autodéfense par l'État." *Déviance et Société* 41, no. 1 (2017): 91–119.

Abrahams, Ray. "Some Thoughts on Vigilantism." In Pratten and Sen, *Global Vigilantes*.

——. *Vigilant Citizens: Vigilantism and the State*. Malden: Polity Press, 1998.

Aguilera Peña, Mario. "Guerra, insurgencia y prácticas judiciales." In *Violencia y estrategias colectivas en la región andina*, edited by Eric Lair and Gonzalo Sanchez Comez, 557–596. Bogotá: Editorial Norma, 2004.

——. *Contrapoder y justicia guerrillera: Fragmentación política y orden insurgente en Colombia (1952–2003)*. Bogotá: IEPRI-Universidad Nacional de Colombia, 2014.

Aldrin, Philippe. *Sociologie politique des rumeurs*. Paris: PUF, 2005.

Ali, Kamran Asdar. "The Strength of the Street Meets the Strength of the State: The 1972 Labor Struggle in Karachi." *International Journal of Middle East Studies* 37, no. 1 (2005): 83–107. http://www.jstor.org/stable/3880083.

Angeli, Claude, and Nicolas Brimo. *Une milice patronale: Peugeot*. Paris: Maspero, 1975.

Antonov, Rostislav. *Primorskie partizany* [The Primorsky Partisans]. Moscow: Fond ROD, 2011.

Apel, Dora. "Lynching Photographs and the Politics of Public Shaming." In Apel and Smith, *Lynching Photographs*.

Apel, Dora, and Shawn Michelle Smith. *Lynching Photographs*. Berkeley: University of California Press, 2007.

204 SELECTED BIBLIOGRAPHY

Aretxaga, Begoña. "Playing Terrorist: Ghastly Plots and the Ghostly State." *Journal of Spanish Cultural Studies* 1, no. 1 (2000): 43–58. https://doi.org/10.1080/713683435.

Athané, François, and Michel Kail. "Sartre au péril du lynchage: L'engagement et le droit." *Lignes*, no. 48 (2015): 179–221. https://doi.org/10.3917/lignes.048.0179.

Avery, Kevin, ed. *Conversations with Clint: Paul Nelson's Lost Interviews with Clint Eastwood, 1979–1983*. London: Continuum, 2011.

Baar, Ronald J., and R. A. Mollan. "The Orthopaedic Consequences of Civil Disturbance in Northern Ireland." *Journal of Bone and Joint Surgery* 71, no. 5 (November 1989): 739–744.

Baczko, Adam. "Juger en situation de guerre civile: Les cours de justice Taleban en Afghanistan." *Politix*, no. 104 (2013): 25–46. https://doi.org/10.3917/pox.104.0025.

Banaji, Shakuntala, and Ram Bhat. *WhatsApp Vigilantes: An Exploration of Citizen Reception and Circulation of WhatsApp Misinformation Linked to Mob Violence in India*. London: London School of Economics, 2019.

Basu, Anustup. "Encounters in the City: Cops, Criminals, and Human Rights in Hindi Films." *Journal of Human Rights* 9, no. 2 (2010): 175–190. https://doi.org/10.1080/14754831003761688.

Bateson, Regina. "The Politics of Vigilantism." *Comparative Political Studies* 54, no 6 (May 2021), pp. 923-955. https://doi.org/10.1177/0010414020957692.

Becker, Howard. *Outsiders: Studies in the Sociology of Deviance*. New York: Free Press of Glencoe, 1963.

Belur, Jyoti. *Permission to Shoot? Police Use of Deadly Force in Democracies*. London: Springer, 2010.

Bérard, Jean. "Tordre ou briser le bâton de la justice? Les mouvements de l'après-68 et les illégalismes des dominants, entre justice populaire et refus de la pénalité (1968–1972)." *Champ pénal* (2013). https://doi.org/10.4000/champpenal.8418.

Berg, Manfred, and Simon Wendt, eds. *Globalizing Lynching History: Vigilantism and Extralegal Punishment from an International Perspective*. New York: Palgrave Macmillan, 2011.

——. "Introduction: Lynching from an International Perspective." In Berg and Wendt, *Globalizing Lynching History*, pp. 1–18.

Berlière, Jean-Marc. "Images de la police: Deux siècles de fantasme?" *Criminocorpus*, January 2009. https://doi.org/10.4000/criminocorpus.206.

Bertelsen, Bjørn Enge. "Multiple Sovereignties and Summary Justice in Mozambique: A Critique of Some Legal Anthropological Terms." *Social Analysis* 53, no. 3 (Winter 2009): 123–147. https://doi.org/10.1177/000276426801200107.

Bertrand, Romain. *Indonésie: La démocratie invisible. Violence, magie et politique à Java*. Paris: Karthala, 2002.

Best, Steven, and Anthony J. Nocella II. *Terrorists or Freedom Fighters? Reflections on the Liberation of Animals*. New York: Lantern Books, 2004.

Binford, Leigh, and Nancy Churchill. "Lynching and States of Fear in Urban Mexico." *Anthropologica* 51, no. 2 (2009): 301–312. https://doi.org/10.2307/25605293.

Bittner, Egon. "Florence Nightingale in Pursuit of Willie Sutton: A Theory of the Police." In *The Potential for Reform of Criminal Justice*, vol. 3, edited by Herbert Jacob, 233–268. Beverly Hills, CA: Sage, 1974.

Bjørgo, Tore, and Miroslav Mareš, eds. *Vigilantism against Migrants and Minorities.* London: Routledge, 2019.

Blom Hansen, Thomas. "Sovereigns beyond the State: On Legality and Authority in Urban India." In *Sovereign Bodies: Citizens, Migrants and States in the Postcolonial World,* edited by Thomas Blom Hansen and Finn Stepputat, 169–191. Princeton, NJ: Princeton University Press, 2005.

Bloom, Joshua, and Waldo E. Martin Jr. *Black against Empire: The History and Politics of the Black Panther Party.* Berkeley: University of California Press, 2013.

Bock, Mary Angela. "Film the Police! Cop-Watching and Its Embodied Narratives." *Journal of Communication* 66, no. 1 (2016): 13–34. https://doi.org/10.1111/jcom.12204.

Bonhomme, Julien. *The Sex Thieves: The Anthropology of a Rumor.* Translated by Dominic Horsfall. Chicago: HAU Books, 2016.

Bourdieu, Pierre. *On the State: Lectures at the Collège de France, 1989–1992.* Translated by David Fernbach. London: Polity Press, 2014.

Bowden, Tom. *Beyond the Limits of the Law: A Comparative Study of the Police in Crisis Politics.* Harmondsworth, UK: Penguin Books, 1978.

Brass, Paul, ed. *Riots and Pogroms.* New York, NYU Press, 1996.

Brinks, Daniel M. *The Judicial Response to Police Killings in Latin America: Inequality and the Rule of Law.* Cambridge: Cambridge University Press, 2007.

Brodeur, Jean-Paul. *The Policing Web.* Oxford: Oxford University Press, 2010.

Brossat, Alain. *Le Corps de l'ennemi: Hyperviolence et démocratie.* Paris: La Fabrique, 1998.

Brown, Richard Maxwell. *Strain of Violence: Historical Studies of American Violence and Vigilantism.* New York: Oxford University Press, 1975.

Brundage, William Fitzhugh. *Lynching in the New South: Georgia and Virginia, 1880–1930.* Urbana: University of Illinois Press, 1993.

Buur, Lars, and Stephen Jensen. "Introduction: Vigilantism and the Policing of Everyday Life in South Africa." *African Studies* 63, no. 2 (2004): 139–152. https://doi.org/10.1080/00020180412331318724.

Caldeira, Teresa P. R. *City of Walls: Crime, Segregation and Citizenship in São Paolo.* Berkeley: University of California Press, 2001.

Caponi, Sandra. "Hygiénisme et réorganisation urbaine au Brésil et en Argentine." *Cahiers du centre de recherches historiques,* no. 33 (2004). https://doi.org/10.4000/ccrh.259.

Carnovale, Vera. "Las ejecuciones selectivas del Ejército Revolucionario del Pueblo: Nociones implicadas en el ejercicio de la justicia revolucionaria." *Caleidoscopio,* no. 21 (2007): 7–42. https://doi.org/10.33064/21crscsh363.

Carrié, Fabien. "Antispécisme." *Encyclopædia Universalis.* Paris: Encyclopædia Universalis, 2015, pp. 179–181.

Carrié, Fabien, and Christophe Traïni, eds. *S'engager pour les animaux.* Paris: La Vie des idées-PUF, 2019.

Carrigan, William D., and Christopher Waldrep, eds. *Swift to Wrath: Lynching in Global Historical Perspective.* Charlottesville: University of Virginia Press, 2013.

Caughey, John. "Their Majesties the Mob." *Pacific Historical Review* 26, no. 3 (1957): 217–234. https://doi.org/10.2307/3636213.

SELECTED BIBLIOGRAPHY

Centro Nacional de Memoria Histórica. *Aniquilar la diferencia: Lesbianas, gays, bisexuales y transgeneristas en el marco del conflict armado colombiano.* Bogotá: Centro Nacional de Memoria Histórica, 2015.

———. *Limpieza social: Una violencia mal nombrada.* Bogotá: CNMH-EIPRI, 2015.

Chacón, Justin Akers, and Mike Davis. *No One Is Illegal: Fighting Violence and State Repression on the U.S.-Mexico Border.* Chicago: Haymarket Books, 2006.

Chamayou, Grégoire. *Manhunts: A Philosophical History.* Translated by Steven Rendall. Princeton, NJ: Princeton University Press, 2012.

Chandavarkar, Rajnarayan. *Imperial Power and Popular Politics: Class, Resistance and the State in India.* Cambridge: Cambridge University Press, 1998.

———. *The Origins of Industrial Capitalism in India: Business Strategies and the Working Classes in Bombay, 1900–1940.* Cambridge: Cambridge University Press, 1994.

Chang, Lennon Y. C., and Andy K. H. Leung. "An Introduction to Cyber Crowdsourcing (Human Flesh Search) in the Greater China Region." In *Cybercrime Risks and Responses: Eastern and Western Perspectives,* edited by Russell G. Smith, Ray Cheung, and Laurie Lau, 240–252. New York: Palgrave Macmillan, 2015.

Chaudhry, M. A. K. *Of All Those Years.* Lahore: Classic, 2006.

Cherstich, Igor, Martin Holbraad, and Nico Tassi. *Anthropologies of Revolution: Forging Time, People and Worlds.* Oakland: University of California Press, 2020.

Chevigny, Paul. *Edge of the Knife: Police Violence in the Americas.* New York: New Press, 1995.

Chowdhury, Nusrat Sabina. *Paradoxes of the Popular: Crowd Politics in Bangladesh.* Stanford, CA: Stanford University Press, 2019.

Chułek, Magdalena. "Mob Justice and Everyday Life: The Case of Nairobi's Kibera and Korogocho Slums." *African Studies* 78, no. 3 (2019): 385–402. https://doi.org/10.108 0/00020184.2018.1519332.

Civico, Aldo. *The Para-State: An Ethnography of Colombia's Death Squads.* Berkeley: University of California Press, 2015.

Codaccioni, Vanessa. "Justice populaire et mimétisme judiciaire: Les maoïstes dans et hors la Cour de sûreté de l'État." *Droit et société,* no. 89 (2015): 17–33. https://doi .org/10.3917/drs.089.0017.

———. *La Légitime Défense: Homicides sécuritaires, crimes racistes et violences policières.* Paris: CNRS Éditions, 2018.

Cohen, Michael. "The Ku Klux Government": Vigilantism, Lynching, and the Repression of the IWW." *Journal for the Study of Radicalism* 1, no 1 (Spring 2007): 31–56. https://doi.org/10.1080/00020184.2018.1519332.

Colas, Dominique. *Le Léninisme.* Paris: PUF, 1998.

Coleman, Gabriella. *Hacker, Hoaxer, Whistleblower, Spy: The Many Faces of Anonymous.* London: Verso, 2014.

Collins, Randall. *Violence: A Micro-Sociological Theory.* Princeton, NJ: Princeton University Press, 2008.

Comaroff, Jean, and John L. Comaroff. *The Truth about Crime: Sovereignty, Knowledge, Social Order.* Chicago: University of Chicago Press, 2016.

Comaroff, John, and Jean Comaroff. "Policing Culture, Cultural Policing: Law and Social Order in Post-colonial Africa." *Law and Social Inquiry* 29, no. 3 (2004): 513–545. https://doi.org/10.1111/j.1747-4469.2004.tb00999.x.

Cooper-Knock, Sarah-Jane. "Policing in Intimate Crowds: Moving Beyond 'The Mob' in South Africa," *African Affairs* 113, no. 453 (2014): 563–582.

Cooper-Knock, Sarah-Jane, and Olly Owen. "Between Vigilantism and Bureaucracy: Improving Our Understanding of Police Work in Nigeria and South Africa." *Theoretical Criminology* 19, no. 3 (2014): 355–375. https://doi.org/10.1177/1362480614557306.

Corbin, Alain. *Le Village des "Cannibales."* Paris: Flammarion, 2009.

Coronel, Sheila S. "Murder as Enterprise: Police Profiteering in Duterte's War on Drugs." In Curato, *A Duterte Reader*, 167–198.

Corporación Colectivo de Abogados. "José Alvear Restrepo." In *José Alvear Restrepo: Una gesta silenciada*. Bogotá: Rodríguez Quito Editores, 2000.

Curato, Nicole. "Politics of Anxiety, Politics of Hope: Penal Populism and Duterte's Rise to Power." *Journal of Current Southeast Asian Affairs* 35, no. 3 (2016): 91–109. https://doi.org/10.1177/186810341603500305.

———, ed. *A Duterte Reader: Critical Essays on Rodrigo Duterte's Early Presidency*. Manila: Bughaw, 2017.

Da Cunha Dupuy, Romane, and Tanguy Quidelleur. "Self-Defence Movements in Burkina Faso: Diffusion and Structuration of Koglweogo Groups." *Noria*, November 2018. https://noria-research.com/self-defence-movements-in-burkina-faso-diffusion-and-structuration-of-koglweogo-groups/

Das, Veena, ed. *Mirrors of Violence: Communities, Riots and Survivors in South Asia*. Delhi: Oxford University Press, 1990.

de Blic, Damien, and Cyril Lemieux. "The Scandal as Test: Elements of Pragmatic Sociology." *Politix*, no. 71 (2005): 9–38. https://doi.org/10.3917/pox.071.0009.

de Castro Trindade, Etelvina Maria. "Modèles et emprunts: L'hygiénisme au Brésil (fin XIXᵉ–début XXᵉ siècle)." In *Les Hygiénistes: Enjeux, modèles et pratiques*, edited by Patrice Bourdelais, 267–296. Paris: Belin, 2001.

de Certeau, Michel. *The Possession at Loudun*. Translated by Michael B. Smith. Chicago, University of Chicago Press, 2000.

Deflem, Mathieu. "Popular Culture and Social Control: The Moral Panic on Music Labeling." *American Journal of Criminal Justice* 45, no. 1 (2020): 2–24. https://doi.org/10.1007/s12103-019-09495-3.

de Gracia, Guillaume. *De sueur et de sang: Mouvements sociaux, résistances populaires et lutte armée dans l'Argentine de Perón*. Paris: Syllepse, 2016.

Deluermoz, Quentin. *Policiers dans la ville: La construction d'un ordre public à Paris (1854–1914)*. Paris: Publications de la Sorbonne, 2012.

de Sousa Santos, Boaventura. "Law: A Map of Misreading. Toward a Postmodern Conception of Law." *Journal of Law and Society* 14, no. 3 (1987): 279–302. https://doi.org/10.2307/1410186.

Dezalay, Yves. "Les courtiers de l'international: Héritiers cosmopolites, mercenaires de l'impérialisme et missionnaires de l'universel." *Actes de la recherche en sciences sociales*, nos. 151–152 (2004): 4–35. https://doi.org/10.3917/arss.151.0004.

Dimenstein, Gilberto. *Brésil, la guerre des enfants*. Paris: Fayard, 1991.

Dimsdale, Thomas J. *The Vigilantes of Montana: Or Popular Justice in the Rocky Mountains*. Butte: McGee Printing, 1950.

Diphoorn, Tessa, and Erella Grassiani, eds. *Security Blurs: The Politics of Plural Security Provision*. New York: Routledge, 2019.

Dudley, Stephen. *Walking Ghosts: Murder and Guerrilla Politics in Colombia*. New York: Routledge, 2005.

Eckert, Julia. "The *Trimurti* of the State: State Violence and the Promises of Order and Destruction." Working Paper no. 80. Berlin: Max Planck Institute for Social Anthropology, Halle, Germany, 2005.

Espinosa Menéndez, Nicolás. "Del control (los castigos insurgentes) a la autonomía (las sanciones comunitarias): Elementos para la transición de la Justicia local en La Sierra de La Macarena." *Agora USB* 16, no. 2 (2016): 407–426. http://www.scielo.org.co/scielo.php?script=sci_arttext&pid=S1657-80312016000200004&lng=en&tlng=es.

———. "La justicia guerrillera en Colombia: Elementos de análisis para los retos de la transición política en una zona de control insurgente (el caso del piedemonte amazónico)." *Estudios Latinoamericanos*, no. 37 (2016): 87–112. https://doi.org/10.22201/cela.24484946e.2016.37.54724.

Ethington, Philip J. *The Public City: The Political Construction of Urban Life in San Francisco, 1850–1900*. Berkeley: University of California Press, 2001.

Falkovsky, Ilya, and Aleksandr Litoy. *Grazhdanskaya voina uzhe nachalas'* [Civil war has already started]. Moscow: Algoritm, 2013.

Fassin, Didier. *Punir: Une passion contemporaine*. Paris: Seuil, 2017.

Favarel-Garrigues, Gilles. "Digital Vigilantism and Anti-paedophile Activism in Russia: Between Civic Involvement in Law Enforcement, Moral Policing and Business Venture." *Global Crime* 21, nos. 3–4 (2020): 306–326. https://doi.org/10.1080/17440572.2019.1676738.

———. "La police russe en procès." *Le Courrier des pays de l'Est*, no. 6 (2005): 66–74.

———. "Vigilante Shows' and Law Enforcement in Russia." *Europe-Asia Studies* 73, no.1 (2021): 221–242. https://doi.org/10.1080/09668136.2020.1862061.

———. "You're a Disgrace to the Uniform!" Lev Protiv's Challenge to the Police in Moscow Streets and on YouTube." *Post-Soviet Affairs* 38, no. 6 (2022): 497–512. https://doi.org/10.1080/1060586X.2022.2093030.

Favarel-Garrigues, Gilles, and Laurent Gayer, eds. "Justiciers hors-la-loi." *Politix*, no. 115 (2016): 9–156.

———. "Violer la loi pour maintenir l'ordre: Le vigilantisme en débat." *Politix*, no. 115 (2016): 9–34. https://doi.org/10.3917/pox.115.0007.

Favarel-Garrigues, Gilles, Samuel Tanner, and Daniel Trottier, eds. "Watchful Citizen: Policing from Below and Digital Vigilantism." Special issue, *Global Crime* 21, nos. 3–4 (2020): 189–331. https://doi.org/10.1080/17440572.2020.1750789.

Febvre, Lucien. "Histoire des sentiments: La Terreur." *Annales* 6, no. 4 (1951): 520–523. https://doi.org/10.3406/ahess.1951.2008.

Fleisher, Michael L. "Sungusungu: State-Sponsored Village Vigilante Groups among the Kuria of Tanzania." *Africa: Journal of the International African Institute* 70, no. 2 (2000): 209–228. https://doi.org/10.3366/afr.2000.70.2.209.

Flores Acuña, Tathiana. *The United Nations Mission in El Salvador: A Humanitarian Law Perspective*. The Hague: Kluwer Law International, 1995.

Foucault, Michel. *Abnormal: Lectures at the Collège de France 1974–1975*. Translated by Graham Burchell. London: Verso, 2003.

———. *Discipline and Punish: Birth of the Prison.* Translated by Alan Sheridan. New York: Vintage, 1995.

———. "On Popular Justice: A Discussion with Maoists." In *Power/Knowledge: Selected Interviews and Other Writings, 1972–1977,* edited by Colin Gordon, 1–36. New York: Pantheon Books, 1980.

———. *Power/Knowledge: Selected Interviews and Other Writings, 1972–1977.* New York: Pantheon, 1980.

———. *"Society Must Be Defended:" Lectures at the Collège de France 1975–76.* Translated by David Macey. New York: Picador, 2006.

Fourchard, Laurent. *Classify, Exclude, Police: Urban Lives in South Africa and Nigeria.* Hoboken, NJ: Wiley, 2021.

———. "Engagements sécuritaires et féminisation du vigilantisme en Afrique du Sud." *Politix,* no. 115 (2016): 57–78. https://doi.org/10.3917/pox.115.0057.

———. "Le vigilantisme contemporain: Violence et légitimité d'une activité policière bon marché." *Critique internationale,* no. 78 (2018): 169–186. https://doi.org/10.3917/crii.078.0169.

Frank, Stephen. "Popular Justice, Community and Culture among the Russian Peasantry, 1870–1990." *Russian Review* 46, no. 3 (1987): 239–265. https://doi.org/10.2307/130562.

Fumerton, Mario. "Rondas Campesinas in the Peruvian Civil War: Peasant Self-Defence Organisations in Ayacucho." *Bulletin of Latin American Research* 20, no. 4 (2001): 470–497. http://www.jstor.org/stable/3339025.

Gabdulhakov, Rashid. "Heroes or Hooligans? Media Portrayal of StopXam (Stop a Douchebag) Vigilantes in Russia." *Laboratorium: Russian Review of Social Research* 11, no. 3 (2020): 16–45. https://doi.org/10.25285/2078-1938-2019-11-3-16-45.

Gaddis, Elijah. *Gruesome Looking Objects: A New History of Lynching and Everyday Things.* Cambridge: Cambridge University Press, 2022.

Gardenier, Matthijs. *Towards a Vigilant Society: From Citizen Participation to Anti-migrant Vigilantism.* Oxford: Oxford University Press, 2023.

Garland, David. *The Culture of Control: Crime and Social Order in Contemporary Society.* Chicago: University of Chicago Press, 2001.

———. "Penal Excess and Surplus Meaning: Public Torture Lynchings in Twentieth Century America." *Law and Society Review* 39, no. 4 (2005): 819–826. https://doi.org/10.1111/j.1540-5893.2005.00245.x.

Gattinara, Pietro Castelli. "Beyond the Hand of the State: Vigilantism against Migrants and Refugees in France." In Bjørgo and Mareš, *Vigilantism against Migrants and Minorities,* pp. 213–227.

Gayer, Laurent. *Karachi: Ordered Disorder and the Struggle for the City.* London: Hurst, 2014.

———. "Militariser les femmes: Doctrines, pratiques et critiques du féminisme martial en Asie du Sud." In *S'émanciper par les armes? Sur la violence politique des femmes,* edited by Caroline Guibet Lafaye and Alexandra Frénod, 151–175. Paris: Presses de l'Inalco, 2019.

Gazit, Nir. "State-Sponsored Vigilantism: Jewish Settlers' Violence in the Occupied Palestinian Territories." *Sociology* 49, no. 3 (2015): 438–454. https://doi.org/10.1177/0038038514526648.

Gerber, Theodore, and Sarah Mendelson. "Public Experiences of Police Violence and Corruption in Contemporary Russia: A Case of Predatory Policing?" *Law and Society Review* 42, no. 1 (March 2008): 1–44. https://doi.org/10.1111/j.1540-5893 .2008.00333.x.

Gill, Lesley. *A Century of Violence in a Red City: Popular Struggle, Counterinsurgency and Human Rights in Colombia.* Durham, NC: Duke University Press, 2016.

———. "The Parastate in Colombia." *Anthropologica* 51, no. 2 (2009): 313–325.

———. "Right There with You: Coca-Cola, Labor Restructuring and Political Violence in Colombia." *Critique of Anthropology* 27, no. 3 (2007): 235–260. https://doi .org/10.1177/0308275X07080354.

Godicheau, François. *La Guerre d'Espagne: République et révolution en Catalogne (1936–1939).* Paris: Odile Jacob, 2004.

Godoy, Angelina Snodgrass. "When 'Justice' Is Criminal: Lynchings in Contemporary Latin America." *Theory and Society* 33, no. 6 (2004): 621–651. https://doi.org/10.1023/ B:RYSO.0000049192.62380.29.

Goldstein, Daniel M. "Flexible Justice: Neoliberal Violence and 'Self-Help' Security in Bolivia." *Critique of Anthropology* 25, no. 4 (2005): 389–411. https://doi .org/10.1177/0308275X05058656.

———. "'In Our Own Hands': Lynching, Justice, and the Law in Bolivia." *American Ethnologist* 30, no. 1 (2003): 22–43. https://doi.org/10.1525/ae.2003.30.1.22.

———. *The Spectacular City: Violence and Performance in Urban Bolivia.* Durham, NC: Duke University Press, 2005.

Goodwin, Jeff. "The Libidinal Constitution of a High-Risk Social Movement: Affectual Ties and Solidarity in the Huk Rebellion, 1946 to 1954." *American Sociological Review* 62, no. 1 (1997): 53–69. https://doi.org/10.2307/2657452.

Grajales, Jacobo. *Gouverner dans la violence: Le paramilitarisme en Colombie.* Paris, Karthala, 2016.

———. "Quand les juges s'en mêlent: Le rôle de la justice dans la démobilisation des groupes paramilitaires en Colombie." *Critique internationale*, no. 70 (2016): 117–136. https://doi.org/10.3917/crii.070.0117.

Guittet, Emmanuel-Pierre. *Antiterrorisme clandestin, antiterrorisme officiel: Chroniques espagnoles de la coopération en Europe.* Montreal: Athena Editions, 2010.

Gutiérrez, María-Teresa. "Proceso de institucionalización de la higiene: Estado, salubridad e higienismo en Colombia en la primera mitad del siglo XX." *Estudios Socio-Juridicos* 12, no. 1 (2010): 73–97. http://www.scielo.org.co/scielo.php?script=sci_art text&pid=S0124-05792010000100005&lng=en&nrm=iso.

Hale, Grace Elizabeth. "Without Sanctuary: Lynching Photography in America." *Journal of American History* 89, no. 3 (December 2002): 989–994. https://doi .org/10.2307/3092350.

Haller, István. *Cazul Hădăreni.* Tîrgu-Mureş: Editura Pro Europa, 1998.

———. *Lynching Is Not a Crime: Mob Violence against Roma in Post-Ceauşescu Romania.* Budapest: ERRC, 1998.

Hamill, Heather. *The Hoods: Crime and Punishment in Belfast.* Princeton, NJ: Princeton University Press, 2011.

Hamm, Mark S., and Jeff Ferrell. "Rap, Cops, and Crime: Clarifying the 'Cop Killer' Controversy." In *Taking Sides: Clashing Views on Controversial Issues in Crime and Criminology*, edited by Richard C. Monk, 23–28. Guilford, UK: Dushkin-McGraw-Hill, 1998.

Hellweg, Joseph. *Hunting the Ethical State: The Benkadi Movement of Côte d'Ivoire*. Chicago: Chicago University Press, 2011.

Henderson, Ernest F. *Select Historical Documents of the Middle Ages*. London: George Bell & Sons, 1896.

Hobsbawm, Eric. *Bandits*. London: Abacus, 2000.

———. "Revolution Is Puritan." *New Society*, May 22, 1969.

Hopkins, Ernest J. *Our Lawless Police: A Study of the Unlawful Enforcement of the Law*. New York: Viking, 1931.

Houte, Arnaud-Dominique. "Citoyens policiers ? Pratiques et imaginaires civiques de la sécurité publique dans la France du second XIXᵉ siècle." *Revue d'histoire du XIXᵉ siècle*, no. 50 (2015): 99–116. https://doi.org/10.4000/rh19.4825.

Huggins, Martha K. "Modernity and Devolution: The Making of Police Death Squads in Modern Brazil." In *Death Squads in Global Perspective: Murder with Deniability*, edited by Bruce B. Campbell and Arthur D. Brenner, 203–228. New York: Palgrave Macmillan, 2000.

Huggins, Martha K., and Myriam P. Mesquita. "Scapegoating Outsiders: The Murders of Street Youth in Modern Brazil." *Policing and Society* 5, no. 4 (1995): 265–280. https://doi.org/10.1080/10439463.1995.9964730.

Hunt, Jennifer, and Peter K. Manning. "The Social Context of Police Lying." *Symbolic Interaction* 14, no. 1 (1991): 51–70. https://doi.org/10.1525/si.1991.14.1.51.

Idrees, Muhummad. "The Abdur Rehman Story (I) Dial 'M' for Murder." In *The Night Was Not Loveless*. Lahore: Rhotas Books, 1991.

Igarashi, Yoshikuni. "Dead Bodies and Living Guns: The United Red Army and Its Deadly Pursuit of Revolution, 1971–1972." *Japanese Studies* 27, no. 2 (2007): 119–137. https://doi.org/10.1080/10371390701494135.

Irvin, Benjamin H. "Tar, Feathers, and the Enemies of American Liberties, 1768–1776." *New England Quarterly* 76, no. 2 (2003): 197–238. https://doi.org/10.2307/1559903.

Jacobs, Carolien, and Christy Schuetze. "'Justice with Our Own Hands': Lynching, Poverty, Witchcraft, and the State in Mozambique." In Berg and Wendt, *Globalizing Lynching History*.

Jaffrelot, Christophe. *Modi's India: Hindu Nationalism and the Rise of Ethnic Democracy*. Translated by Cynthia Schoch. Princeton, NJ: Princeton University Press, 2021.

Jagannathan, Srinath, Rajnish Rai, and Christophe Jaffrelot. "Fear and Violence as Organizational Strategies: The Possibility of a Derridean Lens to Analyze Extrajudicial Police Violence." *Journal of Business Ethics* 175, no 3 (2020): 465–484. https://doi.org/10.1007/s10551-020-04655-6.

Jane, Emma A. "Online Misogyny and Feminist Digilantism." *Continuum* 30, no. 3 (2016): 284–297. https://doi.org/10.1080/10304312.2016.1166560.

Jauregui, Beatrice. "Law and Order: Police Encounter Killings and Routinized Political Violence." In *A Companion to the Anthropology of India*, edited by Isabelle Clark-Decès, 371–388. Oxford: Blackwell, 2011.

———. *Provisional Authority: Police, Order and Security in India*. Chicago: Chicago University Press, 2016.

———. "Just War: The Metaphysics of Police Vigilantism in India." *Conflict and Society* 1, no. 1 (2015): 41–59. https://doi.org/10.3167/arcs.2015.010105.

Jensen, Steffen, and Karl Hapal. "Police Violence and Corruption in the Philippines: Violent Exchange and the War on Drugs." *Journal of Current Southeast Asian Affairs* 37, no. 2 (2018): 39–62. https://doi.org/10.1177/186810341803700202.

Jensen, Steffen, and Anna Braemer Warburg. "Ambiguous Fear in the War on Drugs: A Reconfiguration of Social and Moral Orders in the Philippines." *Journal of Southeast Asian Studies* 5, nos. 1–2 (2020): 5–24. https://doi.org/10.1017/S0022463423420000211.

Jobard, Fabien. *Bavures policières? La force publique et ses usages*. Paris: La découverte, 2002.

———. "Comprendre l'habilitation à l'usage de la force policière." *Déviance et Société* 25, no. 3 (2001): 325–345. https://doi.org/10.3917/ds.253.0325.

———. "Le gibier de police immuable ou changeant?" *Archives de politique criminelle* 32, no. 1 (2010): 93–105.

Jobard, Fabien, and Jacques de Maillard. *Sociologie de la police*. Paris: Armand Colin, 2015.

Johnson, David T., and John Fernquest. "Governing through Killing: The War on Drugs in the Philippines." *Asian Journal of Law and Society* 5, no. 2 (2018): 359–390. https://doi.org/10.1017/als.2018.12.

Johnston, Les. "What Is Vigilantism?" *British Journal of Criminology* 36, no. 2 (Spring 1996): 220–236. https://doi.org/10.1093/oxfordjournals.bjc.a014083.

Jones, Philip E. *The Pakistan People's Party: Rise to Power*. Karachi: Oxford University Press, 2003.

Khalidi, Omar. *Khaki and the Ethnic Violence in India*. Delhi: Three Essays Collective, 2003.

Kim, Linda. "A Law of Unintended Consequences: United States Postal Censorship of Lynching Photographs." *Visual Resources* 28, no. 2 (2012): 171–193. https://doi.org/10.1080/01973762.2012.678812.

Klockars, Carl. "The Dirty Harry Problem." *Annals of the American Academy of Political and Social Science*, no. 452 (1980): 33–47. https://doi.org/10.1177/000271628045200104.

Kloppe-Santamaría, Gema. *In the Vortex of Violence: Lynching, Extralegal Justice, and the State in Post-revolutionary Mexico*. Oakland: University of California Press, 2020.

Kosals, Leonid, and Anastasia Dubova. "Commercialization of Police and Shadow Economy: The Russian Case." *Economic Sociology* 13, no. 2 (2012): 21–28. https://www.econstor.eu/handle/10419/155987.

Kotecha, Kanti C., and James L. Walker. "Police Vigilantes." *Society* 13 (1976): 48–52. https://doi.org/10.1007/BF02693881.

Kotonen, Tommi. "The Soldiers of Odin in Finland." In Bjørgo and Mareš, *Vigilantism against Migrants and Minorities*, pp. 241–256.

Kreuzer, Peter. "'If They Resist, Kill Them All': Police Vigilantism in the Philippines." Peace Research Institute Frankfurt Report no. 142, 2016.

Lamcheck, Jayson S. "A Mandate for Mass Killings? Public Support for Duterte's War on Drugs." In Curato, *A Duterte Reader*, 201–220.

Laruelle, Marlene. "Patriotic Youth Clubs in Russia: Professional Niches, Cultural Capital and Narratives of Social Engagement." *Europe-Asia Studies* 67, no. 1 (2015): 8–27. https://doi.org/10.1080/09668136.2014.986965.

Laryš, Martin, and Miroslav Mareš. "Right-Wing Extremist Violence in the Russian Federation." *Europe-Asia Studies* 63, no. 1 (2011): 129–154. https://doi.org/10.1080/0 9668136.2011.534308.

Lebelley, Frédérique. *Tête à tête*. Paris: Grasset, 1989.

Le Bon, Gustave. *Psychologie des foules*. Paris: Flammarion, 2009.

Lecomte-Tilouine, Marie. "Political Change and Cultural Revolution in a Maoist Model Village, Mid-Western Nepal." In *The Maoist Insurgency in Nepal: Revolution in the Twenty-First Century*, edited by Mahendra Lawoti and Anup K. Pahari, 115–132. Milton Park, UK: Routledge, 2010.

———. "Ruling Social Groups—From Species to Nation: Reflections on Changing Conceptions of Caste and Ethnicity in Nepal." In *Ethnic Activism and Civil Society in South Asia*, edited by David Gellner, 291–336. New Delhi: Sage, 2009.

Le Cour Grandmaison, Romain. "'Vigilar y Limpiar': Identification and Self-Help Justice-Making in Michoacán, Mexico." *Politix* 115, no. 3 (2016). https://doi.org/10.3917/pox.115.0103.

Leech, Garry. *The FARC: The Longest Insurgency*. London: Zed Books, 2011.

Le Goff, Jacques, and Jean-Claude Schmitt, eds. *Le Charivari*. Paris: EHESS-Mouton, 1982.

Le Huérou, Anne. "Police Brutality and Police Reform in Russia and the CIS: Introduction." *Journal of Power Institutions in Post-Soviet Societies*, no. 1, 2012. https://doi.org/10.4000/spa.3813.

León, Juanita. *Country of Bullets: Chronicles of War*. Albuquerque: University of New Mexico Press, 2009.

Linhardt, Dominique, and Cédric Moreau de Bellaing. "Légitime violence? Enquêtes sur la réalité de l'État démocratique." *Revue française de science politique* 55, no. 2 (2005): 269–298. https://doi.org/10.3917/rfsp.552.0269.

López Bermúdez, Andrés. "Las Leyes del Llano, 1952–1953: Conceptos fundamentales." *Dialéctica Libertadora*, no. 8 (2015): 160–176. http://hdl.handle.net/10495/10023.

Lorena Jopson, Teresa. "Revolutionary Justice in the Philippines." *Peace Review* 26, no. 2 (2014): 242–249. https://doi.org/10.1080/10402659.2014.906992.

Loveluck, Benjamin. "Le vigilantisme numérique, entre dénonciation et sanction: Auto-justice en ligne et agencements de la visibilité." *Politix*, no. 115 (2016): 127–155. https://doi.org/10.3917/pox.115.0127.

Lu, Hong, and Terance D. Miethe. *China's Death Penalty: History, Law and Contemporary Practices*. New York: Routledge, 2007.

Lund, Christian. "Twilight Institutions: Public Authority and Local Politics in Africa." *Development and Change* 37, no. 4 (2006): 685–705. https://doi.org/10.1111/j.1467-7660.2006.00497.x.

Maheshwari, Malvika. *Art Attacks: Violence and Offence-Taking in India.* Oxford: Oxford University Press, 2019.

———. "Heroes in the Bedroom: Iconoclash and the Search for Exemplarity in India." *South Asia Multidisciplinary Academic Journal*, no. 4 (2010). https://doi.org/10.4000/samaj.3044.

Mahmud, Khalid. *Pakistan mein Mazdur Tehrik* [The workers' movement in Pakistan]. Lahore: Idarah Fikr-e-Mazdoor Kisan, 1983.

Malik, Anushay. "Public Authority and Local Resistance: Abdur Rehman and the Industrial Workers of Lahore, 1969–1974." *Modern Asian Studies* 52, no. 3 (2018): 815–848. https://doi.org/10.1017/S0026749X16000469.

Mamlyuk, Boris. "The Cold War in Soviet International Legal Discourse." In *International Law and the Cold War*, edited by Matthew Craven, Sundhya Pahuja, and Gerry Simpson, 339–375. Cambridge: Cambridge University Press, 2020.

Marin, Gérard. "Quand le trafic de cocaïne est arrivé à Medellín: Réseaux mafieux, violences et politiques de sécurité (1975–2014)." PhD diss., EHESS, 2014.

Martin, Nicolas. *Politics, Landlords and Islam in Pakistan.* Abingdon, UK: Routledge, 2016.

Massicard, Élise. "Quand les civils maintiennent l'ordre: Configurations vigilantes à Istanbul." *Revue des mondes musulmans et de la Méditerranée*, no. 145 (2019). https://doi.org/10.4000/remmm.10212.

Mathews, Donald D. "The Southern Rite of Human Sacrifice: Lynching in the American South." *Mississippi Quarterly* 61, nos. 1–2 (2008): 27–70. http://www.jstor.org/stable/26476642.

May, Ronald J. *Vigilantes in the Philippines: From Fanatical Cults to Citizens' Organizations.* Manoa: University of Hawaii, 1992.

McCall, John C. "Juju and Justice at the Movies: Nigerian Popular Videos." *African Studies Review* 47, no. 3 (2004): 51–67. https://doi.org/10.1017/S0002020600030444.

McGovern, James R. *Anatomy of a Lynching: The Killing of Claude Neal.* Baton Rouge: Louisiana State University Press, 1992.

Meagher, Kate. "Hijacking Civil Society: The Inside Story of the Bakassi Boys Vigilante Group of South-Eastern Nigeria." *Journal of Modern African Studies* 45, no. 1 (2007): 89–115. https://doi.org/10.1017/S0022278X06002291.

Michel, Joël. *Le Lynchage aux États-Unis.* Paris: La Table ronde, 2008.

Millan, Matteo, and Alessandro Saluppo. *Corporate Policing, Yellow Unionism and Strikebreaking, 1890–1930: In Defence of Freedom.* London: Routledge, 2020.

Minotti–Vu Ngoc, Delphine. "Marginalité et répression en Colombie: Le cas du nettoyage social." PhD diss., Université Stendhal-Grenoble III, 2002.

Monaghan, Rachel. "'An Imperfect Peace': Paramilitary 'Punishments' in Northern Ireland." *Terrorism and Political Violence* 16, no. 3 (2004): 439–461. https://doi.org/10.1080/09546550490509775.

———. "Not Quite Lynching: Informal Justice in Northern Ireland." In Berg and Wendt, *Globalizing Lynching History*, pp. 153–171.

———. "Not Quite Terrorism: Animal Rights Extremism in the United Kingdom." *Studies in Conflict and Terrorism* 36, no. 11 (2013): 933–951. https://doi.org/10.1080/1057 610X.2013.832117.

Moncada, Eduardo. "Varieties of Vigilantism: conceptual discord, meaning and strategies." *Global Crime* 18, no. 4 (2017), pp. 403-423. https://doi.org/10.1080/17440572. 2017.1374183.

Monjardet, Dominique. "À la recherche du travail policier." *Sociologie du travail* 27, no. 4 (1985): 391–407. https://doi.org/10.3406/sotra.1985.2015.

Moretti, Mario. *Brigades rouges: Une histoire italienne. Entretien avec Carla Mosca et Rossana Rossanda.* Paris: Éditions Amsterdam, 2018.

Moroz, Evgueni. "Le néo-paganisme, 'foi ethnique,' contre-culture ou entrisme politique?" In *Le Rouge et le Noir: Extrême-droite et nationalisme en Russie*, edited by Marlène Laruelle, 225–249. Paris: CNRS Éditions, 2007.

Nieves Chaves, Sergio. "La justicia republicana durante la Guerra Civil: Los tribunales especial popular y especial de guardia de Cuenca." In *El pasado que no pasa: La Guerra Civil española a los ochenta años de su finalización*, edited by Eduardo Higueras Castañeda, Ángel Luis López Villaverde, and Sergio Nieves Chaves, 189–206. Cuenca: Ediciones de la Universidad de Castilla–La Mancha, 2020.

Nikolski, Véra. *National-bolchévisme et néo-eurasisme dans la Russie post-soviétique.* Paris: Mare & Martin, 2013.

Ning, Zhang. "The Political Origins of Death Penalty Exceptionalism: Mao Zedong and the Practice of Capital Punishment in Contemporary China." *Punishment and Society* 10 (2008): 117–136. https://doi.org/10.1177/1462474507087195.

Nolte, Insa. "Without Women Nothing Can Succeed: Yoruba Women in the Oodua People's Congress (OPC), Nigeria." *Africa* 78, no. 1 (2008): 84–106.

Ortiz Sarmiento, Carlos Miguel. *La violence en Colombie: Racines historiques et sociales.* Paris: L'Harmattan, 1990.

O'Toole, George. *The Private Sector: Rent-a-Cops, Private Spies and the Police-Industrial Complex.* New York: W. W. Norton, 1978.

Pabón Suárez, Ingrid Carolina. "'Limpieza social' en Bogotá: La construcción del indeseable." PhD diss., Universidad nacional de Colombia, 2015.

Paes Manso, Bruno. *A república das milícias: Dos Esquadrões da Morte à era Bolsonaro* [The republic of militias: Death squads in Brazil]. São Paulo: Todavia, 2020.

Paugam, Serge, Bruno Cousin, Camila Giorgetti, and Jules Naudet. *Ce que les riches pensent des pauvres.* Paris: Seuil, 2019.

Perkins, Christopher. *The United Red Army on Screen: Cinema, Aesthetics and the Politics of Memory.* Basingstoke, UK: Palgrave Macmillan, 2015.

Pfeifer, Michael J., ed. *Global Lynching and Collective Violence*, vol. 1. Chicago: University of Illinois Press, 2017.

———. *The Roots of Rough Justice: Origins of American Lynching.* Urbana: University of Illinois Press, 2001.

———. *Rough Justice: Lynching and American Society, 1874–1947.* Urbana: University of Illinois Press, 2004.

SELECTED BIBLIOGRAPHY

Picard, Nicolas, "L'Application de la peine de mort en France (1906–1981)." PhD diss., Université Paris 1-Panthéon Sorbonne, 2016.

Piccoli, Emmanuelle. *Les Rondes paysannes: Vigilance, politique et justice dans les Andes péruviennes.* Louvain-la-Neuve: L'Harmattan Academia, 2011.

Pratt, John. "Emotive and Ostentatious Punishment: Its Decline and Resurgence in Modern Society." *Punishment and Society* 2, no. 4 (2000): 417–439. https://doi .org/10.1177/14624740022228088.

———. *Penal Populism.* London: Routledge, 2007.

Pratten, David. "'The Thief Eats His Shame': Practice and Power in Nigerian Vigilantism." *Africa* 78, no. 1 (2008): 64–83. https://doi.org/10.3366/E0001972008000053.

Pratten, David, and Atreyee Sen, eds. *Global Vigilantes.* London: Hurst, 2007.

———. "Global Vigilantes: Perspectives on Justice and Violence." In *Global Vigilantes,* edited by David Pratten and Atreyee Sen. London: Hurst, 2007.

Provost, René. *Rebel Courts: The Administration of Justice by Armed Insurgents.* New York: Oxford University Press, 2021.

Ramírez, María Clemencia. *Between the Guerrillas and the State: The Cocalero Movement, Citizenship and Identity in the Colombian Amazon.* Durham, NC: Duke University Press, 2011.

Reeves, Joshua. *Citizen Spies: The Long Rise of America's Surveillance Society.* New York: New York University Press, 2017.

Reiner, Robert. "Media Made Criminality: The Representation of Crime in the Mass media." In *The Oxford Handbook of Criminology,* 3rd ed., edited by Mike Maguire, Rod Morgan, and Robert Reiner, 376–416. Oxford: Oxford University Press, 2002.

Rengo Sekigun jiken no zentai zo o nokosu kai [Commemoration Committee of the Red Army Affair], ed. *Shogen: Rengo Sekigun* [Eye- witness accounts: The Red Army]. Tokyo: Koseisha, 2013.

Reyes, Danilo Andres. "The Spectacle of Violence in Duterte's 'War on Drugs.'" *Journal of Current Southeast Asian Affairs* 35, no. 3 (2016): 111–137. https://doi.org/10.1177/18 6810341603500306.

Roberts, Julian, Loretta J. Stalans, David Indermaur, and Mike Hough. *Penal Populism and Public Opinion: Lessons from Five Countries.* Oxford: Oxford University Press, 2003.

Roizman, Yevgeny. *Gorod bez narkotikov* [A city without drugs]. Yekaterinburg, 2005.

Rojas, Carlos Eduardo, Jr. *La violencia llamada "limpieza social."* Bogotá: Centro de Investigación y Educación Popular, 1994.

Rollier, Paul. "Vies de caïds et justice informelle à Lahore (Pakistan)." *L'Homme,* nos. 219–220 (2016): 63–91. https://doi.org/10.4000/lhomme.29034.

Roman, Meredith L. "U.S. Lynch Law and the Fate of the Soviet Union." In Carrigan and Waldrep, *Swift to Wrath,* pp. 215–236.

Rose, R. S. *The Unpast: Elite Violence and Social Control in Brazil, 1954–2000.* Athens, Ohio University Press, 2005.

Rosenbaum, H. Jon, and Peter C. Sederberg. "Vigilantism: An Analysis of Establishment Violence." *Comparative Politics* 6, no. 4 (1974): 541–570. https://doi.org/10.9783/ 9781512806335-002.

Roy, Srila. *Remembering Revolution: Gender, Violence and Subjectivity in India's Naxalbari Movement*. Delhi: Oxford University Press, 2012.

Rush Smith, Nicholas. *Contradictions of Democracy: Vigilantism and Rights in Post-Apartheid South Africa*. New York: Oxford University Press, 2019.

Rutz, Cynthia Lillian. "*King Lear* and Its Folktale Analogues." PhD diss., University of Chicago, 2013.

Saidon, Gabriela. *La Montonera: Biografía de Norma Arrostito, la primera jefa de la guer-rilla peronista*. Buenos Aires: Sudamericana, 2005.

Sakashita, Fumiko. "Lynching across the Pacific." In Carrigan and Waldrep, *Swift to Wrath*, pp. 181–213.

Sarat, Austin, and Stuart Scheingold, eds. *Cause Lawyering and the State in a Global Era*. New York: Oxford University Press, 2001.

Sarlo, Beatriz. *La pasión y la excepción*. Buenos Aires: Siglo XXI, 2003.

Scheper-Hughes, Nancy. "The Global Traffic in Human Organs." *Current Anthropology* 41, no. 2 (2000): 191–224. https://doi.org/10.1086/300123.

———. "Theft of Life: The Globalization of Organ Stealing Rumours." *Anthropology Today* 12, no. 3 (1996): 3–11. https://doi.org/10.2307/2783143.

Scheper-Hughes, Nancy, and Daniel Hoffman. "Brazilian Apartheid: Street Kids and the Struggle for Urban Space." In *Small Wars: The Cultural Politics of Childhood*, edited by Nancy Scheper-Hughes and Caroline Fishel Sargent, 352–388. Berkeley: University of California Press, 1998.

Scott, James. *Domination and the Arts of Resistance: Hidden Transcripts*. New Haven, NJ: Yale University Press, 1990.

———. "Revolution in the Revolution: Peasants and Commissars." *Theory and Society* 7, nos. 1/2 (1979): 97–134. http://www.jstor.org/stable/657000.

Segrave, Kerry. *Lynchings of Women in the United States: The Recorded Cases, 1851–1946*. Jefferson, NC: McFarland, 2010.

Semukhina, Olga, and Michael Reynolds. *Understanding the Modern Russian Police*. Boca Raton, LA: CRC Press, 2013.

Sen, Atreyee. *Shiv Sena Women: Violence and Communalism in a Bombay Slum*. London: Hurst, 2007.

———. "Un groupe féminin d'autodéfense en Inde: Le 'gang du sari rose.'" *Violence de masse et Résistance—Réseau de recherche*, June 17, 2014. http://resistance/fr/document/un-groupe-fa-minin-dautoda-fense-en-inde-le-gangdu-sari-rose.html.

Shank, Barry. "Fears of the White Unconscious: Music, Race, and Identification in the Censorship of 'Cop Killer.'" *Radical History Review*, no. 66 (1996): 124–145. https://doi.org/10.1215/01636545-1996-66-124.

Shapira, Harel. *Waiting for José: The Minutemen's Pursuit of America*. Princeton, NJ: Princeton University Press, 2013.

Shay, Frank, *Judge Lynch: His First Hundred Years*. New York: Biblo & Tannen, 1969.

Shnirel'man, Viktor. *Porog tolerantnosti: Istoriya i praktika novogo rasizma* [The threshold of tolerance: History and practice of the new racism], vol. 2. Moscow: Novoe literaturnoe obozrenie, 2011.

Shukan, Ioulia. "Defending Ukraine at the Rear of the Armed Conflict in Donbas: Wartime Vigilantism in Odesa (2014–2018)." *Laboratorium: Russian Review of*

Social Research 11, no. 3 (2020): 71–104. https://doi.org/10.25285/2078-1938-2019-11-3-71-104.

Silkey, Sarah. "British Public Debates and the 'Americanization' of Lynching." In Carrigan and Waldrep, *Swift to Wrath*.

Simon, Jonathan. *Governing through Crime: How the War on Crime Transformed American Democracy and Created a Culture of Fear*. New York: Oxford University Press, 2009.

Simonin, Anne. "Les acquittés de la Grande Terreur: Réflexions sur l'amitié dans la République." In *Les Politiques de la Terreur, 1793–1794*, edited by Serge Aberdam, pp. 185–205. Rennes: PUR, 2008.

Simonneau, Damien. "Entre suprématie blanche et cybersécurité: Mutations contemporaines des pratiques de vigilantisme en Arizona." *Politix*, no. 115 (2016): 79–102.

Sinha, Shanta. *Maoists in Andhra Pradesh*. Delhi: Gyan, 2013.

Sivakumaran, Sandesh. "Courts of Armed Opposition Groups: Fair Trials or Summary Justice?" *Journal of International Criminal Justice* 7, no. 3 (2009): 489–513. https://doi.org/10.1093/jicj/mqp039.

Skolnick, Jerome. *Justice Without Trial: Law Enforcement in Democratic Society*. New York: John Wiley & Sons, 1966.

Slipak, Daniela. "La justice de la révolution: *Evita Montonera* dans l'Argentine des années 1970." *Problèmes d'Amérique latine*, no. 93 (2014): 91–108. https://doi.org/10.3917/pal.093.0091.

Smith, Daniel Jordan. "The Bakassi Boys: Vigilantism, Violence and Political Imagination in Nigeria." *Cultural Anthropology* 19, no. 3 (2004): 429–455.

Smith, Shawn Michelle. "The Evidence of Lynching Photographs." In Apel and Smith, *Lynching Photographs*.

Stein, Rebecca. *Screen Shots: State Violence on Camera in Israel and Palestine*. Stanford, CA: Stanford University Press, 2021.

Street, Joe. *Dirty Harry's America: Clint Eastwood, Harry Callahan and the Conservative Backlash*. Gainesville: University Press of Florida, 2016.

Su, Yang. *Collective Killings in Rural China during the Cultural Revolution*. Cambridge: Cambridge University Press, 2012.

Tackett, Timothy. *Par la volonté du peuple: Comment les députés de 1789 sont devenus révolutionnaires*. Paris: Albin Michel, 1997.

Tankebe, Justice. "Self-Help, Policing, and Procedural Justice: Ghanaian Vigilantism and the Rule of Law." *Law and Society Review* 43, no. 2 (2009): 245–270. https://doi.org/10.1111/j.1540-5893.2009.00372.x.

Tanner, Samuel, and Aurélie Campana. "'Watchful Citizens' and Digital Vigilantism: A Case Study of the Far Right in Quebec." *Global Crime* 21, nos. 3‑4 (2020): 262–282. https://doi.org/10.1080/17440572.2019.1609177.

Taussig, Michael. *Defacement: Public Secrecy and the Labor of the Negative*. Stanford, CA: Stanford University Press, 1999.

———. *Law in a Lawless Land: Diary of a Limpieza in Colombia*. Chicago: University of Chicago Press, 2003.

Taylor, Brian. *State Building in Putin's Russia: Policing and Coercion after Communism*. New York: Cambridge University Press, 2011.

Thompson, Edward Palmer. "'Rough Music': Le charivari anglais." *Annales* 27, no. 2 (1972): 285–312.

Thurston, Robert W. *Lynching: American Mob Murder in Global Perspective*. Farnham, UK: Ashgate, 2011.

Tilly, Charles. *Coercion, Capital, and European States, AD 990–1990*. Cambridge, UK: Basil Blackwell, 1990.

——. *The Politics of Collective Violence*. New York: Cambridge University Press, 2003.

——. "War Making and State Making as Organized Crime." In *Bringing the State Back In*, edited by Peter B. Evans, Dietrich Rueschemeyer, and Theda Skocpol, 169–191. Cambridge: Cambridge University Press, 1985.

Tipaldou, Sofia, and Katrin Uba. "Movement Adaptability in Dissimilar Settings: The Far Right in Greece and Russia." *European Societies* 21, no. 4 (2019): 563–582. https://doi.org/10.1080/14616696.2018.1494294.

Traïni, Christophe. "Les formes plurielles d'engagement de la protection animale." In Carrié and Traïni, *S'engager pour les animaux*.

Trottier, Daniel. "Digital Vigilantism as Weaponisation of Visibility." *Philosophy and Technology* 30, no. 1 (2017): 55–72. https://doi.org/10.1007/s13347-016-0216-4.

van Woerkens, Martine. *Le Voyageur étranglé: L'Inde et les Thugs, le colonialisme et l'imaginaire*. Paris: Albin Michel, 1995.

Vasilopoulou, Sofia, and Daphne Halikiopoulou. *The Golden Dawn's "Nationalist Solution": Explaining the Rise of the Far Right in Greece*. New York: Palgrave Macmillan, 2015.

Volkov, Vadim. *Violent Entrepreneurs: The Use of Force in the Making of Russian Capitalism*. Ithaca, NY: Cornell University Press, 2002.

Wahl, Rachel. *Just Violence: Torture and Human Rights in the Eyes of the Police*. Stanford, CA: Stanford University Press, 2017.

Waldrep, Christopher. *The Many Faces of Judge Lynch*. New York: Palgrave Macmillan, 2002.

——. "War of Words: The Controversy over the Definition of Lynching, 1899–1940." *Journal of Southern History* 66, no. 1 (February 2000): 75–100. https://doi.org/10.2307/2587438.

Walsh, Declan. *The Nine Lives of Pakistan: Dispatches from a Divided Nation*. London: Bloomsbury, 2020.

Warouw, Nicolaas. "Community-Based Agencies as the Entrepreneur's Instruments of Control in Post Soeharto's Indonesia." *Asia Pacific Business Review* 12, no. 2 (2006): 193–207. https://doi.org/10.1080/13602380500532313.

Waseem, Zoha. *Insecure Guardians: Enforcement, Encounters and Everyday Policing in Postcolonial Karachi*. London: Hurst, 2022.

Weber, Max. *Essays in Sociology*. London: Routledge, 1948.

——. "L'économie et les ordres." In *Concepts fondamentaux de sociologie*, 225–264. Paris: Gallimard, 2016.

Welsh, Bridget. "Local and National: Keroyokan Mobbing in Indonesia." *Journal of East Asian Studies* 8, no. 3 (2008): 473–504. https://doi.org/10.1017/S1598240800006512.

Whelpton, John. *A History of Nepal*. Cambridge: Cambridge University Press, 2005.

220 SELECTED BIBLIOGRAPHY

White, G. Edward. *Earl Warren: A Public Life*. New York: Oxford University Press, 1982.

Williams, John. "Casualties of Violence in Northern Ireland." *International Journal of Trauma Nursing* 3, no. 3 (1997): 78–82.

Wolf, Sonja. *Mano Dura: The Politics of Gang Control in El Salvador*. Austin: University of Texas Press, 2017.

Wolters, Wendy. "Without Sanctuary: Bearing Witness, Bearing Whiteness." *JAC* 24, no. 2 (2004): 399–425.

Wood, Amy Louise. "Critical Conversation on Donald Mathews's 'The Southern Rite of Human Sacrifice,'" *Journal of Southern Religion* 17 (2015). http://jsreligion.org/issues/vol17/Wood.html.

——. *Lynching and Spectacle: Witnessing Racial Violence in America, 1890–1940*. Chapel Hill: University of North Carolina Press, 2011.

——. "They Never Witnessed Such a Melodrama." *Southern Spaces*, April 27, 2009. https://doi.org/10.18737/M7Z31N.

Yonucu, Deniz. "Urban Vigilantism: a Study of Anti-Terror Law, Politics and Policing in Istanbul." *International Journal of Urban and Regional Research* 42, no. 3 (May 2018), pp. 408-422. https://doi.org/10.1111/1468.2427.12611.

INDEX

ACAB-Land, Marie, 77
Adalet ve Kalkınma Partisi (AKP), 142
Adityanath, Yogi, 140
African National Congress, 16
Ahmedabad Anti-Terrorism Squad, 150
AIDG. *See* Anti-Illegal Drugs Group
AKP. *See* Adalet ve Kalkınma Partisi
Alextime (Makeev, Alexei), 50–51
Ali, Babar, 81
Ali, Hazrat, 147
Ali, Wajid, 81
American Legion, 14
Amor por Medellín, 115
Angre, Ravindra, 150
Animal Liberation Front, 22
Anti-Illegal Drugs Group (AIDG), 151
Anti-Slavery Committee, 12
Anwar, Rao, 128, 145, 147–149
Aramburu, Pedro Eugenio, General, 85
Arbery, Ahmaud, 42, 44
Argentina: Buenos Aires, 85; Timote, 85, 87
Arrostito, Norma, 86

Asociación Campesina de Ganaderos y Agricultores del Magdalena Medio, 110
Association of Southern Women for the Prevention of Lynching, 44
Australia, 1, 23, 25
Autodefensas Unidas de Colombia, 113, 120

Baburova, Anastasia, 69
Bakassi Boys, 16–19, 30
Barriobero, Eduardo, 97
Belgium, 24
Betancur, Belisario, 112
Bharatiya Janata Party (BJP), 21, 31, 140, 157
Bhosale, Praful, 150
Bhutto, Zulfikar Ali, 80, 82, 184n14
Biden, Joe, 43
BJP. *See* Bharatiya Janata Party
Black Lives Matter, 15, 42, 78–79, 149, 159
Black Panther Party, 15, 77
Black Panthers. *See* Black Panther Party
Boko Haram, 16

222 INDEX

Bolivia: Cochabamba, 41, 55
Bolsonaro, Flávio, 142
Bolsonaro, Jair, 8, 141, 152, 157
Bombay's Anti-Terrorism Squad, 132
Borges, Gustavo, 108
BORN. See Boyevaya Organizatsiya Russkikh Natsionalistov
Boss Candrinho, 49–50
Boyevaya Organizatsiya Russkikh Natsionalistov (BORN), 69–70, 72
BP (British Petroleum), 120
Brazil, 8, 111, 112, 113, 117, 127, 130, 141, 152, 155; Timbaúba, 48; Niteroi, 108; Rio de Janeiro, 107–108, 142, 145; São Paulo, 108, 153; Victoria, 108
Brinsley, Ismaaiyl Abdullah, 78
Brown, Foxy, 12, 163n11
Bryan, William, 42
Bush, George, 77

Calaisiens en Colère, 19
Cali Limpia, 111
Callahan, Harry, 130
Cameron, James, 53, 175n97
Canada, 22, 24
carabineros (Chile), 78
Cárdenas, Alvaro, 123
Castaño brothers. See Autodefensas Unidas de Colombia
Castile, Philando, 78
Casy, Jim, 15
charivari, 4, 26, 49
Chile, 77, 78
China, 18, 65, 84, 96–97; Guangxi, 96; Yunnan, 83
Chulavitas, 110
Colombia, 80, 84, 86, 88–94, 99, 102–125; Bogotá, 94, 105, 111, 112, 113, 115, 122; Cali, 94, 112; Ciudad Bolívar, 113, 123; Liborina, 121–122; Medellín, 111, 112, 115, 122, 192n43, 193n66; Pereira, 110, 114, 122; Santa Viviana, 105, 119, 122, 124–125; Serranía de la Macarena, 95; Vista Hermosa, 90
Communist Party of Nepal (Maoist), 93

Communist Party of the Philippines–Marxist Leninist, 88
Creep Catchers, 24

Darwin Crime Rally Protest, 1–2, 6
de los Angeles Iquira, María, 105, 120, 122
Devkota, Khim Lal, 92
Dewèvre, Brigitte, 97
Dimsdale, Thomas, 13
Direct Action Against Drugs. See IRA
Dogar, Khushi Muhammad, 80–82, 92, 184n16
Dolas, Maya, 133, 150
Dozos, 24
Ducran, Gary, 24
Duterte, Rodrigo, 8, 107, 131, 139, 141–145, 151, 152, 157, 158
Dymovsky, Aleksey, 69, 179n43

Eastwood, Clint, 130, 195n15
Ejército de Liberación Nacional (ELN), 99
Ejército Popular de Liberación (EPL), 89
Ejército Revolucionario del Pueblo (ERP), 86
El Salvador, 101, 102, 110, 127–128, 139; San Miguel, 110; Sonsonate, 127
Encounter Squad (Mumbai), 133
Erdoğan, Recep Tayyip, 141
Escritório do Crime, 142
Esquadrão da Morte, 108
Euskadi Ta Askatasuna (ETA), 119
Everest, Wesley, 14

FARC. See Fuerzas Armadas Revolucionarias de Colombia
Fawda, Javed, 153, 200n113
FBI (Federal Bureau of Investigation), 17
Federal Protective Service (Russia), 72
Firmenich, Mario, 86
Fleisher, Michael, 31
Floyd, George, 15, 42, 164n31
Ford, John, 45
Ford, Thomas, 13

INDEX

France, 6, 19, 20, 21, 25, 34, 35, 37, 48, 77, 97, 118, 149, 156, 158, 159, 179n34; Bobigny, 35; Bruay-en-Artois, 97; Calais, 19; Clichy-sous-Bois, 35; Hautefaye, 37; Lens, 98

Frank, Leo, 53

Frente Farabundo Martí para la Liberación Nacional (FMNL), 101–102

Fuerzas Armadas Revolucionarias de Colombia (FARC), 90–100, 112, 120, 187n77, 187n78

Fuerzas Especializadas de Reacción El Savaldor, 128

Gates, Daryl, 132

Gauche prolétarienne, 97–98

Gau Raksha Dal (GRD), 19, 31, 140

Gaviria, César, 120

Glavnoe razvedyvatel'noe upravlenie (GRU), 66

González Martínez, Gil Roberto (pseud. Carafea), 105, 119, 122

Grandmaster Jay (John F. Johnson), 16

GRU. *See* Glavnoe razvedyvatel'noe upravlenie

Grupos Antiterroristas de Liberación (GAL), 118

Guatemala, 109

Guerrero, Edgar, 123

Gulabi Gang, 22

Guthrie, Woody, 9, 14

Hansen, Chris, 24

Hartfield, John, 38

Henao Arango, Luis Jairo, 117

Henao Orrego, John Fredy, 120, 122

Hermandad Hitleriana de Pasto, 120

hindutva, 157

Honduras, 109

Hong Kong, 78

Hopkins, Ernest J., 131

Hukumang Bayan, 94

Human Rights Watch, 101

Hunter, Stinson, 24

hygienist movement. *See* social hygiene

Ibrahim, Dawood, 133, 150

India: Bhagalpur, 137, 139; Dimapur, 56–57; Mumbai (formerly Bombay), 21, 134, 135, 137, 140, 150, 152, 153; Gujarat, 135, 140, 142, 143, 150, 151, 200n108; Kashmir, 134; Nagaland, 56, 57; Punjab, 32, 134; Uttar Pradesh, 135, 140, 147

Indonesia, 45, 47, 125

International Commission of Jurists, 90

International Labor Defense, 44

IRA (Irish Republican Army), 26, 89, 91, 94

Ivachko, Yuri, 66

Japan, 36, 37, 48; Gunma Prefecture, 88

Jee, Ick-Joo, 151

Jewish Community Watch, 25, 29

Jewish Defense League, 15

Johnson, Micah Xavier, 78

Juntas de Acción Communal (JAC), 92, 123

Kavkaz-Tsentr, 71, 180n55

keroyokan, 45

Khan, Aftab Ahmed, 132, 135, 136, 138, 150

Khan, Chaudhry Aslam, 147, 199n94

Khan, Syed Farid, 56–58

Khinshtein, Alexander, 68

Khryushi Protiv, 30

King, Rodney, 77

kneecapping, 26

Knights Templar Cartel, 19

Koglweogo, 24

Kovtun, Aleksandr, 62, 65, 66, 71, 76

Kruel, Amaury, 108

Ku Klux Klan, 18

Lakhiyalov, Murad, 71

Lang, Fritz, 45

Laws of the Llano, 88, 92

Lazutin, Mikhail. *See* Lev Protiv

Le Cocq de Oliveira, Milton, 108

Leroy, Pierre, 97

224 **INDEX**

lesnye bratia, 95
Letzgo Hunting, 24
Levchenko, Anna, 25, 31
Lev Protiv, 28–30, 32
Lévy, Benny (pseud. Victor), 98
Liberal Democratic Party of Russia
  (LDPR), 71
Liberation Tigers of Tamil Eelam
  (LTTE), 95, 188n107
Limonov, Eduard, 67
Lokhandwala operation, 133, 138,
  150
Londoño Arango, Jesus, 121
Long, Gavin Eugene, 78
Losada Valderrama, Ricaurte, 111
Los Angeles Police Department. *See*
  Special Investigation Section
Lubavitch community, 25
Lynch, Charles, 35

Magdalena Medio Limpieza Committee,
  111
Mahendra, King, 92
Makeev, Alexei. *See* Alextime
Mali, 47
maobadi, 90, 92, 93
Mão Negra, 107
Mao Zedong, 83
Markelov, Stanislav, 69
Martsinkevich, Maxim. *See* Tesak
Marulanda Vélez, Manuel (pseud.
  Tirofijo), 99
Mayakovsky, Vladimir, 36
McMichael, Gregory, 42
Medellín, 111–112, 115, 122, 192n43,
  193n66
Medvedev, Dmitry, 69
Mehsud, Naqeebullah, 146–149, 153
Meir Kahane, Rabbi, 15
Mercado, José Raquel, 80, 86
MeToo movement, 22
Mexico, 7, 14, 19–20, 46–48, 50, 58, 76,
  110, 156; Hidalgo State, 48; Mexico
  City, 76; Michoacán State, 19, 110
Minneapolis Freedom Fighters, 15

Minutemen, 12, 14, 19, 23
Moderators, 14
Modi, Narendra, 8, 31, 140–143, 150–152,
  157, 198n69
Montana (vigilantes of), 13–14
Moretti, Mario, 99
Moro, Aldo, 99
Movement Against Illegal Immigration,
  70, 180n49
Mozambique, 48; Beira, 49–50;
  Chimoio, 45
Muerte a Secuestradores, 112
Muttahida Qaumi Movement, 76
M-19, 80, 86, 192n43

Naik, Sudhakarro, 133
National Association for the Advance-
  ment of Colored People (NAACP),
  15, 44
National Bolshevik Party, 67, 178n24
National Socialist Society North, 71
Nayak, Daya, 150
Nepal, 22, 89–90, 92–93, 103
New People's Army (NPA), 88, 94–95, 101
Nieves Ochoa, Martha, 112, 192n43
Nigeria, 16, 18, 131, 156; Aba, 16; Abia
  State, 17; Anambra State, 17
Northern Ireland, 19, 28, 89, 91, 169n116
Not Fucking Around Coalition, 15

oboroten' v pogonakh, 68
Occupy Pedophilia, 10, 32–33, 50
Osborne, John E., 14
Osmeña, Sergio Tomas, 143

Pacoleaks, 78
pájaros, 110, 119, 191n32
Pakistan: 6, 80–82, 100, 126, 128–129,
  133–134, 146, 148–149, 199n91;
  Karachi, 28, 76, 145–149, 152–153,
  197n51; Lahore, 80–82, 84; Lyari, 28;
  Waziristan, 146, 148, 199n89
Pakistan People's Party, 100
Pal, Sampat, 22
Parrott, George, 14

INDEX

Partido Popular, 119
Pashtun Tahafuz Movement, 148–149
Pauletto, André, 34
Pavlensky, Petr, 75
Payne, Justin. *See* Payneful Truth, The
Payneful Truth, The, 24
Pearce, Alanah, 22
Peckinpah, Sam, 101
Penn, Arthur, 45
Peron, Eva, 86
Peron, Juan, 85
Peru, 18, 19, 21, 25, 110
Perverted Justice, 24
Philippines: 8, 20, 88, 94, 101, 107, 128, 131, 139, 141–142, 145, 151–153, 157–159; Cebu City, 143; Davao, 143; Visayan Islands, 94; Tagum City, 143
Posse Comitatus (militia movement), 1
Potter, Will, 54
Primorsky Partisans, 60–62, 65, 67–76, 78–79
Proud Boys, 159
Pyromaniacs (Russian neo-nazi group), 72

QAnon, 18
Qasim, Muhammad, 147
Quayle, Dan, 77

Rasulov, Yasin, 71
Regulators, 11–12, 14
Rehman, Abdur, 81–84, 88, 92, 100–101
Republicans (in Spanish Civil War), 97
Reverbel, Ulysses Pereyra, 87
Restrepo, José Alvear, 92
Richard the Lionheart, 27
Roizman, Yevgeny, 20
Roma (people), 34–35, 38–39, 43–45, 48, 58
rondas campesinas, 19, 168n98
rough music, 4, 26
Russia, 4, 6–7, 10–11, 19–21, 27, 30–31, 49, 60–75, 78–79, 156; Kondopoga,

70; Kirovsky, 65–68; Moscow, 9–10, 28, 30, 32, 50, 63, 67–71, 76; North Caucasus, 64, 67, 71, 73; Oryol, 71–72; Primorye, 60–62, 65, 67–76; Ussuriysk, 61, 66, 72; Vladivostok, 60, 62, 65–66, 71; Yekaterinburg, 20

Sartre, Jean-Paul, 98
Scorsese, Martin, 21
Serviço de Diligências Especiais (SDE), 107–108
Shah, Amit, 140, 142, 150–151
Sharma, Pradeep, 133, 150, 152
Shining Path, 110
Shiv Sena, 21, 152, 167n80
sicarios, 106, 120, 122
Smith, Henry, 54
social cleansing. See *limpieza*
social hygiene, 107, 113–115, 124
Soldiers of Odin, 19, 27
South Africa, 16, 21, 31, 40, 131; Cape Town, 31; Durban, 40
Spain, 118
Special Investigation Section, 132
Sri Lanka, 58, 116, 134
Stannard Baker, Ray, 52
Sterling, Alton, 78
StopKham, 30
Suharto, General, 48–49
Sukhorada, Andrey, 60–65, 67–68, 72, 75–76
Sungusungu, 30–31
Syndicat des commissaires de la police nationale, 159

Taliban, 100, 146, 148
Tanzania, 18, 30
Terre des Hommes, 25
Tesak (Maxim Martsinkevich), 9–11, 27–29, 31–33, 50, 66
This Is Lebanon, 22
Till, Emmett, 54–55
Tirofijo, see Marulanda Vélez, Manuel
TN Rabiot Police Officiel, 77
Trump, Donald, 159

226 INDEX

Turkey, 141
Turma Volante Especial de Repressão aos Assaltos a Mão Armada, 108
Tuskegee Institute, 44

Uçma, Ismet, 142
United Kingdom, 4, 24, 29, 31
United Red Army of Japan, 88
United States, 7, 11–12, 17–19, 22–24, 27, 29, 36–38, 41, 43, 46–47, 51–54, 61, 77–79, 98, 120, 125, 128, 131–132, 149, 157–159; Arizona, 14, 19, 23; Atlanta, 15, 42; Baton Rouge, 78–79; Boston, 17; Brunswick, 42, 44; California, 13, 15; Chicago, 15; Dallas, 78–79; Los Angeles, 77, 132; Minneapolis, 15; Mississippi, 54; New York City, 15, 78; Montana, 13–14; San Francisco, 13, 130; South Carolina, 12, 14, 44; Texas, 43, 48, 54; Vicksburg, 36; Wyoming, 13–14
Uy, Rey, 143

Valle, Juan José, General, 85, 185n40
Vance, Myrtle, 54
Vanzara, Dahyaji Gobari, 150, 151, 200n109
Vargas, Adonai, 122
Vargas, Getulio, 108
vozhdenie, 4
Vyshinsky, Andrey, 93

Warren, Earl, 132
Wen Qainchi, 81, 82, 100
white vanning, 116
Wickersham Commission, 130–131
witchcraft, 5, 21, 30, 45, 47, 49
Without Sanctuary (exhibition), 51–52, 55–56, 58
Wobblies (Industrial Workers of the World), 14

Youth Antidrug Commando, 20, 27

Zemmour, Eric, 158
Zhirinovsky, Vladimir, 71

Printed in the USA
CPSIA information can be obtained
at www.ICGtesting.com
JSHW020004091123
51776JS00001B/1